GW00995132

Conflict Management

A Practical Guide to Developing Negotiation Strategies

Conflict Management

A Practical Guide to Developing Negotiation Strategies

Barbara A. Budjac Corvette, J.D., Ph.D.

National Defense University

PEARSON
Prentice Hall

Upper Saddle River, New Jersey 07458

Library of Congress Cataloging-in-Publication Data

Corvette, Barbara A. Budjac.

Conflict management : a practical guide to developing negotiation strategies / Barbara A. Budjac Corvette
    p.cm.

ISBN 0-13-119323-6

1. Conflict management. 2. Negotiation in business. 3. Strategic planning. 1. Title.

HD42.C678 2006

658.4'053—dc22

2005025179

Director of Production and Manufacturing: Bruce Johnson
Senior Acquisition Editor: Gary Bauer
Editorial Assistant: Jacqueline Knapke
Marketing Manager: Leigh Ann Sims
Managing Editor—Production: Mary Carnis
Manufacturing Buyer: Ilene Sanford
Production Liaison: Denise Brown
Full-Service Production: Judy Ludowitz/Carlisle Publishing Services
Composition: Carlisle Publishing Services
Senior Design Coordinator: Christopher Weigand
Cover Design: Kevin Hall
Cover Printer: Moore Langen
Printer/Binder: Courier Corporation

Copyright © 2007 by Pearson Education, Inc., Upper Saddle River, New Jersey 07458. Pearson Prentice
Hall. All rights reserved. Printed in the United States of America. This publication is protected by
Copyright and permission should be obtained from the publisher prior to any prohibited reproduction,
storage in a retrieval system, or transmission in any form or by any means, electronic, mechanical,
photocopying, recording, or likewise. For information regarding permission(s), write to: Rights and
Permissions Department.

Pearson Prentice Hall™ is a trademark of Pearson Education, Inc.
Pearson® is a registered trademark of Pearson plc
Prentice Hall® is a registered trademark of Pearson Education, Inc.

Pearson Education LTD
Pearson Education Singapore, Pte. Ltd
Pearson Education Canada, Ltd
Pearson Education–Japan

Pearson Education Australia PTY, Limited
Pearson Education North Asia Ltd
Pearson Educatión de Mexico, S.A. de C.V.
Pearson Education Malaysia, Pte. Ltd

ISBN 0-13-119323-6

To human development

Brief Contents

Contents

Preface

Much has been written on negotiation. Compared to other negotiation books, this book is unique in several ways. The reader will likely notice immediately two distinguishing qualities—the emphasis on psychological and sociological factors inherent in the negotiation process and the emphasis on individuality. Another distinguishing quality is the breadth of information and explanation included. Rather than merely setting forth concepts and rules, like so many materials tend to do in this subject, an effort has been made to explore the antecedent to negotiation—conflict—and the ultimate goal of negotiation—persuasion, along with the mechanics of negotiation per se. Further, an effort has been made to explain how the concepts operate in practice. This text is intended to blend theory with practice. Whether you are an undergraduate student or an on-the-job professional, the information in this book will help you understand the art of effective negotiation.

The philosophy underlying this book is that there is not a single script for effecting a successful negotiation. Neither is there a single way to understand, learn, and apply sound principles of negotiation. Like any other human interaction, negotiation is a very personal matter.

This book utilizes theories from psychological and sociological research as a practical guide in challenging preconceived notions and automatic behaviors to transform the reader's perspective and approach. A person cannot be truly effective trying to behave in a manner inconsistent with his or her own unique personality and temperament. The goal for the contents of this book was to cull the best advice from the experience of the author, as well as other recognized experts in conflict, negotiation, and persuasion, and integrate that advice with the tremendous knowledge base available in the fields of psychology and sociology.

While many books ostensibly advocate a win-win approach to negotiation, their contents seem to focus on manipulative and strong-arm tactics not conducive to a cooperative style and not consistent with the interactive style of many personality types. The major focus and purpose of this book are to encourage self-knowledge toward building personalized, effective negotiation strategies. To effect a cooperative, win-win negotiation, one must understand human behavior and communication and, most importantly, must understand oneself. This book contains a wide array of tactics and a knowledge base from which to evaluate the same. It also contains exercises, self-assessment tools, examples, and problem cases on which to practice.

The materials are suitable for academic courses in conflict and negotiation and for practicing professionals and executives. A tremendous effort was made to organize and simplify many complex matters. It is hoped that readers will find these materials to be a practical guide for improving their negotiating expertise in both personal and organizational contexts.

Instructors can request an Instructor's Guide that provides answers to all end-of-chapter assignment material from their local Prentice Hall/Pearson Education representative or visit http://www.prenhall.com.

Acknowledgments

I thank all of my students—practicing attorneys and graduate program participants—who read, studied, and utilized these materials and exercises. They helped me tremendously in testing and finalizing the contents of this book. Special thanks go to Jody Veroff, Ph.D.; Robert Disch, Esq.; Tom and Shari Magrath; George Soncrant, D.O.; and Lisa Spoon for their reviews, comments, input, and testing of materials. I also thank them, along with LaDona Anstine and Marla McFarland, for proofreading, editing, and cross-checking the manuscript prior to publication and for their business research assistance.

I acknowledge my parents for all they provided always and for making me believe that I can do anything I put my mind to doing. I thank Dr. Cocoa for her undying love and devotion. I also give special thanks to Ryan McHenry and Debbie Hoffman.

Special thanks to the reviewers of this text: Jill Tomac, Leadership Resource Group, LLC, Corona Del Mar, CA; Emily Martin, Faulkner State Community College, Bay Minette, AL; Sandra Upton, Cornerstone University, Grand Rapids, MI.

About the Author

Dr. Corvette teaches graduate subjects in conflict, negotiation, human resource management, strategic leadership, organizational transformation, executive skill development, psychology, and law. She also authors and teaches professional training seminars on negotiation in various locations throughout the country. She has been on the faculty of George Washington University in Washington, D.C.; Averett University in Washington, D.C., and Virginia; Saint Augustine's College in Raleigh, North Carolina; and Southwestern College in Winfield and Wichita, Kansas. She is currently Professor of Behavioral Science at the Industrial College of the Armed Forces, National Defense University.

She holds a Ph.D. and M.A. in Human Development from The Fielding Institute in Santa Barbara, California, and a J.D. and an M.B.A. from George Washington University in Washington, D.C. She is a certified clinical sociologist specializing in conflict resolution and organizations. She is an attorney-at-law, licensed in Virginia, and a certified public accountant.

Through her careers in law and executive management, Dr. Corvette accumulated much experience in conflict resolution and negotiation. Her professional experience includes sixteen years in commercial law including mergers and acquisitions, taxation, and litigation; seven years in the practice of accounting; and several years in organizational development. She has served in the diverse positions of controller, vice president of finance, general counsel, chief operating officer, independent consultant, and expert witness.

The contents of this book and the views expressed are solely those of the author and do not reflect the official policy, an endorsement by, or the position of the Industrial college of the Armed Forces, the National Defense University, the Department of Defense, or the U.S. Government.

Introduction

This brief introduction explains the organization of the book and provides a guide for getting you started toward the goal of building personalized, effective negotiation strategies. In this book, we approach negotiation in a broad sense as human interaction. In so doing, we may think of negotiation as being understood and affected by all that affects human interaction generally.

Separating human interaction from the human beings involved is impossible! Individuals differ in how they take in information, how they perceive, how they process information, and how they learn. Those differences and others that we explore affect reactions, decisions, and communication. Interaction is personal. Negotiation is personal.

Because of the personal nature of negotiation and the necessity of interacting with other persons when negotiating, the first step in learning how to negotiate effectively is to increase your knowledge of self and others. A major focus of this book is to assist the reader in gaining that knowledge. Another focus of this book is to explore the full spectrum of negotiation. That is, we look at conflict as the antecedent to negotiation. We, of course, study negotiation itself. Our study of negotiation, however, stresses the art of persuasion— the ultimate or essential purpose of negotiation!

Many psychological and sociological principles and theories have sought to assist us in understanding people—individuals and their interactions. We review several of those theories that provide insight into how we know ourselves and others, as well as how we persuade others.

In chapters 1 through 7, we examine basic negotiation behavior characteristics and how they affect interaction and communication. Chapter 1 will assist you in designing your personal plan for improvement. In chapter 2, you will have the opportunity to assess key aspects of your personality that affect your negotiation behavior. Chapter 3 reviews major schools of thought on conflict and allows you to assess your attitude and approach using conflict, chaos, complexity, and systems theories. We examine ways to diagnose, analyze, manage, and use conflict. Chapter 4 combines personality and conflict approach with negotiation styles, and chapter 5 describes negotiating temperaments. We identify behavior that may be expected from certain temperaments. Again, you will have the opportunity to assess yourself. In chapter 6, we review principles of effective communication and forces that draw people together, as well as those that push them apart. Cultural and gender differences are discussed in chapter 7.

In chapters 8, 9, and 10, we analyze interests and goals in negotiation and take a closer look at selected psychological theories that aid in understanding the importance of perception and power in negotiation. We also review how to prepare for psychological games in negotiation.

In chapter 11, you will have the opportunity to determine your assertion index. We examine passivity, hostility, and anger control and provide exercises to build your constructive assertion skills. In chapter 12, we study additional theories from cognitive psychology relative to the principles of persuasion and provide guidelines that will assist in building your skills.

In chapters 13 and 14, we further apply the psychological and sociological factors covered in previous chapters to the negotiation framework. We identify the stages of the process, introduce and define concepts and terms that are used to study the process in detail, and identify general principles of effective negotiation and mistakes commonly made. We also address preparation for specific negotiations in chapter 14.

In chapters 15 and 16, we provide negotiation tactics used to develop alternative techniques and strategies. You will learn when and how various tactics are used as well as how to deal with and respond to the use of these alternatives by your counterpart. Our examination includes ethical considerations and the use of teams in negotiation.

In chapter 17, we link the foregoing knowledge base to two powerful areas of human interaction—leadership and public relations. We briefly explain how effective negotiation skills are necessary to effective public relations and leadership. In chapter 18, we address modes of third-party intervention in conflict. The materials are aimed toward both assisting you in choosing such alternatives and in building your intervention skills.

In chapter 19, we cover concepts to assist you in personalizing negotiating tactics and techniques. We integrate the psychological, sociological, and negotiating principles addressed in the preceding chapters. In chapter 20, we provide keys for your continued use in evaluating your negotiating effectiveness. The material in appendix A directs you to supplemental resources. In addition to the many exercises and cases throughout the text, appendix B contains several negotiation cases for your use in developing your skills.

As you study these materials, your learning will be enhanced if you embrace the following guiding principles:

- I will apply abject honesty in assessing my current attitudes, values, beliefs, personality characteristics, and habits.
- I believe in my ability to learn and grow.
- Improving my effectiveness in human interaction and negotiation will take study, understanding, and *practice, practice, practice*.

Have fun and learn. Remember that you have your own unique personal power and the power to develop as you choose.

Chapter 1

Defining Negotiation and Its Components

PERFORMANCE COMPETENCIES FOR THIS CHAPTER

- To understand the definition and magnitude of negotiation
- To understand that there are limits to what is negotiable
- To identify the components of negotiation performance
- To identify the steps necessary to develop your effective personal negotiating power

"All
the world's
a stage."

William Shakespeare

ALL HUMAN INTERACTION IS NEGOTIATION

Whatever the nature of your business, profession, or current pursuits, you encounter conflict and you negotiate. Life is filled with human interaction and human interaction is essentially a negotiating arena. Other people influence our emotions and behavior, and we influence the emotions and behavior of others. We participate in a continuum of perceiving others and forming attitudes toward people, things, and concepts while others are perceiving and forming attitudes about us.

In the course of our daily business, professional, and personal lives, we regularly seek to affect the attitudes and behavior of others. At times we seek approval, recognition, or affection. At times we seek to cause action by others. At times we seek to gain the right or privilege to take certain actions ourselves. At times we seek to obtain money or other tangible value. In our interactions with friends, family, clients, employees, employers, contractors, service providers, professionals, merchants, and business associates, we use information and knowledge to get what we want. Negotiation is that process of influencing others in order to get what we want.

We negotiate much more often than we may realize. Effective, ethical negotiation is not intimidation, nor is it chiseling or trickery. Rather, effective negotiation is using knowledge of self and others combined with analysis of information and time, thereby tapping the power to affect behavior. The application of that knowledge and information comprises the personal power to win in any negotiation. In effective, ethical negotiation, both sides win. That concept is merely a restatement of the business tenet that it is not a good deal unless it is a good deal for all sides.

It is, perhaps, easiest to accept the notion in the foregoing and come to a definition of negotiation by further considering what negotiation is not. Negotiation is not a game. Negotiation is not always a formal process nor in a formal setting. Negotiation is not limited to business transactions. Negotiation is not conducted solely for tangible things we can see and touch. Negotiation is not simply using power-over tactics—shouting louder or bullying better. Negotiation is not a prescribed set of universally applicable maxims or precepts. That having been said, however, it must be noted that power-over tactics are sometimes used in ostensible negotiation; and, there are indeed, rules and customs often observed in negotiation.

Negotiation is the process of interacting with the goal of obtaining agreement or the result you desire.

KEY TERM
Negotiation is an effort to influence or persuade.

It is an interpersonal skill that is not the province of any particular profession. However, it is extremely important to personal interaction, business and organizational management success, and leadership.

Negotiation is an art. Negotiation may also be considered scientific—having principles and methods that are used systematically through training and experience. Many people believe that negotiation is difficult and that it is just easier to avoid it or always compromise their desires. Others believe that if someone would just tell them the rules they could be effective! There are few universally applicable rules. The rules that do exist provide only general guidelines that must be applied to specific circumstances and specific individuals.

Negotiation is complex and interdisciplinary. It encompasses conflict assessment, management, and resolution. Negotiation is complex primarily because it happens between human beings! Above all, negotiation is personal and individual. It is subject to, understood, and effectuated by the same psychological and sociological principles and theories that govern social interactions generally. Once one understands the application of those principles, negotiation becomes much less complex and intimidating.

After understanding what it is, it is easy to see the magnitude of negotiation. Every day in all aspects of our lives we negotiate. Think of one time today when you tried to influence someone. Perhaps it was a family member. Perhaps it was a coworker. Perhaps it was your boss. Perhaps it was a stranger. You may have tried to cause someone to behave in a particular way. You may have tried to cause someone to think in a particular way. If so, you were negotiating. Do you recall a time when you wanted someone to think you not rude? If you attempted to affect that person's opinion—to have them agree with your self-perception—you were negotiating.

As human beings we seek psychological consistency and balance. We want things to make sense. We want our way. We want to be satisfied. While there is much to explore in that vein, it will suffice for this chapter to understand that the conflict inherent in the need for psychological consistency triggers attempts to influence. That is, it triggers the need or opportunity to negotiate. Have you ever considered that life would be simple but for human beings?

KEY CONCEPT
All interaction is negotiation.

The pervasiveness of negotiation underscores its importance. The good news, however, is that you have ample opportunity to apply what you learn about negotiation. You may—and should— practice every day. Improving your interactions generally will also improve your negotiation effectiveness.

THE PERSONAL NATURE OF NEGOTIATION

The heart of negotiation may be said to be the heart of the individuals involved. What is commonly referred to as the heart is usually what makes negotiation feel difficult. Our emotions, temperament, disposition, and other aspects of our personalities give each of us unique needs, interests, goals, and perspectives. Our needs and desires invoke our ego and our self-concept as well as our fears. These attributes, or phenomena, are actually based in the brain, of course.

It is not uncommon for people to believe that they negotiate effectively on behalf of others while not doing so well for themselves. Why the difference? We may say the heart or, more appropriately, the ego is the difference. It is, to a great extent. However, it is probable that if we are ineffective as our own advocates, we are probably not performing at our maximum effectiveness for others either. Once you learn to understand yourself, you will get to the heart of negotiating. It will take some effort but your results will be satisfying.

HOT TIP!
Practice negotiation in personal settings.

NOT EVERYTHING IS NEGOTIABLE

It seems common to hear that everything is negotiable. Well, that is just not true! Would you sell your child or your pet? Would you compromise the health of your child or your pet? If you said, "No," then you see that, contrary to popular statements that everything is negotiable, it is *not*! If you said, "Yes," then recognize that negotiation requires a minimum of two people and that your counterpart is likely to hold some things to be nonnegotiable. If your reaction here is that these examples are extreme, ponder the issue further. If one has no values, beliefs, or options, then everything might be negotiable. The key here is to identify your personal ethics, moral code, and values as you consider negotiation options.

In addition to those abiding factors, each potential negotiation must be analyzed to determine whether or not the matter *should* be negotiated. If there is not a potential for a **mutual beneficial exchange** that leaves the parties better off than *not* negotiating, then the matter should *not* be negotiated. This principle should become clear as you proceed through your study of negotiation and begin to prepare for each negotiation.

KEY POINT
Identify alternatives prior to negotiating.

CONSCIOUS AND UNCONSCIOUS DETERMINANTS OF YOUR NEGOTIATION PERFORMANCE

Facts and circumstances, including relative power, as well as time constraints, of course, affect negotiation options and outcomes. However, our human interaction is affected by who we are and with whom we interact. Personality and temperament, values and beliefs, perception, attitudes, style of learning, motivation, way of thinking, style of communication, approach to conflict, fears, and much more determine who we are in any human interaction. We are shaped by our experiences. We often unconsciously adopt the attributes of significant others in our life. Each one of us has a unique combination of attributes that serve as the base for our personal power.

We are not always conscious of these attributes and characteristics or the other factors inherent in negotiation. We must know who we are if we are to use our strengths. We must know who we are if we want to consciously develop the attributes we desire. We must also be aware of certain psychological phenomena that may cause us to believe things that are not so. Sometimes we suffer from distortions in our perceptions and thinking that cause us to miss opportunities and make poor choices in negotiation.

WHAT YOU DO NOT KNOW WILL HURT YOU

In addition to causing poor choices, what we do not know can hurt us in other, more subtle ways. Even if we are not conscious of our everyday negotiation interactions, we develop patterns and habits. We are also subject to what is called *social learning* (Bandura 1977). We learn both by observing and doing. In the negotiating arena, this can mean that we imitate the behaviors of those with whom we have negotiated previously. We are particularly likely to adopt behavior exhibited by others that we view as generating a positive outcome for them.

Therefore, if you have often felt like the loser in prior negotiations, you may begin to utilize the same tactics that were used to gain an advantage over you. There are several problems associated with doing so. Feeling like a loser reflects a competitive, gamelike, or win/lose approach. While that is one of the four approaches available for negotiation, it is usually the most inappropriate and ineffective one. Perhaps you felt like your prior negotiations were fair for both sides and you, therefore, have fallen into a pattern of compromising. While such an approach is not competitive, it, too, is not usually the most appropriate or effective approach. Perhaps you have been met in the past with individuals unwilling to negotiate and now you find yourself falling into a pattern of avoidance. Obviously, you cannot get what you want unless you try.

Another problem in copying the negotiating behavior of others is that you are a different person and those tactics may not work well for you. The tactics may actually be inappropriate but worked on you for any number of reasons—lack of preparation, lack of confidence, fear, the particular situation or circumstances, to name a few.

These patterns are difficult to change. Until we become conscious of our self and our actions, we cannot assess the extent of our effectiveness. Our level of experience is irrelevant to this quest. A person who has been negotiating formally for twenty years is not necessarily being effective. She may have been making the same mistakes for twenty years! If we get different results for others than for ourselves, we need to examine why.

COMPONENTS OF NEGOTIATION PERFORMANCE

The components of negotiation performance, then, include personality, approach, style, temperament, perceptions, interests, goals, needs, values, and powers—of all parties involved. Additional components include the substantive issues, the nature of the conflict, the effects of the conflict, and the alternatives for all parties involved. Components also include the persuasive abilities of all parties involved.

HOW TO DEVELOP YOUR EFFECTIVE PERSONAL NEGOTIATING POWER

Knowledge of human behavior is essential to achieving effective negotiation skills. Effective negotiation requires knowledge of self in all of the aspects noted in the preceding subsections as well as knowledge of others. You must know yourself before you may know or understand others. You must become aware of your thought patterns and how they affect your goals and behaviors. You must become aware of your behaviors and how you are perceived by others. You must also acquire knowledge of the nature of conflict, principles of communication and persuasion, and methods for gathering and analyzing information. Effective negotiation also requires critical thinking and creativity.

Psychological and sociological theories provide insight into how we know ourselves and others. The study of psychological and sociological principles combined with self-assessment and practice will guide you to increased effectiveness. Practice of your new knowledge on your own account—where your heart and ego are involved—will generate the greatest gain because it is there where you can discover who you are and your greatest fears. Since you negotiate every day, use those everyday experiences on your own behalf to apply your knowledge and practice your skills.

> **"It is easier to be wise for others than for ourselves."**
>
> *La Rochefoucauld*

The study of principles of communication and persuasion combined with self-assessment and practice will guide us to increased effectiveness. The study of conflict combined with an assessment of our approach to conflict—and practice—will also guide us to increased effectiveness.

Critical thinking requires an inquisitive mind—asking why and how. It requires openness to options. It requires knowing oneself—one's biases, prejudices, and beliefs. It requires challenging preconceptions and assumptions. It requires multifarious, empathetic, comparative, and integrative thinking. The effectiveness of and the mutual gain derived in a negotiation correspond with the level of creativity applied.

A GENERAL PLAN TO DEVELOP YOUR EFFECTIVE PERSONALIZED NEGOTIATION STRATEGIES

Presented in the following list are fifteen steps that will enable you to use your personal negotiating power.

1. Practice critical thinking and empathy.
2. Study and understand key principles from psychological, sociological, communication, and conflict theories.
3. Know yourself.
4. Understand the dynamics of conflict.
5. Know major negotiation styles and temperaments and how to interact with each of them.
6. Communicate effectively, allowing for differing perceptions, biases, and prejudices.

7. Acknowledge cultural and contextual expectations.
8. Understand the dynamics of power.
9. Identify interests and goals.
10. Be assertive.
11. Be persuasive.
12. Be thoroughly prepared and avoid common mistakes.
13. Use tactics that suit you and understand tactics used by others.
14. Know when to walk away as well as when and how to use third-party help.
15. Know how to evaluate your performance and target improvements.

After mastering these fifteen items, then you must—

Practice. Evaluate. Practice. Evaluate.
Change?
Practice. Evaluate. *Practice.*

A Beginning

Start working on your critical thinking and self-knowledge by asking yourself the following two questions.

- What do I know?
- How do I know what I know?

> "To be absolutely certain about something, one must know everything or nothing about it."
>
> *Henry A. Kissinger*

Performance Checklist

✓ All human interaction is negotiation. Negotiation is the process of interacting with a goal and encompasses conflict management and resolution.

✓ Not everything is negotiable. Not everything should be negotiated.

✓ The components of negotiation include the individual personalities involved, interests, goals, needs, values, perceptions, power, substantive issues, alternatives, context, communication, and persuasion. What we do not know about ourselves and our habits may lessen our effectiveness and inhibit our development.

✓ Critical steps in becoming more effective in negotiation are to know yourself, understand the process of conflict and negotiation, control yourself, and do what feels natural for you. Developing personalized negotiation strategies requires critical thinking and creativity, self-assessment, study, application of knowledge, and practice.

Key Terms, Phrases, and Concepts

Negotiation

Mutual Beneficial Exchange

Unconscious Determinants of Negotiation Performance

Review Questions

Mark each of questions 1 through 5 as True (T) or False (F) and answer questions 6 through 10.

T F 1. All human interaction may be considered negotiation.
_____

T F 2. Negotiation is an effort to influence. _____

T F 3. Negotiation is an art and a science. _____

T F 4. Everything is negotiable. _____

T F 5. Everything should be negotiated. _____

6. Explain how and why negotiation is not subject to fixed rules or methods. _____

7. Why is your personal life a good place to practice building your negotiation skills? _____

8. How can your ego interfere with your negotiation performance? _____

9. What kinds of things or factors of which you may not currently be aware may affect your negotiation performance? Why? _____

10. List ten components of negotiation performance.
_____

Case 1.1

Assume that you own and operate a business. Your production this year was based on prior years' experience. You have been left, however, with 100,000 unsold units on hand. You have been selling your product at $5 each and expected the same price for these 100,000 units. You have exhausted all avenues you can think of for disposing of your excess product. You do not have the storage capacity for keeping these units in inventory while you continue production.

This morning a giant retail organization contacted you urgently seeking the type of product you produce to fill deficits in their supply. They offer to pay you $3 per unit.

Case Discussion Questions

1. How would you assess whether or not you should negotiate? Identify the factors you would consider and the overall rule you would apply.

2. What factors can you readily identify that will affect your negotiation options and outcomes?

3. What unconscious factors might also affect your negotiation performance?

Chapter 2

Personality

PERFORMANCE COMPETENCIES FOR THIS CHAPTER

- To learn what comprises personality
- To learn key aspects of major personality theories most relevant to conflict, negotiation, and persuasion
- To assess key aspects of *your* personality

"Thales was asked what was most difficult to man; he answered: 'To know one's self.'"

Diogenes

In this chapter we review aspects of personality that relate to the dynamics of conflict, negotiation, and persuasion. Major personality theories are synthesized and presented for your use in self-understanding. First, we define personality and then proceed to specific characteristics that impact your negotiation behavior. You are urged to assess your personality relative to the factors and characteristics presented here. In this chapter you assess yourself. Later chapters address the effects of the various personality characteristics. What you learn from this chapter will serve as the foundation referenced throughout this book in developing your personal negotiation strategies.

WHY IT IS IMPORTANT TO KNOW YOUR PERSONALITY

"Every man has three characters— that which he exhibits, that which he has, and that which he thinks he has."

Alphonse Karr

People interact in negotiation. "Human interaction" may more appropriately be one word. It is difficult to separate the interaction from the people. Your negotiating success depends upon an accurate understanding of and use of your unique personality type and style of interaction as well as an accurate perception and understanding of others' personality types and styles. Knowing yourself is a prerequisite to knowing others. Knowing yourself is also a prerequisite for tapping your personal power to maximize your effectiveness in any human interaction.

DEFINING PERSONALITY: ONE SIZE DOES NOT FIT ALL

Personality may be described as the dynamic, developing system of an individual's distinctive emotional, cognitive, and spiritual attributes. That definition purposefully does not *limit* personality to characteristic behaviors and/or thoughts, because there abound many perceptions of what should be deemed characteristic.[1] Nevertheless, we will be discussing matters in terms of characteristics.

---

[1] This definition also recognizes the predominant view on nature versus nurture—that personality is the result of a dynamic interaction among genes and environment (including the situation).

There exist many schools of thought and approaches to analyzing personality. It is neither possible nor necessary to review personality exhaustively here. We address key portions of those theories most relevant to the dynamics of human interaction generally and negotiation particularly. We view personality from a human development perspective. Implicit in such a view is the recognition that personality changes (or can change) over the life span. You have the power and ability to develop traits, characteristics, and aspects of your self. Also implicit in such a view is that behavior occurs (or may occur) relative to circumstances. You may demonstrate varying aspects or characteristics of your personality in varying circumstances and/or with varying other people. Culture also affects development of certain personality characteristics. Having knowledge of these variations is a prerequisite to assessing the reasons and propriety for variations—and to changing your behavior.

FACETS OF PERSONALITY THAT AFFECT YOUR NEGOTIATION APPROACH AND TEMPERAMENT

In this section we investigate key facets of personality that affect your interaction in negotiation: emotional stability; conscientiousness; locus of control; self-monitoring; competitiveness and types A and B; need for achievement, power, and affiliation; Machiavellianism; Jungian personality preferences of extroversion, introversion, cognitive processing style, and orientation to others; learning style; right-brain/left-brain dominance; creativity; charisma; and emotional intelligence.

Everyone possesses each of the facets and traits to some degree. You will find that some traits are similar to each other. You may even think that some describe the same trait or characteristic by a different name. Examining each of them will help you to find your personal negotiating style and power as well as help you to identify and develop into the negotiator you desire to be. You will likely find a balance in the combination of traits and characteristics you possess and exhibit. Your task here is to assess the relative strength of each in order to gain understanding of particular strengths and weaknesses in your interactions. As you study each section, try to honestly assess yourself. A profile form (exhibit 2-1) is included for use in recording your self-assessments.

Exhibit 2-1

Personal Profile of Negotiating Personality Attributes

Personal profile of negotiating personality attributes.

Emotional stability	High _____	Moderate _____	Relatively low _____
Conscientiousness	High _____	Moderate _____	Relatively low _____
Internal locus of control	High _____	Moderate _____	Relatively low _____
External locus of control	High _____	Moderate _____	Relatively low _____

Locus of control is primarily   Internal _____   External _____

Self-monitoring	High _____	Moderate _____	Relatively low _____
Type A	High _____	Moderate _____	Relatively low _____
Type B	High _____	Moderate _____	Relatively low _____
Competitiveness	High _____	Moderate _____	Relatively low _____
Achievement need	High _____	Moderate _____	Relatively low _____
Personal power need	High _____	Moderate _____	Relatively low _____
Social power need	High _____	Moderate _____	Relatively low _____
Affiliation need	High _____	Moderate _____	Relatively low _____

Among the need for achievement, personal power, social power, and affiliation, the strongest is:

Achievement _____   Personal _____   Social _____   Affiliation _____

Machiavellianism	High _____	Moderate _____	Relatively low _____
Personal source of energy		Extroverted _____	Introverted _____
Preference for taking in information		Sensing _____	Intuiting _____
Preference in rational functioning		Thinking _____	Feeling _____
Preference for external interaction		Judging _____	Perceiving _____

Primary learning style   Accommodating _____
                                Diverging _____
                                Converging _____
                                Assimilating _____

Preference for activities utilizing   Right brain _____   Left brain _____

Creativity	High _____	Moderate _____	Fairly low _____
Charisma	High _____	Moderate _____	Fairly low _____
Emotional intelligence	High _____	Moderate _____	Fairly low _____

Consistency check

Review your profile for sense and consistency. Note the following expected relationships:

Accommodating learning style with sensing

Assimilating learning style with intuiting

Left-brain dominance and sensing and thinking

Right-brain dominance and intuiting and feeling

Right-brain dominance and creativity

LEARNING THEORY AND ASSESSING YOURSELF

None of the characteristics should be viewed as good or bad but merely as different! As you assess yourself, try not to react to the particular terms used by theorists to identify various traits and attributes. Try to understand the nature of and behavioral impact of the personality facets. Also recognize that we each have a tendency to see ourselves as already possessing traits we admire and that we tend to dislike things about us that we have designated as wanting to change. Honesty is necessary.

Tests and scales have been developed for measuring most of the facets of personality addressed here. Some are published, and some are not.[2] Some are statistically validated, while others are not. Although the exercises offered here are not of the magnitude to assure general reliability, they are designed to assist you in your private introspection.[3]

> **"He who knows himself best esteems himself least."**
>
> *H. G. Bohn*

EMOTIONAL STABILITY AND CONSCIENTIOUSNESS

The terms **emotional stability** and **conscientiousness** come from what is well known as the *Big Five model* (Digman 1990) of personality theory.[4] Reflect on the following statements and decide whether they are usually more descriptive or less descriptive of you. It may be helpful to also ask someone else to tell you how descriptive these statements are of you.

- I worry a lot.
- I experience distress and tension often.
- I get upset rather easily and quickly.
- I tend to be moody.
- I do not remain calm in tense situations.
- I get nervous easily.
- I often find it difficult to control my temper.

---

[2] Most such tests may be administered only by professionals licensed in the state where you reside, and assessment materials may be difficult to find. However, the material in appendix A will guide you in locating relevant material.

[3] It is recognized that when an individual makes him/herself public, as, for example, in a questionnaire to be scored by another, it is possible to skew the results (see, e.g., Schwarz 1999). If one attempts to present a desired self, the results are not accurate. It is quite possible that educated, honest self-assessment is the most reliable of all assessments.

[4] See also Hurtz and Donovan (2000); and Raymark, Schmidt, and Guion (1997).

This first dimension of personality is used to describe your behavior under distress. If, more often than not, you remain unchanged, calm, collected, and confident when confronted with unexpected stressors, then you should probably assess yourself as having high emotional stability. If, on the other hand, unexpected stressors typically cause you to feel very anxious, nervous, or tense or cause you to lose confidence or otherwise change your behavior in negative ways and you found the foregoing statements to be fairly descriptive of you, then you might assess yourself as having relatively low emotional stability.

Now consider the next group of statements and decide whether they are more or less descriptive of your typical behavior. Again, the assessment of someone who has substantial experience with you may help.

- I am always careful and thorough.
- I plan.
- I organize.
- I am efficient.
- I am reliable.
- I am industrious.
- I persevere and follow things through to completion.

If you *typically* are not dependable, are easily distracted or disorganized, miss deadlines, procrastinate, abandon or fail to complete projects, tasks, or assignments, then you should probably assess yourself relatively low on conscientiousness. If you are very dependable, organized and focused, always meet deadlines, complete projects and plans, and seek high levels of competence and believe that the foregoing statements describe your usual behavior very well, you should probably assess yourself extremely high on conscientiousness.

LOCUS OF CONTROL

Please complete Exercise 2-1 prior to reading further.

Exercise 2.1

Think of three times recently when things did not go your way or did not turn out as well as you had hoped. Write down each one.

Next, consider the first incident. What is your *immediate* thought to explain the disappointing outcome? Do *not* think long about this. Simply record your first thought.

Do the same with incidents 2 and 3.

Now, think of two more incidents and, again, record your reasons for the outcome in each.

The term **locus of control** is used to describe the extent to which a person believes she/he is the master of what happens to her/him (Rotter 1966). Those who believe that they are in control are said to have an *internal* locus of control, while those who believe that what happens to them is the result of happenstance or the actions of others are said to have an *external* locus of control. You do not have to believe that you are the master of all things and all fate in order to have an internal locus of control. A good indication of an internal locus of control would be your taking responsibility for a poor performance evaluation. Individuals with an extremely high internal locus of control also tend to accept responsibility for actions of others under their control, such as subordinates. A good indication of an external locus of control would be your regularly attributing poor performance to reasons outside of yourself, such as interference from others or unfairness of others.

If in exercise 2.1 you consistently attributed the reasons for the outcome to factors external to you, you might assess yourself with an external locus of control. On the other hand, if you consistently attributed the reasons to things in your control, you should assess yourself with an internal locus of control.

SELF-MONITORING

You might think of **self-monitoring** as your chameleon factor. However, do not conclude that it is necessarily a negative trait. Self-monitoring is the term used to describe an individual's ability to adapt or change behavior based on circumstantial or situational factors (Snyder 1987).[5] It is also possibly related to emotional intelligence, which we discuss later in this chapter. People with a high degree of self-monitoring adjust their behavior to suit the people, circumstances, and situation; people with a low degree of self-monitoring remain consistent in their demeanor, expressed attitudes, and behavior despite any situational cues that may indicate otherwise. If you are typically conscious of external cues and react to them by modifying your expressions, behavior, or demeanor, you

---

[5] See also Day, Schletcher, Unckless, and Hiller (2002). (Note that there is not yet a large amount of research on self-monitoring.)

should probably assess yourself as a relatively high self-monitor. If your behavior, expressions, and demeanor remain consistent across very different situations and with very different individuals and external circumstances, then you should probably assess yourself as a very low self-monitor. If you pride yourself in consistent behavior—always being true to yourself—you are likely to be a low self-monitor.

COMPETITIVENESS AND TYPES A AND B

Do you eat rapidly? Do you walk rapidly? Do you often focus on obstacles and become impatient with them? Do you try to do more than one thing at a time? Do you place time pressure on yourself? Are you obsessed with time? Do you readily know how long each of your regular daily tasks takes? Do you find relaxation difficult? Do you evaluate your performance and success in terms of quantifiable things, such as earnings and personal possessions? Do you like to discuss your accomplishments and acquisitions?

Are you able to relax without feeling guilty? Would it be correct to say that you feel no need to wear a watch? Do you feel like there is ample time to accomplish your goals? Do you rarely think in terms of time expended? Do you rarely discuss your achievements?

One measure of personality is known as **Type A and B** (Friedman and Rosenman 1974). If you answered "yes" to most of the questions in the first paragraph of this subsection, then you are likely a Type A personality. If you answered "no" to most of those questions and are more aligned with the sentiments expressed in the second paragraph, then you are likely a Type B personality.

Competitiveness is a characteristic most often associated with Type A personalities. It is common for Type A individuals to have a high level of competitiveness. However, individuals exhibit Type A or B behaviors in varying degrees. Furthermore, some individuals who possess Type A tendencies such as time urgency, speed, and impatience do not necessarily focus on competing with *others*. They sometimes are competing with themselves. Therefore, in addition to assessing whether you are more A or more B, you should separately assess your level of competitiveness with others. A desire to win and the penchant for focusing on quantifiable material accomplishments are the strongest indicators of high competitiveness.

HOT TIP!
Be sure to assess whether you compete more with yourself or with others.

NEEDS FOR ACHIEVEMENT, POWER, AND AFFILIATION

David McClelland's needs theory of motivation (McClelland 1961, 1975) also addresses aspects of personality relevant to our purpose here. He and his associates investigated certain behavior relative to the **needs for achievement, power, and affiliation.**[6] Everyone has some level of all three needs; however, it is the strength of each need relative to the others that may affect behavior and negotiation performance.

Those with a high need for achievement are driven to excel. They also tend to seek responsibility—wanting credit for solutions, and they seek feedback. High achievers are typically moderate risk takers.

While the need for power may be analyzed in two veins—personal and social, our focus here is on the need for personal power. Those with a high need for personal power seek power over others. They seek to control or cause behavior in others. Social power, on the other hand, is the power to enable others to excel and the power to create a greater good.

Those with a high need for affiliation seek pleasant, friendly interactions and relationships. They seek cooperation and mutual understanding. They may tend to move away from competitive interactions.

In assessing the relative strength of these needs, you may consider what you would prefer others say about you after you depart this life. Would you most like to be described in terms of your material accomplishments? Would your greatest satisfaction come from being described as a warm and caring person? Would you like to be recognized for having helped others succeed?

In addition to thinking about how you feel you identify with each of these needs, you may learn about the relative strength of these needs in your personality by examining how you assess others and how you explain the stories and motives of others. These can be about real people you know, or they can be stories you fabricate about strangers in magazines or photographs. Since we project our own motives onto others, what you imagine and understand about others will disclose something about you. Look for themes in your stories about what is happening and what will happen. If you find frequent focus on friendship, affiliation, and love, it

---

[6] See also Atkinson and Raynor (1974).

may be a reflection of your relatively high need for affiliation. If you find frequent focus on control and influence over others, it may be a reflection of your relatively high need for personal power. Finally, if you find frequent focus on accomplishment and responsibility, it may be a reflection of your relatively high need for achievement.

MACHIAVELLIANISM

Machiavellianism is named for Niccolo Machiavelli and seems to be closely related to values and ethics.[7] It is the name used to measure the extent of one's motivation for personal gain. It measures one's willingness to place self-interest above all other interests. A person with a high level of Machiavellianism believes that the end *always* justifies the means. Such a person approaches situations with a high level of competitiveness and wile. A high level of Machiavellianism is related to manipulative and deceptive behavior. Due to the nature of this trait, questionnaires to measure it are apt to produce inaccurate results! You may look into yourself to assess your level of this trait.

JUNGIAN PERSONALITY PREFERENCES

Our focus in this section is on the theories of personality that originated with Carl Jung. Although Jung's work extends far beyond what we use here, he analyzed four key dimensions of personality that are particularly relevant to understanding human interaction in general and negotiation in particular.

Jung (1968) analyzed four dimensions of personality: (1) our **personal source of energy,** (2) our **manner of taking in information,** (3) our **style of processing information** and/or making decisions, and (4) our **style of structuring or interacting with the outside world.** Jung coined a term to describe the two most opposite extremes of each dimension. While each of us possesses aspects of both extremes, according to Jung, we are born with a predisposition for a preference as to each dimension. Those preferences derive from a combination of genetics and early experience.

Most individuals retain a preference even while developing their opposite capacities. The degree to which these predispositions develop depends upon one's environment, including the amount and significance of your contact with people of the same or different

---

[7] This concept of personality is based on Niccolo Machiavelli's *The Prince*. See Christie and Geis (1970).

preferences as well as the type of activities you undertake. These preferences affect what we perceive, what we come to know, how we learn and know, and how we approach negotiation.

The opposite of each preference is present in the unconscious and can influence your behavior. Often such displays of nonpreference behaviors are viewed by others as aberrations. Most individuals do possess a preference, although individuals differ in the relative strength of their preferences. Knowing your preferences is necessary for improving your negotiation communication. Furthermore, when under distress or experiencing some loss of self-control, you will unconsciously revert to your preferences.

Jung's terms for the two preferences in each dimension are (1) *extroversion* and *introversion* (E and I), (2) *sensing* and *intuiting* (S and N), (3) *thinking* and *feeling* (T and F), and (4) *perceiving* and *judging* (P and J). Jung's work has been popularized by others. The Myers-Briggs type indicator (MBTI) is widely recognized and is built on Jung's work.[8] The following material is intended to provide a general framework for your informal determination of preferences.

EXTROVERSION/INTROVERSION: PERSONAL SOURCE OF ENERGY

Extroverts tend to verbalize much of what they observe and judge. They are energized by people and action, and they become tired when they spend too much time alone. They would rather talk than listen, and they sometimes speak before they think. Extroverts prefer to work in groups, like to test ideas on others, and like affirmation from others. They often talk until the answer or solution comes to them.

Jung's (1968) original theory described a person's energy source as also related to the person's view of the world. Accordingly, extroverts take an external and objective view and introverts take an internal and subjective view.

Introverts tend to keep their observations and judgments to themselves. They are energized by thoughts and ideas and can become drained by prolonged, intense interaction with several people. Introverts prefer listening over talking and often regret, after the

---

[8] Another popular application that is built upon Jung's work and the MBTI is *Type Talk* (Kroeger and Theusen 1988). The MBTI is a psychological instrument available through individuals trained and licensed to administer the test. It must be noted that, despite its widespread use, there still lacks valid evidence for the MBTI. The categories and terms used here are substantially consistent with both Jung and MBTI. It is also noted here that Jung preferred to spell the word as extra*vert; however, the common preferred spelling is used through this book.

fact, not having spoken up. They think before they talk, often deferring a response. Introverts get rejuvenated by time alone with their thoughts and often feel a need to be alone after extended time with several people. Introverts prefer to generate ideas or work through problems alone. They are perceived as good listeners and often as shy or reserved. Introverts also tend to be annoyed when someone states the obvious or restates something that has already been said.

Descriptive words that should assist your self-assessment are presented in the following lists. In combination with the foregoing explanation, use the following words to determine whether you are *more or less* an extrovert or an introvert. If a scale existed between the two extremes, would you place yourself more toward the E or the I?

Extrovert (E)	Introvert (I)
Sociability	Territoriality
Interaction	Concentration
External	Internal
Breadth	Depth
Extensive	Intensive
Multiple relationships	Limited relationships
External events	Internal reactions
Gregarious	Reflective
Speaks, then thinks	Thinks, then speaks

COGNITIVE PROCESSING STYLE: HOW WE TAKE IN AND PROCESS INFORMATION

Here we will look at the second and third dimensions of personality according to Jung's theory—sensing/intuiting and thinking/feeling. Sensing and intuiting designate opposite styles of taking in information. Thinking and feeling designate opposite styles of processing information. The function of taking in information is nonrational, while the function of processing that information is rational.

Sensing/Intuiting

Sensors tend to be quite literal in their observations about the world as well as in their perceptions and data gathering. They are practical and realistic and enjoy the tactile part of life. Sensors prefer tangible, hands-on experiences. They like precision and sequential presentations. They know by reference to physical, external, and objective sources. They feel certain about those things that come from the five senses—taste, touch, sight, hearing, and smell. They prefer facts and details to interpretation of meaning. They prefer specific questions and specific answers. Sensors concentrate on the present and would rather act than think. They get frustrated when instructions are not clear or when details are left to later. They are more comfortable learning subjects and skills that are conducive to precise rules or formulas, such as mathematics, accounting, engineering, and other *objective* knowledge, than they are with learning subjects such as philosophy, human behavior, religion, and similar areas wherein *subjectivity*, multiple approaches, and uncertainty more abound.

Intuitors can be figurative. As information is gained through the five senses, intuitors take it in and look for meanings and relationships. They know by reference to nonphysical, internal, and subjective sources. They prefer to look at the grand scheme of things. They prefer a holistic approach, trying to organize information into theoretical frameworks. Intuitors like to find the underlying meaning rather than accepting things at face value. They tend to think about several things at once. They may be accused of being absent-minded. They find details boring. Approximations and randomness do not bother the intuitor. That there may not be one correct answer does not bother an intuitor.

The list of words that follows is provided as additional assistance in identifying your preference on this dimension. Decide whether you are closer to the S or the N.

Sensor (S)	Intuitor (N)
Literal	Interpretative
Present	Future
Tangible	Conceptual/theoretical
Perspiration (doing)	Inspiration (thinking)
Concrete	Abstract
Sequential	Multiple
Fact	Fantasy
Practicality	Ingenuity
Specific	General

Thinking/Feeling

Note that Jung's terms here were not intended to describe one preference for thinking and another for feeling. This preference describes two types of rational processing. The names are not to imply that thinking connotes intellect or logic and feeling connotes emotions. Rather, the two distinguish the approach to and relative values used in decision making. Both are rational, intellectual functions. Ideas create feelings. Feelings create ideas. The terms denote two processes for the same function—processing information and making decisions.

Thinkers prefer to be detached and analytical in making decisions. They try to use objective criteria and guidelines. They strive for clarity and what they believe is justice. They try not to get personally involved in decisions. Thinkers are often called firm minded. They stay cool and calm when others get upset. When thinkers see others as wrong, thinkers may say so, regardless of the others' feelings. It is more important for thinkers to be right than to be liked. They are sometimes viewed as cold or uncaring. Thinkers remember numbers more easily than they remember faces and names.

Feelers use interpersonal involvement and subjective value and criteria in making decisions. The impact and consequences of decisions are important to feelers. They are often referred to as tenderhearted. They try to identify with others and be empathetic. Feelers often overextend themselves to meet the needs of other people. They do not hesitate to apologize for or rescind something they said that hurt another's feelings. They are sometimes criticized for being fuzzy or indirect due to their concern for others' feelings. They prefer harmony over clarity and tend to put a great deal of love into their efforts. Feelers take things personally. One may say that they lead with their heart.

The following lists may assist you in identifying your preference on this dimension. Decide whether you identify more with the T words or the F words.

Thinker (T)	Feeler (F)
Objective	Subjective
Firm minded	Fair hearted
Rules	Circumstances
Absolutism	Persuasion
Just	Humane
Clarity	Harmony
Critical	Empathetic
Policies	Values
Detached	Involved

ORIENTATION TO OTHERS

We have distinguished information-gathering preferences—sensing and intuiting. We have distinguished decision-making or information-processing preferences—thinking and feeling. We have distinguished energy sources and preferences—extroverting and introverting. This last of the four dimensions distinguishes how one relates to the outer, or external, world both verbally and behaviorally.

Perceiver/Judger

Perceivers prefer a flexible, spontaneous, adaptive, and responsive environment. For them, sticking to decisions creates anxiety. They prefer to wait and see what needs to be done. They are easily distracted. They love to explore. They are often accused of being disorganized. They believe that creativity is more important than order and that if work is not fun it probably is not worth doing.

Judgers prefer a structured, scheduled, ordered, planned, and controlled environment. They have a place for everything and everything in its place. They are decisive and deliberate. They make decisions with minimal stress. Judgers plan their work and follow their plan. Their view is that there is a correct way and an incorrect way of doing everything. They like to complete things. When something pops up to interfere with their plan, they experience annoyance and anxiety. Judgers are always waiting for others who fail to be on time. They believe that if everyone would simply do as they are supposed to, life would be great. They are often accused of being angry when they are merely stating their opinions—or frustrations.

The following lists will assist you in identifying this preference.

Perceiver (P)	Judger (J)
Pending	Firm
Indefinite	Decided
Flexible	Fixed
Adapt	Control
Defer	Complete
Respond	Anticipate
Random	Structured
Tentative	Definite
Spontaneous	Planned
What deadline?	Meets deadline

LEARNING STYLE: WHAT YOU SEE AND HOW YOU KNOW

Learning may be defined as the process of acquiring a relatively permanent change in understanding, attitude, knowledge, information, ability, and/or skill (Wittrock 1977). There are many ways to learn and many ways of knowing. No single theory fully explains learning. Nor does any single theory account for all individual differences. Human learning is complex. Several theories and measurement instruments have been developed to assess cognitive processing, learning, and perception.[9] In the preceding subsections, we addressed Jungian psychology in terms of how we take in information and how we process that information or come to decisions. Here we borrow from the Kolb learning style model (Kolb 1984, 1985) to assess your dominant or preferred **learning style,** which is another way to assess how you take in and process information.

The Kolb inventory attempts to measure certain aspects of perception and cognitive processing and then categorizes individuals according to four major learning types. The four types are accommodators, divergers, convergers, and assimilators.

- *Accommodators* learn best by hands-on activity—by doing. They take in information primarily through their senses and apply it concretely. An accommodator would learn to play tennis by simply picking up a racket and going for it. It is believed that accommodators are also likely to invite new experiences and take risks. Typically, accommodators use trial-and-error techniques and are able to adapt relatively quickly to new information and new situations. It is also thought that accommodators like to gather information by talking with others and like to influence others. Since they rely on experience as their teacher, accommodators tend to ignore information that conflicts with their own experiences and views. Accommodators also may miss deadlines due to their dislike of structure and procedure. This learning style is closely aligned with the Jungian preferences for extroversion and sensing.

- *Divergers* also take in information primarily through their senses, but they reflect on the information—seeking meaning rather than concrete application. Divergers may learn tennis by trying it followed by thinking about the meaning or effect of their actions, seeking understanding of how to play. It is believed that divergers tend to be concerned about the feelings of others and to seek harmony. Typically, divergers excel in being able to appreciate multiple views and hold multiple perspectives. They are also typically imaginative, have broad interests, and work well in groups.

---

[9] For further information on some of these theories and instruments, see Dyrud (1997) and Feder (1996). For a more thorough discussion of adult cognition see Cavanaugh and Blanchard-Fields (2002).

- *Convergers* take in information through abstract conceptualization and then apply it in active, concrete experience. They learn
  by thinking and then doing. Convergers would learn to play tennis by first reading an instruction book on the game and then
  picking up a racket to apply the information gained. They tend
  to thrive on efficiency and timeliness—seeking results and
  conclusion. They also, however, tend to seek simple or single
  solutions—the one best answer. Thus, convergers may not work
  particularly well in groups and may not excel in creativity. Further, convergers' penchant for decisiveness may cause them to
  sacrifice quality for quantity at times.
- *Assimilators* take in information through abstract conceptualization and process the information reflectively—seeking meaning,
  interrelationships, and integration. They learn by abstract conceptualization and reflective observation. Assimilators would
  learn tennis by reading and thinking about it and visualizing the
  play. Assimilators typically tend to value order, continuity, and
  expert opinion. They excel in the theoretical. They are rational
  and logical thinkers—able to reason both deductively and induc-
  tively. Assimilators prefer to work alone and may sometimes be
  overly cautious. This learning style is closely aligned with the
  Jungian preferences for introversion and intuiting.

RIGHT-BRAIN/LEFT-BRAIN DOMINANCE

The brain consists of two hemispheres connected by fibers called
corpus callosum. Each half, or hemisphere, is covered by a cerebral
cortex—known as gray matter—that controls sensory and motor
processing, perception, and cognitive functioning. The left side of
the brain controls the right side of the body, while the right side of
the brain controls the left side of the body. The left side of the brain
is also the center for speech, language, verbal memory, hearing,
logic, mathematical processes, detail, and planning. The right side of
the brain is the center for processing nonlinguistic hearing/sounds,
visuospatial processing, touch sensations, emotions, relational and
conceptual thought, analogous thinking, and creativity.

Most adults have a preference for left or right activities or may
be said to be dominated by the left or right side of the brain. Those
who are strongly left-hemisphere dominant are detail-oriented and
attach importance to logical thinking and objectivity. Those who are
right-hemisphere dominated are big-picture oriented and attach

importance to analogous thinking and subjectivity. If you have ever wondered why many accomplished musicians with traditional musical training are unable to play by ear and many who have never studied music and cannot read music are able to play beautifully by ear, it is because the two functions are controlled by different sides of the brain. Playing music by ear is a right-brain function, while reading music is a left-brain function.

You may see a relationship between the sensing/intuiting and thinking/feeling preferences we have discussed. That is, sensing and thinking are activities that utilize the left brain, while intuiting and feeling are activities that utilize the right brain. This information about brain function is intended to assist you with those assessments, as is the creativity discussion that follows.

CREATIVITY

Creativity is that ability to see what others do not see. It is a right-brain function; however, just as with the other characteristics addressed here, creativity can be developed; and, just as with the other characteristics addressed here, creativity varies among individuals. Traits and skills that may be linked to creativity include openness to new experiences and new ideas, fondness for complexity, the ability to think critically as well as integratively, the ability to see multiple views, and a high level of self-confidence. You may see similarities to the intuitive preference we have discussed as well as to the cognitive style of assimilators and divergers already discussed. Persons who are intuitors, assimilators, and/or divergers may find it easier to develop their creativity. The ability to think creatively is a valuable skill in negotiation.

CHARISMA

Charisma is somewhat like sex appeal—difficult to describe, but you know it when you feel it! Furthermore, like sex appeal, charisma is not the same to all individuals. Charisma is a personal force that draws people—that causes people to like, admire, and agree.

You will, perhaps, obtain the most useful information on your level of charisma by querying your friends. You may ask them the following questions:

- Do I pay close attention when you are talking?
- Do you trust me?

"A charismatic CEO can win every argument regardless of the facts. A noncharismatic CEO has to win on the merits of the argument."

Jim Collins, author of Good to Great

- Do you understand what I say?
- Do I appear too fearful of failure?
- Do I help you attain your goals?
- Do you respect my views?
- Do I respect you and your feelings?
- Am I competent?
- Am I persuasive?
- Do you like to be with me?

It is possible to learn to be charismatic. Key attributes associated with charisma include vision, energy, and the expression of empathy (Nadler and Tushman 1990; Waldman and Yammarino 1999). One may focus on developing those attributes to become charismatic.

EMOTIONAL INTELLIGENCE

The term **emotional intelligence** is used to describe an individual's ability to excel in human interaction. Certain competencies have been suggested to comprise emotional intelligence (see Davies, Stankov, and Roberts 1998). The development of self-knowledge, self-management, self-motivation, and empathy will increase your emotional intelligence (EI).

Performance Checklist

✓ Personality is the package of an individual's distinctive emotional, cognitive, and spiritual attributes.

✓ Facets of your personality that affect your negotiation include emotional stability, conscientiousness, locus of control, self-monitoring, competitiveness, Type A and B, need for achievement, need for power, need for affiliation, Machiavellianism, extroversion, introversion, sensing, intuiting, thinking, feeling, perceiving, judging, learning style, right-brain/left-brain dominance, creativity, charisma, and emotional intelligence. Since facets of personality may change with age and in response to environmental changes, you should assess yourself periodically.

✓ Your negotiating success depends upon understanding and using your unique personality as well as perceiving and understanding the personalities of others. You must know yourself to tap your personal power. You must understand yourself before you can understand others. Using your learning from this chapter you should review your profile recorded on exhibit 2-1 according to the consistency check provided on the form.

Key Terms, Phrases, and Concepts

Emotional Stability

Conscientiousness

Locus of Control

Self-Monitoring

Type A and B

Competitiveness

Needs for Achievement, Power, and Affiliation

Personal Source of Energy

Manner of Taking in Information

Style of Processing Information

Style of Structuring or Interacting with the Outside World

Learning Style

Right-Brain/Left-Brain Dominance

Emotional Intelligence

Review Questions

Mark each of questions 1 and 2 as True (T) or False (F) and answer questions 3 through 10.

T F 1. It is not possible to change any aspect of one's personality.

T F 2. It is possible to change your characteristic behaviors.

3. Consider the question "What do I know and how do I know it?" in light of how you take in information.

4. Consider how you know what you know in light of your learning style.

5. Develop a working definition of *personality* in your own words.

6. Describe in your own words your primary learning style.

7. Identify a left-brain activity that you do well.

8. Identify a right-brain activity that you do well.

9. Critically evaluate the behavioral differences that may be observed when comparing a person with a high level of competitiveness with others to a person who has high competitiveness with herself.

10. Critically evaluate the difference between a need for personal power and a need for social power.

Case 2.1

Since your goal is to learn how to identify key personality characteristics when interacting in live situations, rather than presenting a written case here, you are asked to tune into a television program or movie for a live case. Watch for ten to fifteen minutes. You may also recall an experience or a vignette from memory. Try to identify in each character as many of the personality and behavioral characteristics studied in this chapter as you can.

Case Discussion Questions

1. Was the task difficult?

2. Did you find it difficult to differentiate among or between any aspects? If so, you might study those aspects again.

3. Were the overwhelming majority of the personality aspects identified the same or similar to your personality aspects? If so, you may want to reflect on why and do the case again.

Chapter 3

Conflict

"On a cold winter's day, a group of porcupines huddled together to stay warm and keep from freezing. But soon they felt one another's quills and moved apart. When the need for warmth brought them closer together again, their quills again forced them apart. They were driven back and forth . . . until . . . [they found] maximum of warmth and a minimum of pain."

Arthur Schopenhauer

PERFORMANCE COMPETENCIES FOR THIS CHAPTER

- To learn the nature of conflict and its relationship to negotiation
- To assess your personal approach to conflict
- To use systems thinking to diagnose and analyze conflict
- To understand the difference between managing, resolving, and avoiding conflict

Conflict is the antecedent of negotiation. We seek to change someone's opinion because it conflicts with ours. We seek to change someone's behavior because it conflicts with what we want. We seek to cause someone to give us something or do something for us because something conflicts with our ability to satisfy our need or otherwise get what we want by ourselves. Our view and analysis of conflict, therefore, directly affects negotiation approach and strategy.

As with most things in life, individuals develop attitudes and ways of thinking that often result in habits or patterns of behavior when dealing with conflict. Attitudes and patterns can interfere with attaining maximum negotiation effectiveness by clouding assessment of the situation and frustrating choice of appropriate strategies.

Before it is possible to develop an effective negotiation strategy, it is necessary to correctly diagnose the conflict. Before it is possible to correctly diagnose the conflict, it is necessary that we recognize our predispositions for dealing with conflict. The propriety of strategy varies with the nature of the conflict, the circumstances, and the individuals involved. Armed with self-knowledge and basic conflict assessment tools, we may proceed to develop personal strategies that work to solve the right problem.

In this chapter you will have the opportunity to examine your approach to conflict. Following that, we proceed to a discussion of the nature of conflict, diagnostic tools, and alternative strategies. The strategies discussed in this chapter will serve as a foundation for integrating your personality and temperament with effective negotiation techniques in later chapters. Interested readers may find the supplemental resources referenced in the footnotes in this chapter helpful for continued study.[1]

FIRST THINGS FIRST

Before we begin our study, please complete the following exercises.

Exercise 3.1

Write down on a sheet of paper the first few things that come to your mind when asked, "What is negotiation?"

- Do *not* ponder this. Take only 30 to 45 seconds to respond.

---

[1] Individuals interested in advanced study may want to regularly check these journals for articles of interest: *Journal of Conflict Resolution, Journal of Social Issues, Negotiation Journal Peace and Change.*

Exercise 3.2

Write down on a sheet of paper the first things that come to your mind when you hear the word *conflict*.

- Again, do not think hard. Take only 30 to 45 seconds to respond.

Now put those thoughts aside while we begin to explore the subject of conflict.

CONFLICT: WHAT IS IT? WHERE IS IT?

Conflict exists wherever and whenever there is an **incompatibility** of cognitions or emotions within individuals or between individuals. It arises in personal relationships, in business and professional relationships, in organizations, between groups and organizations, and between nations. Note that the definition implies as necessary a real or **perceived interdependence.** Conflict may be real or perceived. That is where the concept of cognition comes into our definition. Our thoughts—cognitions—include what we believe. Our beliefs are our beliefs—what we think we know—whether or not based in reality. In interpersonal interaction, perception is more important than reality. What we think—perceive—affects our behavior, attitude, and communication. We further explore the phenomenon of perception and its role in negotiation elsewhere in this book.

> **KEY POINT**
> If every conflict were truly a *real* incompatibility, then negotiation would be little more than an exercise in frustration!

If what you seek is truly not possible, you are either focusing on the wrong problem or selecting the wrong solution. The keys for purposes of developing your negotiation skills are to underscore the words *interdependence* and *perceived.* If there is no interdependence, there is little the parties can or will do for each other, which is another way of saying that not everything is negotiable. If the negotiation has no potential to benefit you, you should not negotiate. In such circumstances, a nonnegotiated option is the better alternative.

It is the perception or belief that opposing needs, wishes, ideas, interests, and goals exist that create what we commonly call conflict. Conflict is everywhere, and it is inevitable. It arises from many sources. In addition to being the antecedent for negotiation, conflict may also arise during negotiation.

The subject of conflict is large and complex. Conflict, if misdiagnosed or misdirected, can lead to a spiral of antagonistic interaction and aggravated, destructive behavior. Here we address only the most important issues relevant to developing effective negotiation skills. What we address, however, should assist you in all of your interactions.

Your Personal Approach to Negotiation and Conflict

Compare your automatic responses to the word *negotiation* in Exercise 3.1 to the words in the following lists to determine whether your current approach to negotiation is positive or negative.

Positive Approach	Negative Approach
Interaction	Contest
Mutual benefit	Win or lose
Interdependence	Control
Opportunity	Problem
Difference	Dispute
Exchange	Struggle
Persuade	Manipulate
Exciting	Frightening
Stimulating	Tension
Challenging	Difficult

The "wild card" is the word *conflict*. If one of your responses was the word *conflict*, you must assess your view of conflict to decide if, for you, it constitutes a negative or positive approach to negotiation.

Compare your automatic responses to the word *conflict* in Exercise 3.2 to the groups of words shown next to determine whether your current approach to conflict is positive or negative.

Positive Approach	Negative Approach
Strengthening	Destructive
Developmental	Pain
Growth	War
Courageous	Hostility
Helpful	Threat
Exciting	Violence
Stimulating	Competition
Creative	Anger
Energizing	Distress
Clarifying	Alienation
Enriching	Hopeless
Good	Bad

Many perceive negotiation as conflict; but, if that comes with a negative attitude or view, it can produce an **aversive drivelike state**, which produces rigid thinking. Rigid thinking lessens the ability to see trade-offs necessary to integrate a win-win solution. A negative approach reduces general cognitive ability and creativity—the key skills necessary for successful resolution of conflict. It is advisable to try to think in terms of interdependence and mutuality. Our attitudes toward conflict and, therefore, negotiation develop from social learning in the context of our families and prior experiences.

If you already hold a positive view toward negotiation and conflict, you will find such a view helpful in developing your personal negotiation effectiveness. If—as is the case for many individuals—you have a negative view of either or both, you will be well served to work on revising your view.

ANOTHER EXERCISE IN ATTITUDE

Suppose that someone offered you a coin toss proposition. He offers to flip a quarter while you call heads or tails. If you make the call correctly, he will give you one million dollars. If you call the toss incorrectly, you must pay him one hundred thousand dollars. What is your first impulse? First thought? Do you take the chance?

Analyze your thought process. Do you think the guy is crazy to give you ten-to-one odds on a fifty-fifty chance? Is your immediate thought what you will do with a million dollars or how you will feel giving up one hundred thousand dollars? Can you afford to give up one hundred thousand dollars?

Your first thought may reflect your general positive or negative attitude. The evaluation of whether or not you can afford losing, of course, should ultimately determine whether or not you may consider taking this chance.

THE TERMS ATTITUDE, VIEW, APPROACH, AND STYLE

You may think of the term approach, used in the preceding section, as synonymous with your general view and attitude toward conflict and negotiation. In chapter 4 we discuss alternative styles of negotiation, or particular approaches to particular interactions. Your view of conflict and negotiation, along with key personality characteristics, affects your instinctive choice of interaction style. The next section provides information that should prove helpful in honing your personal approach to, or view of, conflict and negotiation generally.

SOCIOLOGICAL SCHOOLS OF THOUGHT ON CONFLICT

There are three widely recognized schools of thought on conflict. The **traditional view** is that conflict is bad and should be avoided. This general approach to conflict fosters both avoidance and competitive behavior in interaction. This is the view that many people learn unconsciously, and it is a view that causes anxiety about negotiation and fosters avoidant negotiating styles. Such unconscious negative learning is predominant in Western cultures and is related to cultural norms and values. During our early years, we may be taught behaviors that perpetuate the traditional view. Admonitions that may sound familiar and teach us that conflict is bad and should be avoided include phrases such as: "If you can't say anything nice, don't say anything at all"; "Don't start a fight"; "Be nice—just get along."

The **human relations school of thought,** the second of the three, views conflict as natural and sometimes functional and other times dysfunctional. If the words you used in the exercises earlier in this chapter were neutral to positive, you may fit into the human relations view. According to this view, conflict *can* be a mechanism through which views and opinions are made known and through which an opportunity for creativity and persuasion is born. Conflict can also increase communication and integration. This general approach to conflict encourages maintaining an open mind toward conflict. If you are able to begin to focus on the more positive aspects of conflict, you will expand and improve your negotiating strategies.

The third school of thought, the **interactionist view,** holds that conflict is inevitable *and* that maintaining and managing a certain degree of it can actually be helpful. This general approach to conflict is to embrace it. This school of thought views conflict as a positive force except when it is misdiagnosed, improperly avoided, or mismanaged. Some examples of positive effects from conflict include multiple views, diversity in all respects, cohesion, meeting deadlines, and creativity. Even though this is a positive view of conflict and one that, if adopted, will aid in developing effective negotiation strategies, it is important to recognize that there are two keys. One key is correct diagnosis. The other is the appropriate strategy and action.

If your responses in the exercises earlier in this chapter were mostly positive, you may already hold an interactionist view of conflict. Such a view will assist you in effective negotiation strategies.

CONSTRUCTIVE AND DESTRUCTIVE CONFLICT

Conflict may be constructive or destructive, and conflict approach may be constructive or destructive. A general negative, avoidant, or competitive approach or attitude is often destructive. As stated earlier, often we learn unconsciously to hold a destructive view of conflict through our early interactions. Destructive patterns that we develop result in missed opportunities, frustration of goals, and other personal negative repercussions.[2] In organizational contexts, further negative repercussions may include lower productivity, lower morale, increased destructive political behavior, reduced cohesion, absenteeism, and turnover.[3]

One example of a destructive conflict would be that of two departments within the same organization that are unable to work together. Suppose that the cost accounting department is hostile toward the production department, and vice versa. Such a situation may arise from disagreements between the two department heads. The disagreement may stem from a personal dislike, a misunderstanding, a prior business interaction, or from a number of other potential sources. It is typical for sentiments of the head to filter through the personnel in the department. Chain reactions and patterns often develop. The negative, or destructive, repercussions may range from late and inaccurate reporting to intentional sabotage and gamesmanship.

Another example of a destructive conflict is one that arises from zero-sum reward systems. When there is a fixed amount to be divided based upon some person's or persons' perspective of deservedness, employees are placed into a competition. In such a context, many destructive behaviors may emerge.

An example of a constructive conflict would be an ethics committee composed of individuals from varying areas of expertise and

[2] See Dunn and Tucker (1993); Jaycox and Repetti (1993); Jones (1992); McGonagle, Kessler, and Gotlib (1993); and Young-Eisendrath (1993).
[3] See Hathaway (1995); Kolb and Putnam (1992); and Yorbrough and Wilmot (1995). Political behavior is that which occurs outside of formal or accepted boundaries. While some political behavior may not produce harm, illegitimate and destructive political behavior includes protests, sabotage, and harmful coalitions.

constituencies, such as one member representing community interests and one member representing shareholder interests. Differences of perspective and values create conflict. This type of conflict, unless mismanaged, produces valuable additional information as well as multiple minds for analyses. It is the type of conflict that produces well-thought-out decisions with knowledge of impact.

Another constructive conflict would be a contest among employees for valuable suggestions. Although there would be competition for generating the best ideas, the competition is directed toward the common goal of organizational effectiveness.

CONFLICT, CHAOS, AND COMPLEXITY THEORIES

Key sociological conflict theorists emphasize that conflict is both inevitable and necessary for the continued existence of a social group. Social groups exist in all aspects of life and may be any size of two individuals or more. The use of conflict theory here is for understanding and managing the constructive, positive effects of conflict, as well as for understanding, avoiding, and/or resolving destructive conflict.

According to conflict theory, conflict serves a communication function that can aid in consensus and integration. Conflict theories also focus on power and domination in social structures. Conflict unconfronted may lead to partial or complete disintegration or undesirable change through subversive acts or open demonstration of hostilities. Signs and behaviors exemplified in a negative, destructive spiral include increasingly critical language, defensive language, diverting communication to third parties, unhealthy coalitions through biased or false communications to third parties, and openly aggressive or hostile behavior—even violence.

Chaos and complexity theories inform us that behavior may develop into a system or patterns. The system may have an intended and visible structure that may be competitive, avoidant, or collaborative. A system may also, in effect, have an invisible order. A system—even a dyad, or two individuals—will come to a functioning level, whether or not such level is optimal or desired. You have seen an exemplification of this if you have ever observed or known a relationship marked by chronic bickering or fighting. Feedback can produce growth or chaos. In complexity theory, feedback is referred to as a recursive loop. The lesson here from chaos and complexity theories is to think long term in our analysis of conflict. Change is predictable given a long-term view and adequate understanding of conflict. The system drives behavior, and key interrelationships influence behavior over time. Intervention with a short-term view may produce worse problems than those that were addressed.

A SYSTEMS APPROACH TO CONFLICT DIAGNOSIS

The science and study of parts, elements, relationships, rules, and processes inherent in models or systems have produced a variety of systems theories. Various systems theories have been applied to understanding social systems. Applied here is a combination of communication systems theory, conflict theory, critical theory, chaos theory, and symbolic interactionism.[4] The underlying theme of communication systems theories, while less precise than other models, is relational and probabilistic. While it is not necessary to master the field of **systems theory,** you will increase your effectiveness by developing a **systems approach** and perspective to conflict diagnosis and negotiation strategizing. First we review certain principles derived from systems theory. Then we apply those principles to conflict diagnosis. Later in this book, we address the dynamics of personal conflict approach and formal system structure.

Structural functionalism and general systems theory both assume self-correcting phenomena. A social system automatically responds to disruption in ways that tend to maintain the stability of the system, or the status quo. A system can create and sustain conflict. Systems and relationships are held together by consensus and conflict.

Communication systems theories (and most others) hold that systems are open and that, in fact, a closed system will ultimately cease to exist. Systems are comprised of subsystems or subparts, and there is a dynamic interaction between and among the parts as well as with external factors.

For our purposes here, systems *thinking* is most important. Systems thinking may be described as a theoretical perspective that recognizes parts, subsystems, interrelationships, and interdependencies while maintaining a holistic approach in examining and understanding. Systems thinking is divergent thinking—with no boundaries—as opposed to convergent thinking toward a single problem or answer. Individuals with an intuitive preference and those who favor a divergent learning style as discussed in chapter 2 will find systems thinking rather natural. On the other hand, convergent learners will likely resist a systems approach.

[4] The interested reader is referred to Checkland (1981); Coser (1977); Lemert (1993); Ritzer (1992); and Senge (1990) for further study.

A systems theory approach includes an analysis of cause-and-effect relationships but does not assume that the whole is equal to the sum of its parts. A systems theory approach also includes the element of feedback analysis. It also includes analysis of the system itself—ways in which structure, roles, and rules create or sustain conflict. As applied to conflict and negotiation, our thinking should focus on constructive change.

In diagnosing or assessing conflict, utilize the foregoing perspective and principles and begin by tracking backward. Determination of how the system is creating or sustaining conflict requires identification and analysis of chain reactions and interactions. Cooperation is necessary to sustain conflict. These elements may be found by observation and communication. Seek to find actions, reactions, and interactions. Seek to discover impressions and misperceptions. Assess what is perpetuating the conflict. Identify system rules that are adding to or sustaining the conflict. Identify who and what benefits from the conflict. Determine what is attained by the conflict that might be attained in an alternative, constructive manner. Look for patterns, communication gaps, and cause-and-effect relationships.

Identification of individual roles and functions served, both formal and informal, is necessary in diagnosis. Identify subsystem roles, functions, and relationships. One approach useful in identifying roles and functions is to draw a **sociogram.**[5] The analysis may be done with or without a diagram. Key sociogram terms follow.

Social network: a group of individuals linked in interaction

Cluster: subgroups of the social network

Prescribed clusters: formal groups defined by the greater system

Emergent clusters: informal groups not formally recognized by the system

Isolate: an individual not connected to any social network

Bridge: an individual who links clusters by being a member of each

Liaison: an individual who interacts with two or more clusters but is *not* a member

Star: individuals with many links in the system

Clique: an informal, relatively permanent subgroup

Coalition: a temporary subgroup

---

[5] Jacob Moreno created the technique of sociometry for studying group interactions (Moreno 1947).

CONFLICT DIAGNOSIS EXAMPLE

We can use the interdepartmental hostility between production and accounting mentioned earlier in this chapter as an example of destructive conflict to illustrate the diagnosis process. A partial organization chart is depicted in Exhibit 3-1 for use in creating a sociogram.

First we should consider what is likely to happen if the chief operating officer (COO) approaches the conflict by issuing an edict of compliance or, worse, by taking one side or the other. Even without further knowledge of the situation, we know that at least one of the parties will be unhappy with such action. Such a move is likely to generate more conflict and polarize the parties further.

EXHIBIT 3-1
Organization Chart

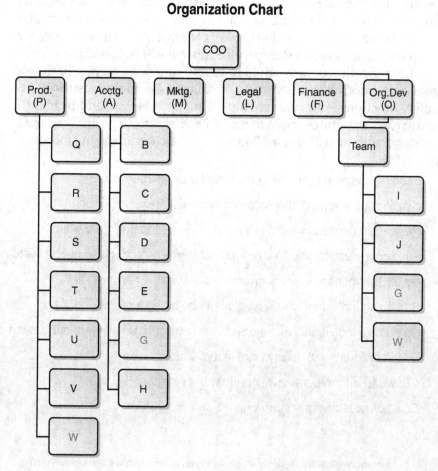

If nothing is done, the system is likely to continue to sustain the conflict. The conflict is not likely to go away by itself. The COO will want to diagnose the conflict and the system prior to any negotiation. Is it necessary for either P or A, the parties in conflict, to diagnose the conflict prior to addressing the conflict? If they are smart, it is! Unless information is gathered, it is not possible to be sure that the right problem is addressed; nor is it likely that a right solution will be offered. If one of them were to approach the other with an open-ended question to state the problem, the reciprocal question back not only would be fair but also should be expected.

Through observation and inquiry, we may uncover causes for the conflict. The original cause is not as important as acute causes reflected in chain reactions and patterns. We should look for positive and negative effects and attributes of the system that affect the conflict. We want to resolve the conflict and eliminate the next occurrence.

A sociogram of the relationships is presented in Exhibit 3-2. The sociogram in Exhibit 3-2 shows the entire organization as a social network. Production and accounting are also social networks. The production department, the accounting department, and each of the other departments in the organization are prescribed clusters. The organizational development team is both a prescribed cluster and a coalition. Both G and W are bridges. The chief operating officer is the only star in our abbreviated example, for the sake of keeping our example simple. Through interviews and observations, we find that S, T, and B are close social friends who like each other and also would enjoy working together. They constitute a clique and an emergent cluster, and they provide informal links between the departments in conflict. Thus, they are liaisons. Individuals G, W, S, T, and B are key sources of information for our diagnosis. It appears that they may have interests in resolving the conflict as well.

The personnel in each of the two departments in conflict also constitute emergent clusters. They have come to consensus about the interdepartmental conflict and function outside of their formal role to sustain it. In our hypothetical example, the culture of the organization is competitive, with little interpersonal trust. Those aspects of the system are also perpetuating the conflict behavior. The culture is conducive to competing or avoiding.

The individuals in the conflict are likely gaining personal satisfaction in the form of revenge on the other group. They are enjoying team spirit in the nature of a contest. Each department's consent to the conflict sustains the conflict. System stability is

Exhibit 3-2

A Sociogram of all Sample Organization Personnel

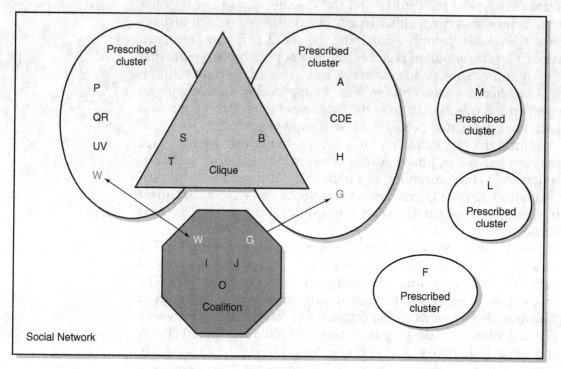

Code: Rectangle = Social network
         Circle   = Prescribed cluster
         Triangle = Clique
         Octagon = Coalition
Key roles: Liaisons   = S, T, and B
         Bridges   = W and G

maintained in the status quo. In this case, however, it is not the optimal functioning level for the system. Although minimal operational requirements may be met, overall organizational performance is compromised. The organization, of course, is losing. Due to lack of cooperation, useful information is not being shared between the groups. There are also likely to be detrimental effects on the organizational development team, due to the membership of G and W—members of opposing sides of our conflict.

Even though there is some integration in each department from the team spirit produced by the conflict, individuals are likely weary and frustrated in their work. In our hypothetical example, we find no constructive effects from the conflict. If there were constructive effects, we would use a strategy to manage a portion of the conflict toward maintaining those constructive ends.

The conflict presents itself as personal. That is, A says that P is impossible and is not a team player. P says that A does not do her job and is extremely unpleasant to be around. We learn, however, that the more acute causes are faulty perceptions and lack of knowledge. P did not receive the updated cost standards until a week into the last three production periods. He believes that A is purposely trying to cause P to fail. The competitive culture feeds that perception. We also learn that P withheld vital information from A that caused A's cost report to be embarrassingly incorrect last month. P's retaliatory chain reaction is an example of a negative pattern development.

Before considering our diagnosis complete we would also look for interactions with marketing (M), legal (L), and finance (F). We would look for coalitions related to the conflict that might exist outside of the production and marketing departments. Further, we would investigate external interactions affecting the conflict and the organization.

Last, we gather enough information to open communication between the parties to persuade them that the original late reports from A were due solely to lack of staff. Key members of A's staff were detailed to a special task force. A prior systemic analysis would have disclosed this pending conflict in advance. The system—and probably the COO—helped to create and sustain the conflict by avoiding recognition of the true conflict—dual tasking with inadequate staff.

SYSTEMS THINKING IN SIMPLE AND COMPLEX CONTEXTS

To further illustrate systems theory, we may apply systems thinking to the conflict inherent in asking for a raise. We first ask whether there is a conflict. Employee, boss, other employees, and the organization are interdependent, and there is at least the perception that granting a raise is incompatible with maintaining a low-expense budget. A holistic approach will assist in preparing for the negotiation.

We should gather information that will help us analyze the relative equity of receiving or not receiving the raise. Using a holistic approach, we recognize that a raise may tend to disrupt the system and that the system will exert pressure to maintain the status quo. The formal system may include specific rules regarding the timing and amount of raises. The formal system may also include performance evaluation measures based upon expenditure or profit levels. Our boss's compensation may be tied to such a system.

We recognize that the compensation of others and the general compensation policies are interrelated and interdependent with our compensation. We may also recognize that our obtaining a raise may cause others to ask for raises. We should also recognize that our boss will search for cause and effect. We must identify the cause for our request—other than that we simply would like more money to spend! Perhaps we have taken on additional responsibilities. Perhaps the market price for our services has increased substantially since the time of our original employment. Perhaps others in relevant jobs equivalent to the value of ours receive more pay than we do.

Our justification may also relate to the potential effect of having our raise request denied. We may quit, because denial is unfair. If denied, we may move to another employer at the pay rate we are requesting. If we quit, the key project on which our boss's compensation depends may fail.

As a result of systems thinking, we are able to gather information necessary to evaluate our options and formulate our strategy. The approach is useful in any context, from the most simple to the most complex. Since a systems approach requires looking at parts of the system or problem, it actually reduces apparent complexity. It facilitates the discovery of the actual problem needing attention. Very often, conflict resolution efforts fail because the wrong problem is attacked.

MANAGING, RESOLVING, AND AVOIDING CONFLICT THROUGH NEGOTIATION

KEY POINT
Strategies for addressing conflict include managing, resolving, and avoiding.

Managing is using the conflict for constructive purposes. Managing conflict constructively may be approached in a compromising or a collaborative style, but it must entail a positive attitude or view. Resolving is getting rid of the conflict. Resolution may be approached in three styles of interaction—competing, compromising, and collaborating. Avoiding is doing nothing. Even under the interactionist view, some conflict is best avoided. Styles are addressed further elsewhere in this book; here we focus on conflict strategies.

Maintaining and managing conflict—or even creating conflict—are appropriate when you want to create constructive results such as increased creativity, more diversity, higher productivity, or less groupthink. As already stated, managing conflict is using it for constructive purposes. Groupthink is the name for the phenomenon wherein individuals become so concerned for the feelings of members that differences of opinion are not voiced. Those concepts are addressed elsewhere in this book.

Resolving conflict is the best course of action when behaviors are destructive, the conflict is destructive, or unwanted results stem from the conflict. If you have a conflict with someone with whom you must interact every day and every day you experience a stomachache when confronted with this person, the conflict must be resolved. If a conflict between purchasing and accounting has resulted in a failure to exchange information necessary for accurate reporting, the conflict must be resolved. Resolution will enable the system to function effectively.

Avoidance, at least on a temporary basis, may very well be the best choice when emotions are high, when tempers are too hot, when you are unsure of the appropriate action, or when the substantive issue is minor. Avoidance may also be the most effective strategy when the conflict is constructive and there are no destructive consequences flowing from it. For example, if two work groups have conflict between them similar to team spirit that causes them to compete with each other in productivity and the conflict does not rise to the level that impedes necessary communication, then the conflict is constructive. In such a case, if it is not broken, do not fix it!

Avoiding resolution of destructive interpersonal conflict often precipitates a negative spiral of increasing negativity and destruction. It gets worse! However, avoidance may be the best choice when, based upon your complete assessment and diagnosis, the effects of any action you may take are likely to produce results no better than, or harm greater than, currently exists.

In selecting the best overall goal and strategy, it is necessary to focus on interdependence rather than power over others, mutual empathy and communication, and potential constructive effects. Sometimes, even when avoidance is the appropriate external strategy, you may need to manage or resolve the conflict internally. When there is, in fact, no interdependence, the conflict is likely to be solely internal to one party. One party may wish things were different but may be faced with choosing avoidance, management, or resolution to deal with the internal conflict. A negative internal spiral may result when one-sided destructive conflict is avoided. For example, if you are on the losing side of a competitive interaction, you are left to resolve internal conflict. If you carry resentment or harbor anger and discomfort, you invite a personal negative spiral.

In resolving conflict, you have three potential goals: (1) try to change the other person; (2) try to change the situation; or (3) try to change yourself. Changing the other person is unlikely to work! Your focus should not be on the other person but on the other person's opinions and behaviors. You may develop your skills in understanding and communicating with the other person. Changing the situation, however, includes changing the perceptions, opinions, and behavior of the other. Changing yourself is to change your assessment, perception, and opinions and to accept the outcome.

Thus, with goal 1 being unrealistic, we are left with using negotiation and persuasion to accomplish goals 2 and 3. Developing an effective strategy requires a correct diagnosis of the nature, source, and effects of the conflict; consideration of the others involved; identification of your goals; knowledge of self; an appropriate style; understanding of perception and power; and the development of your personal techniques. When choices 1 and 2 are inappropriate or impossible, you are left with the third alternative, which may require that you alter your perception and understanding in accepting that not everything is negotiable.

COMPLETING YOUR CONFLICT APPROACH ASSESSMENT AND PLAN

You are urged to reflect on the attitudes and behaviors of your immediate family members during your childhood and now. Using

EXHIBIT 3-3
Personal Summary of Conflict Approach Assessment and Plan

My attitude toward conflict is

Mostly positive _____   More negative than positive_____

Fairly to very negative _____

I plan to work toward having a more open and positive attitude toward conflict:

Yes _____   No _____

The conflict attitude of my immediate family during my childhood was

Mostly positive _____   More negative than positive _____

Fairly to very negative _____

The conflict strategy used most often in my immediate family during my childhood was

Avoidance _____   Management _____   Resolution _____

The conflict strategy used most often by the organizations with which I have been involved is/was

Avoidance _____   Management _____   Resolution _____

I regularly use systems thinking when diagnosing and analyzing conflict:

Yes _____   No _____

I plan to work toward using a systems approach in diagnosing and analyzing conflict:

Yes _____   No _____

those reflections along with the results of the exercises done at the beginning of this chapter and your learning from this chapter, complete the personal summary of conflict approach assessment and plan presented in Exhibit 3-3.

PRACTICE

Three brief problems are presented here for your practice in assessing conflict and the choice of conflict strategy. Following these problems, you will have an opportunity to tackle a substantial conflict diagnosis exercise presented in Case 3.1 at the end of the chapter.

Problem 1

Two work associates consistently differ in their approach and recommendations regarding systems utilized in the department and projects undertaken in the department.

Is this conflict constructive or destructive?

What would you do to discover destructive and constructive elements and effects?

Which strategy would you use—avoidance, management, or resolution?

> **Tips:** Are they respectful and courteous in their disagreements? Does the conflict add information and enrich decisions? The destructive parts should be resolved. The constructive parts should be managed.

Problem 2

You have a dispute with a contractor. He refuses to take an action that he says is not required by the contract.

Is this constructive or destructive conflict?

What strategy will you use? Why?

> **Tip:** If you avoid, the conflict will get worse. There appears to be no constructive portion to manage here. This conflict must be resolved.

Problem 3

You believe that your boss insulted you and placed you in a bad light in the eyes of your peers. You are livid.

Is this constructive or destructive conflict?

Which strategy will be most effective? Why?

Tip: You are probably best advised to avoid temporarily. Once you regain self-control, this conflict begs for resolution.

Performance Checklist

✓ Conflict is inevitable and pervasive in all aspects of life. Conflict is both constructive and destructive. Approaches to conflict may be constructive and destructive. The existence of conflict is what precipitates efforts to negotiate and persuade.

✓ Most individuals have preexisting attitudes toward conflict that are either positive or negative and, therefore, constructive or destructive, respectively. One's attitude or approach affects choice of strategy.

✓ Conflict, chaos, and complexity theories assist in understanding conflict. Systems thinking is helpful for diagnosing conflict and in developing effective conflict strategies. It entails divergent thinking, open communication, and a search for interdependencies and interrelationships.

✓ Strategies for dealing with conflict include avoidance, management, and resolution. Goals of conflict resolution may be to change others, to change the situation, or to change yourself. Only the latter two are realistic but include changing the perceptions and opinions of others. Destructive internal conflicts require internal resolution. Interpersonal conflict is sometimes best avoided either temporarily or permanently. Constructive interpersonal conflict should be managed. Destructive interpersonal conflict should be resolved. A form is included at the end of this chapter (Exhibit 3-3) to summarize your conflict approach assessments. References to supplemental reading on the subject of conflict are contained in footnote 1 to this chapter.

Key Terms, Phrases, and Concepts

Incompatibility

Perceived Interdependence

Aversive Drivelike State

Attitude/View

Approach/Style

Traditional View

Human Relations School of Thought

Interactionist View

Constructive and Destructive Conflict

Conflict, Chaos, and Complexity Theories

Systems Theory/Systems Approach

Sociogram

Review Questions

Mark each of questions 1 through 5 as True (T) or False (F) and answer questions 6 through 10.

T F 1. Systems thinking recognizes subsystems, interrelationships, and interdependence while maintaining a holistic approach.

T F 2. Systems thinking is divergent thinking.

T F 3. Divergent thinking entails multiple perspectives and might be viewed as multidirectional.

T F 4. Convergent thinking is focused on finding a single or best view or answer.

T F 5. Creativity is associated with divergent thinking and not with convergent thinking.

   6. Develop a working definition of *conflict* in your own words.

   7. Describe the approach one should take in diagnosing conflict. How does your approach incorporate systems thinking?

   8. Identify two situations in which avoiding may be an appropriate or effective conflict strategy.

   9. Describe situations in which conflict may be best managed through compromise or collaboration.

   10. Identify one case or situation in which conflict may best be resolved through competition.

Case 3.1

American Dream Holdings, Ltd. (ADHL), is the 100 percent owner of eighty-eight subsidiary corporations, some of which operate in virtually every state of the United States and many of which operate in a limited number of states. One of the subsidiary corporations, EFC Corp., is the general partner of two thousand limited partnerships with operations scattered around the world. EFC Corp. is the flagship and largest of ADHL's subsidiary companies. ADHL also has 20 to 50 percent ownership interests in other business operations. ADHL is owned by two individuals: one, Mr. Major, with 80 percent, and the other, Mr. Minor, with 20 percent. The individual owners operate additional businesses not under the ADHL umbrella. Such additional businesses are considered affiliates. ADHL provides legal, financial, and administrative services including payroll and human resource management to all of its subsidiaries as well as to many affiliates. ADHL collects a monthly fee for such services. The fee is based on estimated needs for the services and is due regardless of the number of hours actually spent on a particular company's matters. ADHL does not assess or collect supplemental fees for work done in excess of the estimate. The group of eighty-eight subsidiaries and ADHL employ two thousand individual employees. All employees participate in the year-end bonus plan that is based upon group net profit attainment. The organizational structure including departmental organization is dictated by ADHL executives. The chief operating officer of ADHL, Ms. Iwon, was initially selected and hired by the 80 percent owner to be EFC Corp.'s senior vice president. EFC Corp.'s chief operating officer, Mr. Toolate, was selected and hired by the 20 percent owner approximately two months after Ms. Iwon was hired. Approximately one year after Mr. Toolate was hired, Ms. Iwon orchestrated a reorganization that included her being promoted to the parent holding company position. EFC Corp. is perpetually three months behind in paying fees to ADHL. EFC Corp. is recalcitrant in distributing financial reports to ADHL.

Case Discussion Questions

1. Using a systems approach, identify the system or systems and their subsystems as well as the various relationships and interdependencies you see. You may utilize a drawing such as a sociogram if you like.

2. Using a systems approach, identify the various conflicts in the case including describing *how* each is a conflict. Be sure to note how each conflict you identify meets the definition of a conflict.

3. Continue your diagnosis and assessment by analyzing the function served by or the effect of each conflict in the case; assessing whether the system structure is competitive, avoidant, or collaborative; and determining your strategy and/or strategies.

Chapter 4

Negotiation Style

"There are two
statements about
human beings that
are true. That all
human beings are
alike and that all
are different."

Mark Van Doren

PERFORMANCE COMPETENCIES FOR THIS CHAPTER

- To learn the four major negotiation styles
- To learn how personality affects negotiation style
- To assess your natural and habitual negotiation styles
- To learn how to choose the appropriate style
- To identify steps toward developing effective negotiation styles

Your general view of or attitude toward conflict affects your approach to negotiation. *Style* is the term used to describe your approach to a *particular* negotiation. That style is affected by your general approach to conflict as well as certain personality characteristics. Within styles of negotiation we see temperaments, which further refine styles in terms of more specific aspects of interaction. This chapter is devoted to negotiation styles, and the next chapter addresses negotiation temperaments.

The first section of this chapter contains four exercises to aid in assessing your negotiation style. Following those exercises, negotiation styles are discussed along with information for analyzing your evaluation results. The balance of the chapter addresses matters of choosing and developing effective negotiation styles.

ASSESS YOUR NATURAL AND HABITUAL NEGOTIATION STYLES

Exercise 4.1

Free Money Exercise

SITUATION 1

Suppose that you and a friend are walking together. A stranger approaches you and offers to give the two of you one hundred thousand dollars. There are no strings attached. The only requirement, however, is that you have five minutes to decide how the two of you will share the money. If you cannot agree within five minutes, no money will change hands.

What is your impulse in response to situation 1? What is your concept of fairness? Does fairness enter into your thoughts at all? Do you offer to split the money equally?

What do you do if your friend objects to sharing the money equally? What if your friend says that she is in greater need of money and should, therefore, receive 75 to 80 percent, or all of the money? What if your friend is in dire need of that amount of money to pay a debt or to pay for urgent medical surgery? What if you are in dire need of the money?

Do your thoughts of fairness change in response to changed facts? Do you begrudgingly take whatever you can get? Do you adopt an even-split-or-nothing attitude?

Make a note of your approach and performance:

_____

_____

_____

_____

SITUATION 2

Amend the scenario slightly. Suppose a stranger approaches you individually and says that he has just received a sum of money. The stranger further tells you that he must give you a portion of the money in order to keep any of it. The stranger refuses to tell you the total amount of money.

What is your first impulse?

In situation 2, do you immediately focus on the amount of money the stranger may be keeping, or is your first reaction to be happy with whatever amount you receive—even one dollar?

Make a note here of your approach and performance:

_____

_____

_____

_____

We will revisit your responses later in this chapter. First, it will be useful to complete the questionnaire in Exercise 4.2. Assessing your natural negotiation style is a necessary step in developing effective, personalized negotiation strategies. Following the assessment, you will have the opportunity to consider aspects of your personality that impact your negotiation style.

Exercise 4.2

Negotiation Style Assessment Exercise

Complete the assessment instrument in Exhibit 4-1. Then proceed through the chapter. Analysis of the results will be discussed later in the chapter.

EXHIBIT 4-1

Negotiation Style Assessment Instrument

You may use the following twenty-eight statements to assess your current negotiation style. You should undertake the assessment by first entering your responses in column A for your general assessment. Next, and prior to calculating any scores, cover your prior assessment answers and undertake the assessment four additional times, each time with a particular person in mind from different aspects of your life as reflected in the definitions for columns B, C, D, and E. Instructions for scoring and analyzing your results are provided at the end of the assessment exercise.

Use the scale of 1 to 5 that follows in recording your responses.

1 = never; 2 = seldom; 3 = occasionally; 4 = very frequently; 5 = always.

Column definitions: A: General assessment responding to your overall behavior
B: A professional or business associate
C: A social friend
D: A family member
E: A new acquaintance

Assessment Statements   E D C B A

1. Making people happy is a paramount goal in my interactions.

2. When my ideas differ from others' ideas, I argue for acceptance of mine.

3. When the other person says something to which I do not agree, I say "Maybe you are right" or "I don't know."

4. I am not reluctant to share information and expertise with others.

5. When I have the power to decide, I exercise my options without extended discussion.

6. When someone disagrees with me, I change the subject or say "Whatever" or "Okay."

7. It is important for me to know what others value and need.

8. If someone tells me he or she needs something from me, I rearrange things to get it to him or her.

9. If I want to pay $100 and the other wants to receive $200, my resolution is to offer to pay $150.

10. I get uncomfortable when people get upset or disagree with me.

11. I think that information is power.

12. When someone proposes something different than what I have in mind, I find out more about that person's position.

13. When someone calls when I am in the middle of a project, I stop what I am doing and tend to his or her needs.

14. I think that most disagreements are contests over who is correct.

Exhibit 4-1 continued

Assessment Statements

E D C B A

15. When someone gets upset with me for something I said, I change my statement to make him or her feel better.

16. I find ways to make the other person happy while I still get my way.

17. I keep things to myself that I think will upset someone.

18. I will go to a restaurant to make the other person happy, even if I don't like the food there.

19. I enjoy letting others know the power I have.

20. When someone disagrees with me, I try to find out his or her reasoning.

21. I think it is advantageous for me when someone is afraid of me.

22. I try to structure my statements with the goal of winning the argument.

23. Giving others what they want is compatible with getting what I want.

24. I do things I don't want to do in order to keep things peaceful.

25. I feel bad when I disappoint the other person.

26. I think that both parties should give some when they disagree.

27. When I propose an idea to which the other person disagrees, I don't press the matter.

28. I think that differences of opinion or differences in what people want provide opportunities that help me.

Negotiation Style Assessment Instrument Scoring

Record your scores by question number and total as indicated in the following chart.

General Assessment from Column A

#3 ___ + #6 ___ + #10 ___ + #15 ___ + #17 ___ + #24 ___ + #27 ___ = Style A total ___

#2 ___ + #5 ___ + #11 ___ + #14 ___ + #19 ___ + #21 ___ + #22 ___ = Style C total ___

#1 ___ + #8 ___ + #9 ___ + #13 ___ + #18 ___ + #25 ___ + #26 ___ = Style AC total ___

#4 ___ + #7 ___ + #12 ___ + #16 ___ + #20 ___ + #23 ___ + #28 ___ = Style CC total ___

Assessment for Person B, Column B

#3 ___ + #6 ___ + #10 ___ + #15 ___ + #17 ___ + #24 ___ + #27 ___ = Style A total ___

#2 ___ + #5 ___ + #11 ___ + #14 ___ + #19 ___ + #21 ___ + #22 ___ = Style C total ___

#1 ___ + #8 ___ + #9 ___ + #13 ___ + #18 ___ + #25 ___ + #26 ___ = Style AC total ___

#4 ___ + #7 ___ + #12 ___ + #16 ___ + #20 ___ + #23 ___ + #28 ___ = Style CC total ___

Assessment for Person C, Column C

#3 ___ + #6 ___ + #10 ___ + #15 ___ + #17 ___ + #24 ___ + #27 ___ = Style A total ___

#2 ___ + #5 ___ + #11 ___ + #14 ___ + #19 ___ + #21 ___ + #22 ___ = Style C total ___

#1 ___ + #8 ___ + #9 ___ + #13 ___ + #18 ___ + #25 ___ + #26 ___ = Style AC total ___

#4 ___ + #7 ___ + #12 ___ + #16 ___ + #20 ___ + #23 ___ + #28 ___ = Style CC total ___

Assessment for Person D, Column D

#3 ___ + #6 ___ + #10 ___ + #15 ___ + #17 ___ + #24 ___ + #27 ___ = Style A total ___

#2 ___ + #5 ___ + #11 ___ + #14 ___ + #19 ___ + #21 ___ + #22 ___ = Style C total ___

#1 ___ + #8 ___ + #9 ___ + #13 ___ + #18 ___ + #25 ___ + #26 ___ = Style AC total ___

#4 ___ + #7 ___ + #12 ___ + #16 ___ + #20 ___ + #23 ___ + #28 ___ = Style CC total ___

Assessment for Person E, Column E

#3 ___ + #6 ___ + #10 ___ + #15 ___ + #17 ___ + #24 ___ + #27 ___ = Style A total ___

#2 ___ + #5 ___ + #11 ___ + #14 ___ + #19 ___ + #21 ___ + #22 ___ = Style C total ___

#1 ___ + #8 ___ + #9 ___ + #13 ___ + #18 ___ + #25 ___ + #26 ___ = Style AC total ___

Adapted in part from M. A. Rahim and N. R. Mager, "Confirmatory Factor Analyses of the Styles of Handling Interpersonal Conflict: First-Order Factor Model and Its Invariance across Groups," *Journal of Applied Psychology* 80, no. 1 (1995): 122–32.

Exercise 4.3

A Game

This game will provide further information with which to assess your natural tendencies and habits in connection with negotiation style. The game is played with a group of people. A minimum group size of ten people is preferable. There must be a moderator. The moderator selects as many numbers as there are people playing and secretly assigns values to the numbers. Each player randomly draws a number out of a hat. The relative values of the numbers are not known because the values assigned are not known; that is, no one knows whether he or she holds a high or low number. The theoretical prize is the value of the paper drawn. *But,* in order to win anything, there is one requirement. That requirement is to establish a partnership with *at least* one other player. Any player who fails to establish a partnership is out of the game. No one is permitted to show another the paper drawn. It is permissible to tell another person what was drawn, but there cannot be verification of truth by looking at the paper. Each pair or group of partners is to determine its sharing agreement. Partners may agree that each will collect the amount represented by his or her individual number, or they may agree to share in any other manner. Each partner must decide with whom to form a partnership, whether or not to disclose his or her number, and whether or not to believe disclosures made to him or her.

Make a note of your approach and performance in the game:

_____

_____

_____

_____

ANALYSIS OF GAME OUTCOME

Your approach to this game may provide information about your degree of competitiveness or cooperation in negotiation as well as your tendencies toward being general or specific in negotiation. In addition to your self-assessment, you should ask for your partner's perceptions of your approach.

FOUR MAJOR NEGOTIATION STYLES

In this section, we review the four major styles of negotiation along with how certain aspects of your personality may affect your tendencies toward one or more of them.

AVOIDANCE

In chapter 3, we discussed **avoidance** as a potential goal or strategy in addressing conflict. Avoidance is also a negotiating style. Avoidance is retreating or withdrawing. It is failing to engage. It may be to ignore the existence of a conflict in its entirety. Avoidance may be, however, total or partial. That is, one might seek to negotiate but not be able to bring oneself to address the substance of the conflict toward resolution.

A major deficiency of avoiding is that it causes missed opportunities and missed benefits. With no engagement, there can be no resolution. With avoidance, you avoid getting what you want. The approach ignores a search for common ground and mutually beneficial exchange.

Behavior that exemplifies the avoidance style includes sulking, making sarcastic comments, holding in your true feelings, or refraining from talking about a matter. If your general attitude toward conflict is relatively negative, you may be prone to the avoidance style in negotiation. If in situation 1 of Exercise 4.1, the Free Money Exercise, your impulse was to say nothing and let the other person make the sharing decision, you exhibited avoidance behavior. If your conduct was similar in Exercise 4.3, A Game, in that you found it difficult to initiate partnership discussions or did not express your feelings, you exhibited avoidance behavior.

One aspect of personality that may have some relationship to this negotiation style is locus of control. If you have a relatively high external locus of control, that aspect of personality may present obstacles in confronting conflict. If you believe that you cannot affect outcomes, you are less likely to try. A low level of assertiveness may also trigger avoidance behavior. Assertion is addressed in depth elsewhere in this book.

ADVERSARIAL / COMPETITIVE

The **adversarial** or **competitive** style of negotiation is a win/lose approach. Along with this style usually comes difficulty in refraining

from engaging at every conflict opportunity. Underlying the competitive approach is a perspective that resources are limited—a zero-sum perspective. The competitive style may range from mildly adversarial to extremely aggressive.

A primary deficiency of a competitive approach is that one party loses. It may be you! Furthermore, a focus on winning or being correct is likely to cause one to miss information and possibilities that may, in fact, be self-beneficial.

Behavior that exemplifies the competitive style includes making remarks with no regard for the other's feelings or position, always having a retort, refusing to back down, discussing differences in front of other uninvolved people, belittling the other, using accusatory language and power-over tactics, having no regard for the interests or goals of the other, and manipulation. It is characterized by criticizing, defensiveness, stonewalling, and contempt on both sides. This style is self-centered. If this style continues far enough on the continuum, other behaviors may include trickery and even violence.

A negative attitude toward conflict generally may tend toward either an avoidance style or a competitive style—or both. You may avoid when you think you cannot win, and you may engage in every opportunity for a contest. If in situation 2 of Exercise 4.1, the Free Money Exercise, your goal was to get your share of the money without regard to the needs expressed by your friend, you exhibited a competitive style. If your conduct in Exercise 4.3, A Game, focused on trying to get the most that you could to the exclusion of considering options, you exhibited competitive behavior.

If you assess yourself high on the Type A personality characteristic of competitiveness, you may be prone to the competitive style of negotiation. Other personality characteristics that may influence a tendency toward this style include a high need for personal power, a high need for achievement, and a high level of Machiavellianism. Another flag for your consideration is your assessment on emotional stability. Those with a low level of emotional stability are more likely to lose their temper and lose control generally. A loss of control and a high level of anxiety may make things ripe for adopting a win/lose approach.

ACCOMMODATING/COMPROMISING

The **accommodating** or **compromising** negotiation style is to give up part of what you want at the request of the other. It is a middle-of-the road approach focused on meeting the needs of others without totally giving up one's own needs. It can be closely related to avoidance; that is, giving in without considering other, more creative options is to avoid negotiating further. Compromising is giving in. It is distinctly different than collaborating, which is explained in the next section of this chapter. It is not unwise to prepare a compromise position as a backup, provided that such position is nevertheless better than your nonnegotiated alternatives.

Behavior that exemplifies this style is splitting the difference and agreeing openly while being internally dissatisfied. If your natural style of negotiation tends to be compromising, you may have a relatively neutral view toward conflict generally. If in Exercise 4.1, the Free Money Exercise, your impulse was to share equally or to allow your friend in need to take the greater share, you exhibited the compromising negotiation style. If your conduct was similar to that in Exercise 4.3, A Game, you exhibited avoidance behavior.

Two aspects of personality that may be related to this style are the need for affiliation and an external locus of control. Those with a high need for affiliation are drawn to satisfy the needs of others. A very high external locus of control combined with a high need for affiliation would be consistent with wanting to please and believing that one could not do better anyway.

> "Compromise makes a good umbrella, but a poor roof; it is a temporary expedient, often wise in party politics, almost sure to be unwise in statesmanship."
>
> *Lowell*

COOPERATIVE/COLLABORATIVE

The difference between compromise and **cooperative** or **collaborative** negotiation is that in compromise you are giving up something while in cooperation you are finding a way to get the other person *and* yourself what you *both* want. This type of negotiation is consistent with a win/win approach—seeing the possibility of a second pie or, perhaps, a cake! It is the opposite of a zero-sum approach. This style entails collaborating creatively to meet mutual goals.

Key behaviors that exemplify this approach are listening and expressing your feelings and desires. If your general attitude toward conflict is positive, you are likely to be able to adopt a collaborative style. If in Exercises 4.1 and 4.3 you tried to find mutual satisfaction, you exhibited a collaborative style.

A strong internal locus of control and a feeling preference are personality characteristics that serve this style well, because they are consistent with finding a solution and considering the views of others, respectively. Type B personalities will typically be more comfortable with this style than will Type A personalities. Other personality characteristics helpful in developing this style include high emotional stability and a high need for achievement, provided that they are not combined with a high level of competitiveness. A high need for social power is also naturally consistent with a collaborative style.

DISTRIBUTION VERSUS INTEGRATION

Conflict approaches and negotiation styles may also be understood in the context of distribution and integration. **Distribution** is allocating limited resources or limited benefits. **Integration** is to remove limitations. They may be best understood by examining the underlying perspective of each. A distributive style incorporates an underlying view that needs and goals of the parties are incompatible. An integrative style incorporates an underlying view that needs and goals of the parties are different. Perhaps both parties do not want to share the pie. Perhaps one party prefers cake. The first views the glass as half empty, while the latter views the glass as half full. An integrative style entails open thinking that facilitates finding mutual satisfaction.

Competition and compromising negotiation styles are distributive in nature. Collaborative negotiation is integrative. Integration is more difficult than competing or compromising. Integration requires an open mind and some creativity.

ANALYZING ASSESSMENT RESULTS

In Exercise 4.2, which includes the Negotiation Style Assessment Instrument, the style designations represent the four major styles discussed. The letter A is avoidance; the letter C is competitive; the letters AC designate accommodating/compromising; and the letters CC designate cooperative/collaborative.

Review the scores for A, C, AC, and CC on the assessment instrument relative to each other. If you find that your highest score across all five assessments is consistently one type, that style represents your primary or dominant negotiation style. If your high score varies among the five assessments, the results indicate that you use different styles with different persons or in different areas of your life.

In each case, analyze why you use a particular approach. There may indeed be sound reasons for variations across assessments. Relative values and goals often affect choice of appropriate style.

Prior experiences and behavior modeled by significant others also impact negotiation style tendencies. Evaluate how your family history, your family's approach to conflict, and your work experiences compare with the results of your assessments.

A frequent use of avoidance or compromise may also stem from unassertiveness. In a different way, a competitive style is also unassertive.

Now review your learning thus far and complete the profile form presented in Exhibit 4-2. The form provides a place to summarize your assessments from all of the preceding exercises in this chapter, as well as to record a few related personality factors noted in the previous sections of this chapter.

CHOOSING THE APPROPRIATE STYLE

Often all four styles will be used within one negotiation. In complex matters containing many issues, you may compromise on certain pieces while using collaboration as your primary style to satisfy the primary, or overall, needs and wants of both parties. There may be some issues not important in the overall goal that are too hot to negotiate and that you will, therefore, avoid. There are, however, relatively few situations for which the competitive style would be the best choice. The collaborative style is usually the most effective choice. We use contingency theory to aid in the choice of style in the next section of this chapter.

KEY POINT
There is no single negotiation style that is most appropriate across every negotiation.

Avoiding may be most effective when emotions are high or when the matter in conflict is trivial or of low value relative to the likely cost of engaging the other person. If, for example, your boss has said to you that if you say one more word you will be fired, avoidance may be the appropriate choice! The problem with avoidance is that, by definition, there will be no resolution or agreement.

A competitive style may be appropriate in an emergency, particularly if you have special expertise that will save others from harm. This style may also be appropriate when there is no relationship between the parties and you are aware that the other party is clearly competing. An example would be buying an automobile. Sometimes a competitive style is expected and is the only realistic option.

EXHIBIT 4-2

Profile of Negotiating Style Assessment

In exercise 4.1, the Free Money Exercise, my attitude and/or behavior were

Avoidant ___   Competitive ___   Accommodating/compromising ___   Collaborative ___

In situation 2, my attitude and/or behavior were

Avoidant ___   Competitive ___   Accommodating/compromising ___   Collaborative ___

In exercise 4.3, A Game, my attitude and behavior were

Avoidant ___   Competitive ___   Accommodating/compromising ___   Collaborative ___

My dominant style assessment was

In general:	Avoidant ___	Competitive ___	Accommodating ___	Collaborative ___
In business:	Avoidant ___	Competitive ___	Accommodating ___	Collaborative ___
In social setting:	Avoidant ___	Competitive ___	Accommodating ___	Collaborative ___
In family:	Avoidant ___	Competitive ___	Accommodating ___	Collaborative ___
With a stranger:	Avoidant ___	Competitive ___	Accommodating ___	Collaborative ___

My locus of control is distinctly	External ___ [A] [AC]	Internal ___ [CC]
My need for affiliation is	High ___ [AC]	Moderate or Low ___
My Type A competitiveness is	High ___ [C]	Moderate or Low ___
My need for personal power is	High ___ [C]	Moderate or Low ___
My need for social power is	High ___ [CC]	Moderate or Low ___
My need for achievement is	High ___ [C]	Moderate or Low ___
My emotional stability is	High ___ [CC]	Moderate or Low ___ [C]
My creativity is	High ___ [CC]	Moderate or Low ___
I have a feeling preference.	Yes ___ [CC]	No ___

[A]   May relate to avoidance style
[C]   May relate to compromise style
[AC] May relate to collaborative style
[CC] May relate to competitive style

Accommodating, or compromising, sometimes is the best option presented. If no better option is available and a nonnegotiated option is not better, then compromising is appropriate. This style may also be appropriate when the relationship between the parties is more important than the issues. As noted earlier, it is also sound practice to hold a compromise position as a next-to-best last resort.

There is rarely a case for which collaboration is not the most effective style. The difficulty with collaboration is that it requires the most creativity and the most effort. Furthermore, for some people, it will feel out of character.

Your natural negotiation style is strongly influenced by your view of conflict and your personality. If you see negotiation as conflict, see conflict as negative, and score relatively high on Type A competitiveness, for example, you may engage unwittingly in competitive and avoidant styles. The goal is to understand your tendencies and develop your personal style.

As you completed the assessment instrument presented in Exercise 4.2, you may have found that your style varies from person to person or situation to situation. This may be the result of personality tendencies and habit or conscious choice. We discuss later how to make a conscious, effective choice consistent with your personality and temperament.

CONTINGENCY THEORY

Contingency theory is a term used to refer to a broad base of literature that addresses contextual factors influencing organization structure and management. It is, however, helpful in analyzing negotiation styles and strategies. Just as in organizational management, negotiation entails a myriad of factors—contextual, situational, factual, and interpersonal. The appropriate strategy, style, and tactics are contingent on the mix of those factors.

Also consistent with contingency theory is the notion of anticipating change and adapting to change. Such is the case with negotiation. While it is necessary to plan, it is critical to remain flexible and to understand how to react to unanticipated factors. Flexibility will feel natural to those with a perceiving preference. Those with a judging preference are likely to be more resistant to flexibility. The contingency analysis of negotiation is summarized in the following section.

DEVELOPING EFFECTIVE STYLES

Using the appropriate option requires knowledge and development of self and evaluative thought regarding the particular people and circumstances involved. Two vignettes follow for your practice in evaluating style choice.

PRACTICE

Retrospective Vignette 1

Think of an occasion when someone interacted with you in a competitive manner. Try to reconstruct the sequence of events, conversation, and emotions. Was the style appropriate in the circumstances? What happened? Was any common ground found? Were additional issues discovered? Did you give the person what he or she wanted? Was the style effective in solving a problem? What effect was there on the relationship?

Retrospective Vignette 2

Think of another occasion when you interacted with someone in a competitive manner. Again, try to reconstruct the entire scene. How did it go? Was your style appropriate? Did you get what you wanted? Was another style more appropriate on retrospection?

LEARNING CREATIVITY

It is worth noting again that the collaborative style is most often the best choice, particularly in the long term. Personal characteristics conducive to a collaborate approach include high emotional stability, high need for social power, high internal locus of control, a feeling preference, and creativity. It is possible to develop any behavior characteristic including emotional stability and creativity.

Those with an intuitive preference, as well as assimilators and divergers, may find it easier to tackle building creativity. Among the things you can do to increase your creativity are to work cryptograms or to develop them. You may also build your creativity by challenging your assumptions every day. Look for different meanings in old things and places. As you review your interpersonal interactions and prior negotiations, consider what you might have done differently. Evaluate the effectiveness of your course of action. Be open. Be optimistic.

Dynamic Interaction among Personality, Interests, Goals, Context, and Others

The optimum negotiation strategy will be determined by the dynamic interaction of each party's unique personality, style of interaction, temperament, perception of the other's style and temperament, perception of the issues in conflict, culture, values, needs, goals, powers, time constraints, expertise, and preparation. The first two have been addressed in this and the prior two chapters. The other items are addressed in later chapters. Your unique personality pervades each of these items. Your self-knowledge will aid you in developing alternative styles as well as in using your natural style to its optimum. Creativity will always help you to find a mutually satisfying agreement.

Performance Checklist

✓ The four major negotiation styles are avoiding, competing, accommodating/compromising, and cooperating/collaborating. Competing and compromising are distributive in nature, and collaborating is integrative.

✓ Personality affects an individual's comfort with particular styles. The personal attributes of emotional stability, internal locus of control, feeling preference, and creativity are particularly helpful in collaborative negotiation. An external locus of control may be associated with the avoidance style. High needs for personal power and achievement as well as high Machiavellianism and low emotional stability may be associated with a competitive style. High need for affiliation and external locus of control may be associated with a compromising style.

✓ Most individuals have a natural or habitual predominant style. Your personal assessment done in Exercise 4.2 should demonstrate your predominant style.

✓ Each of the four styles is appropriate at times. The choice depends upon relative interests, goals, values, and personality fit. The collaborative style is usually most effective.

✓ Practicing applying your learning from this chapter is a step toward developing effective negotiation strategies.

Key Terms, Phrases, and Concepts

Avoidance

Adversarial/Competitive

Accommodating/Compromising

Cooperative/Collaborative

Distribution

Integration

Contingency Theory

Review Questions

Mark each of questions 1 through 4 as True (T) or False (F) and answer questions 5 through 10.

T F 1. Avoidance is sometimes the most effective style.

T F 2. An adversarial style is sometimes most appropriate.

T F 3. A competitive style and approach limit solutions.

T F 4. A negative attitude toward conflict is most closely associated with the avoidance and competitive styles.

5. Think about why collaborating is the most difficult.

6. Think about why collaborating is most often the most effective style to use.

7. Think about what steps you may take and what plan you develop to increase your creativity.

8. Why would increasing your creative skill increase your negotiation effectiveness?

9. Identify at least two of your personality characteristics that will assist you in performing effective negotiation.

10. Identify at least two of your personality characteristics that will require your focused attention and/or control in order to increase your negotiation effectiveness.

Case 4.1

You (or your company) desire to purchase a business. Assume that there exists adequate external support for a purchase price value of between two and three times annual earnings.

Case Discussion Questions

1. Which negotiation style would you choose?

2. Why is that style appropriate?

3. What factors and issues can you think of that may facilitate a collaborative style?

Case 4.2

You desire your work team to complete a project within the next two weeks. Doing so will necessitate a great number of extra hours. In the past, all of the individuals involved have expressed dislike for overtime and have gone to great lengths to avoid it.

Case Discussion Questions

1. Which negotiation style would you choose?

2. Why is that style appropriate?

3. What factors and issues can you think of that may indicate that a collaborative style would be effective?

Chapter 5

Key Negotiating Temperaments

"If I knew you and you
knew me,
If both of us could
clearly see,
And with an inner
sight divine
The meaning of your
heart and mine,
I'm sure that we would
differ less,
And clasp our hands in
friendliness,
Our thoughts would
pleasantly agree
If I knew you and you
knew me."

Nixon Waterman

PERFORMANCE COMPETENCIES FOR THIS CHAPTER

- To learn how your personality affects your negotiating temperament
- To learn the four key negotiating temperaments
- To identify behavioral expectations associated with each negotiating temperament
- To assess your unique negotiating temperament

A person's negotiating success depends upon an accurate under-standing and use of his/her own unique personality type and style of interaction as well as an accurate perception and understanding of the other's personality and style. This chapter discusses combi-nations of particular personality characteristics that combine into four major negotiation temperaments. We discuss how personality and temperament differences present challenges in the negotiation process and how to recognize behavior characteristics of the four major temperaments. Tips on communicating with the various tem-peraments are included elsewhere in this book.

CATEGORIZING PERSONALITIES

At first it may seem inconsistent to say that we are each unique while at the same time to say that we can identify personality types. To be certain, each of us is a unique package of traits, characteris-tics, experiences, and perspectives. Further, there are no absolutes in the facets used here. We focus on specific facets of personality that, in combination with each other, can be understood as an indi-vidual's negotiation temperament. The temperaments described here are not to be interpreted as descriptive of an individual's entire personality.

Everyone possesses and exhibits each facet from time to time and to some extent. Preferences may also change with environment, effort, and maturity. People may utilize various traits according to need and circumstances. Caution is advised in making sweeping or immutable generalizations of people. Nonetheless, much complex-ity and diversity can be understood by studying and understand-ing basic interaction temperaments. Those temperaments reflect a core of characteristics that affect perceptions and behavior. Even though no two people are precisely the same, that core regularly presents itself in human interaction.

Whether we like to admit it or not, we categorize people regularly—both strangers and those we know. Expressions such as "slow," "bigmouthed," "uptight," "laid-back," "control freak," to name a few, may sound familiar. Perhaps the most interesting aspect of categorizing people is that our categorization of others is affected by and reflects on who we are. In fact, we are most likely to label those most different from us.

Often, we label people quickly. We also label people based upon accumulated experience with them. We all come to know what to expect from people with whom we often interact, and we conduct ourselves accordingly in an effort to maximize our satisfaction and happiness. In the negotiating arena, we must do the same thing; however, at least in the formal setting or in negotiating with someone we just met, we are not afforded the time to accumulate experience with that person. Rather, at the negotiating table we must quickly recognize and adapt to the personality with whom we must deal. Knowledge of personality and the dimensions of human behavior inherent in temperament provides the power to interact effectively.

"... **Let people be different.**"

David Grayson

Personality typing, or labeling, is not negative. There are no good or bad personality types.[1] Typecasting is a method to celebrate and creatively use differences between people. In fact, typecasting removes negative assumptions and attitudes, replacing them with a constructive understanding, thereby enhancing communication. Thus, it enables one to resist the tendency to view certain behavior of others as intentionally personal or offensive. Increased knowledge and understanding help us to control our own behavior so that we may reach our negotiation goal.

FOUR MAIN ALTERNATIVE PREFERENCES

According to psychological theory—most preeminently Carl Jung, we each possess preferences in four key areas of personality.[2] Those areas describe our personal source of energy—extroversion/ introversion, the way we take in information—sensing/intuiting, the way we process information—thinking/feeling, and the way we structure and interact with the outside world—judging/perceiving. The possible combinations of those four preferences create sixteen personality types.[3] Fortunately, we can condense the task here to understanding how to recognize two preference areas, or four combinations, in others and how to deal with four key negotiating temperaments.

Our personal source of energy is easily kept secret from those who do not know us well. Our way of thinking, likewise, is difficult

---

[1] All types of pathologies and personality disorders are excluded from the discussion here.

[2] Chapter 2 provides explanation of each facet of personality addressed here.

[3] Jung's original theory (1968) described extroversion and introversion so profoundly different from each other as to analyze each of the other preference areas under the umbrellas of extroversion and introversion. Thus, Jung analyzed eighteen personality types.

for others to assess. While extroverts and introverts often experience communication difficulties that are discussed in chapter 6, those two areas of personality are not critical in identifying primary negotiating temperaments of others. However, your level of extroversion or introversion, as well as your preference for thinking or feeling, will help in understanding your *own* behavior. Here we look at the second and fourth preference areas.

The way we take in information and the way we interact with the outside world are evident in key negotiating temperaments. It can become fairly easy to identify another's preference for taking in information. The way we interact with our outside world is the most difficult preference to hide from others. In this chapter we look at the four combinations of sensing/intuiting (S/N) and judging/perceiving (J/P) and how they present themselves in negotiation. You will learn how to identify those preferences and how to improve your negotiating skill with that knowledge.

PERCEIVING OTHERS

Perception is a process of active participation. Individuals select and organize stimuli differently and categorize and interpret differently. We discuss perception and communication more fully in other chapters. Here we briefly touch on differences in selecting stimuli. Sensors prefer precision and detail, while intuitors prefer abstraction and generality. Thus, they see and perceive differently. A sensor would see trees where an intuitor would see a forest.

What is sometimes viewed as an offensive or difficult behavior is merely a reflection of a personality comprised of components opposite to one's own. Sensors and intuitors see different things, and judgers and perceivers approach the world and interact in different ways. Judgers reveal their position and opinions while perceivers do not. Judgers anticipate and expect decisions while perceivers defer decisions. Abstraction and distraction to one are reflection and interrelating to another. While one responds to approaching deadlines (judger), another sees no date or end at all (perceiver). Annoying detail to one (an intuitor) is the tangible substance of importance to another (a sensor). What is justice to one (a thinker) is relative and subjective to another (a feeler).

We tend to expect others to be like us. Our expectations affect our perceptions, and our perceptions affect interpretation and assignment of meaning. Attempts to communicate without recognizing these differences can lead to frustration and even anger. We tend

KEY TERM
Perception
is the selection and organization of stimuli.

to take offense when someone does not act as we expect. Understanding our opposites will change our expectations of others and enhance communication. To be effective in negotiation, you must recognize and relate to people who see the world through lenses different from your own, who gather and process information in a manner different from your own, and whose values and needs are different from your own.

BEHAVIOR EXPECTATIONS

Research has demonstrated that one or two key traits are most determinative of how a person interacts with others. These characteristics of interaction have been referred to as *temperament*.[4]

The single most important trait affecting interpersonal interaction is how a person takes in information. We regularly hear expressions of the communication difficulty presented by conflicting traits. For example, how often have you said, "I don't know where you're coming from"? If two people are not "reading off the same page," how can they have a meaningful discussion or come to agreement? Therefore, it is most helpful to know whether a person is a sensor or an intuitor. The other of the two key traits most relevant to negotiation interaction is how a person relates to the world, or his or her lifestyle orientation—the judger versus perceiver preference.

In negotiation, before agreement we need a meeting of the minds. We must know what each side has communicated. We must ensure that we are working on the same issues, and we must relate our positions and decisions to each other in a way that will be understood. Only then may there be agreement.

The more we know about the other preferences and other aspects of personality, the better will be our ability to be effective. It is noted that the four negotiating temperaments we discuss do not fully describe all human temperaments because the interplay of the other two preference categories and other characteristics have significant effect on an individual's total personality and temperament. Nevertheless, a closer look at the two key preference categories provides a great deal of information for negotiation effectiveness.

---

[4] Other behaviorists and psychologists have analyzed personality traits in terms of temperaments (see, e.g., Keirsey and Bates 1978). The organization and analysis here differ from the general literature on temperaments.

FOUR KEY NEGOTIATING TEMPERAMENTS

The sections that follow present profiles of four negotiating temperaments, how to recognize them, how they are typically perceived, and what behavior to expect from each. If you can develop your knowledge as well as your listening and observation skills adequately to recognize one or two of the key preferences in others, you will be able to interact more effectively in the negotiation process.

HARMONIZER (PACIFIER)

The **harmonizer** is the intuitive-perceiving (N/P) combination. The harmonizer sees the big picture and approaches problems with a broad perspective, organizing information into concepts and theories. Harmonizers have a tendency to discuss multiple issues together or move freely from one to another, because they see the interrelatedness of matters in their search for meaning and a grand scheme.

• Harmonizer (pacifier)

It is nearly impossible to get the harmonizer to focus on details, unless you can appeal to his or her need for harmony or elevate the details to an adequate level of importance in the grand scheme. It is difficult to disagree with the harmonizer due to his or her usually excellent persuasive ability and ability to generate creative alternatives. It is also tough to pressure harmonizers, because they tend to defer decisions and are not pressured by time deadlines. It is usually possible to distract a harmonizer and move to a different issue when something is moving in the wrong direction.

The harmonizer shares perceptions without making or looking for judgment. Miscommunication can occur if these perceptions are considered as decisions. Many harmonizers openly demonstrate their concern for others and may even take criticism personally. Others appear more aloof.

The best way to get along with a harmonizer is to show appreciation for his or her creative concepts and alternatives and to propose an equally broad alternative theory. Harmonizers are probably most easily recognized at the negotiating table by their general, theoretical, and open-ended approach.

The harmonizer may, either when out of control or as an intentional maneuver, become the **pacifier.** Once the pacifier shows up at the negotiating table, there is not likely to be resolution.

N/J

CONTROLLER (BULL)

• Controller
(Bull)

Impatient for decision ✗

The **controller** is the intuitive-judging (N/J) combination. The controller, due to his or her intuitive preference (like the harmonizer), also sees the big picture and approaches problems with a broad perspective, organizing information into concepts and theories. Although as the controller takes in information he or she sees the interrelatedness of matters in a search for meaning, the controller's need for closure causes him or her to remain focused on the topic or task at hand rather than becoming scattered or leaving loose ends.

The controller has an organized plan and is impatient for decision and resolution. The controller is firm, decisive, and deliberate. These negotiators thrive on structure and order, possess stubborn resolve in the *rightness* of their positions, and want things their way.

Even though controlling, these individuals do not seek conflict but seek harmony or, at least, calm. Many of them also have a desire to help others. However, since controllers hold strong opinions, they can become (or appear to be) argumentative.

Miscommunication or disagreements can quickly escalate with a controller. They have a tendency to view things as fixed, right-wrong, and black-white. In communicating with a controller, it is best to allow time for him or her to moan in private as alternatives are introduced. The best way to get along with a controller is to evidence a desire to come to agreement. Controllers are probably most easily recognized at the negotiating table by their sense of the big picture combined with their resolve.

The controller, when out of control, may become the **bull.** Once the bull appears, there is likely to be no resolution.

PRAGMATIST (STREET FIGHTER)

• Pragmatist
(Intimidator)

SJ

The **pragmatist** is the sensing-judging (S/J) combination. The pragmatist sees details, focuses on specifics, and approaches things sequentially. Pragmatists take things literally rather than conceptually. They like facts and figures as well as concrete, tangible results. They are practical, realistic, and bottom-line oriented. One is often able to deduce their conservative financial philosophy.

Pragmatists view themselves as objective. Like the bull, they are organized and impatient for resolution. Pragmatists are also firm, decisive, and deliberate—possessing stubborn resolve in their positions.

Given their difficulty in seeing the big picture, their focus on details, and their determination to be *right*, pragmatists can usually see little reason for accepting alternatives or giving concessions. Disagreements with the pragmatist can quickly escalate, and the pragmatist can become abrasive and argumentative.

Either due to loss of control or as an intentional maneuver, the pragmatist turned **street fighter** views the negotiation as a win/lose proposition. The street fighter wants to win at all cost.

The best way to get along with the pragmatist is to utilize facts and figures and to demonstrate a concern for the bottom line. The best way to deal with the street fighter is to allow him or her time to cool off. Pragmatists are relatively easy to spot by their focus on details combined with stubborn resolve.

ACTION SEEKER (HIGH ROLLER)

• Action Seeker (High Roller)

The **action seeker** is the sensing-perceiving (S/P) combination. The action seeker sees details, looks at specifics, and approaches things sequentially. Action seekers also take things literally rather than conceptually.

Action seekers avoid both theory and planning. They are *not* impatient for resolution. Although they are able to defer decisions and adapt to new information, they do have a strong sense of the here and now. They are hands-on people.

Action seekers are spontaneous and action-oriented and seek thrills and gratification. They may allow excitement to take precedence over careful thought. Thus, when action seekers go out of control, they may either win or lose *big*.

In communication, remember that action seekers often share perceptions that may sound like but that are *not* judgments or decisions. The best way to communicate with the action seeker or the **high roller** (the action seeker out of control) is to utilize facts and figures and to occasionally encourage him or her to discuss personal interests in order to tone down the runaway enthusiasm.

Since they do not thrive on order or completion, action seekers can be easily distracted. Action seekers disdain rules, and they are unpredictable. In addition to recognizing their detailed approach, you can spot an action seeker by some hyperactivity.

OTHER INDICATIVE AND RELATED FACETS OF PERSONALITY

Due to the complexity of personality, it is helpful to consider other facets of personality that may be related to negotiating temperament. As stated elsewhere in this book, right-brain/left-brain dominance is related to learning style and to the sensing/intuiting preference. Right-brain dominance is related to the intuiting preference, while left-brain dominance is related to the sensing preference. The accommodator style of learning is associated with sensing (and with extroversion), while the assimilator style of learning is associated with intuiting (and with introversion).

There may be a similarity between a high level of conscientiousness and judging preference (J) behavior. Similarly, Type A personality characteristics may exhibit themselves as similar to judging preference (J) behavior.

Emotional stability, competitiveness, the need for power, the need for affiliation, the need for achievement, and the other two learning styles of converging and diverging may also relate to negotiation temperament when combined with other facets. Those potential effects are noted in the assessment section that follows.

ASSESSING YOUR PRIMARY NEGOTIATING TEMPERAMENT

You should utilize your personality assessments completed elsewhere in this book along with the preceding temperament profiles to fully analyze your primary negotiating temperament. You may find that you relate somewhat to more than one temperament. If you score high in self-monitoring, you may think that you see yourself in all four temperaments. It is important to assess your primary, natural, negotiating temperament. It is easier and more effective to utilize what comes naturally, and it is what comes naturally that takes over when we are under distress or out of control. Knowing how you will behave is necessary to developing effective strategies.

To find your primary temperament, focus first on the manner in which you take in information. Consider your right-brain/left-brain dominance, learning style, and sensing/intuiting to determine your preference. You will notice that, after such determination, you should fit within one of two profiles. Some of the correlations already noted may assist you and provide you with added information about yourself.

If you are a harmonizer who is also very high on the need for affiliation or the need for social power, and low on conscientiousness, you should take special care to avoid becoming the pacifier in negotiations. If you are an action seeker with low conscientiousness or low emotional stability, take care not to become the high roller. If you have a judging preference and also have a high need for personal power and a high level of competitiveness, you may be prone to becoming the bull or the street fighter. You should exercise particular caution in controlling your negotiation interactions if you also have a low level of emotional stability to add to that mixture.

If your learning style is either converging or diverging and you are unsure of your negotiation temperament, consider three additional facets. If you are a converger and are also high in need for achievement, competitiveness, or conscientiousness, you may fit the controller profile. If you are a diverging style of learner and are also relatively low on conscientiousness and need for achievement, you may fit the action seeker profile. A form is provided in Exhibit 5-1 to record your temperament assessment.

Performance Checklist

- ✓ Certain aspects of personality relate particularly to interaction style. Preferences for taking in information and structuring the outside world exhibit themselves in negotiating temperaments. Right-brain/left-brain dominance; learning style; conscientiousness; Type A characteristics; emotional stability; and needs for power, achievement, and affiliation may also relate to temperament.

- ✓ The four key negotiation temperaments are the harmonizer (pacifier), the controller (bull), the pragmatist (street fighter), and the action seeker (high roller). The parenthetical names describe the temperament out of control.

- ✓ Temperament affects perceptions, interpretations, and certain behaviors. It is possible to recognize each temperament by paying attention to approach. Harmonizers are general and open-ended; controllers are general and resolved; pragmatists are specific and resolved; and action seekers are specific and open-ended.

- ✓ You should record your negotiation temperament assessment in the form provided in Exhibit 5-1 using the knowledge gained thus far.

Exhibit 5-1
Negotiating Temperament Assessment Form

My primary negotiating temperament is

Harmonizer _____   Controller _____   Pragmatist _____   Action seeker _____

I am a harmonizer who also has

High need for affiliation _____

High need for social power _____

Low conscientiousness _____

If one or more of the preceding are true, I will focus on not being a pacifier _____

I am a controller who also has

High competitiveness _____

High need for personal power _____

Moderate to low emotional stability _____

If two or more of the preceding are true, I will focus on not being a bull _____

I am a pragmatist who also has

High competitiveness _____

High need for personal power _____

Moderate to low emotional stability _____

If two or more of the preceding are true, I will focus on not being a street fighter _____

I am an action seeker who also has

Moderate to low conscientiousness _____

Moderate to low emotional stability _____

If one or both of the preceding are true, I will focus on not being a high roller _____

Key Terms, Phrases, and Concepts

Perception

Harmonizer (pacifier)

Controller (bull)

Pragmatist (street fighter)

Action Seeker (high-roller)

Review Questions

Mark each of questions 1 and 2 as True (T) or False (F) and answer questions 3 through 10.

T F 1. The four key negotiating temperaments reflect four possible combinations of two personality preferences.

T F 2. Understanding two personality preferences is all that is necessary to master negotiating behavior.

3. A negotiator who moves freely from one issue to another or discusses multiple issues together is exemplifying the temperament of a/an _____.

4. A negotiator who focuses on specifics and details might be one of which two temperaments? _____ or _____.

5. A negotiator who likes detail and is also focused on resolution exemplifies the temperament of a/an _____.

6. The negotiating temperament that is likely most unpredictable is the _____.

7. Why are harmonizers and controllers prone to organize information into concepts and theories? What aspects of personality relate to such behavior?

8. What personality characteristics or traits must a harmonizer be sure to keep in check or under control? Why?

9. What personality characteristics or traits must an action seeker be sure to keep under control? Why?

10. Think of a recent interaction you were party to. Imagine yourself in the eyes of the other party. Which negotiating temperament did you exhibit?

Case 5.1

Ventura Capital is a financier who specializes in capitalizing start-up companies. Andy Preneur is a would-be entrepreneur. He needs capital to start his new business. Andy and Ventura have been negotiating a potential agreement over the last few months. It seems there is only one item unresolved. Ventura wants her investment to remain in the company and earn a preferred dividend of 5 percent, even if Andy no longer needs the money. Andy wants the right to buy out Ventura's interest at any time as long as the 5 percent return is paid. Role-play this case with another person. When you finish, address the following questions.

Case Discussion Questions

1. Which of the four key temperaments was most clearly displayed by the other person? Identify specific comments and behaviors to support your assessment.

2. Which of the four key temperaments do you think your comments and behaviors most clearly displayed?

3. Do you agree with each other's self and other assessments? If not, why do you think you see the behaviors differently?

Chapter 6

Communicating
in Negotiation

- To understand communication as a process
- To learn rules for effective listening and speaking in negotiation
- To learn communication filtering techniques for negotiation
- To recognize signs of destructive conflict in negotiation and what to do when they arise
- To learn to watch body language in negotiation
- To be cautious in written and electronic negotiation

> "It is a great misfortune neither to have enough wit to talk well nor enough judgment to be silent."
>
> *La Bruyere*

Do you communicate when you speak, or do you just make noise? Is what is written here communication, or just noise? Communication is essential for negotiating success. The opening quotation summarizes the essence of negotiation communication. Your goal should be to say the right things in the right ways at the right times and to hear. What you say must be understood as you intend it to be effective. Saying the right things in the right ways is necessary for your message to be understood. Hearing the other parties is necessary for you to say the right things at the right times. Communication is a two-way process.

Communication is the effective transfer of intended meaning. If the transfer falls short of that, it is just noise. The process of communication can be understood in parts. Noise can arise in any of the parts. Noise can arise from several factors. However, much noise comes from interpersonal differences in key aspects of personality discussed previously in this book.

We are naturally able to interact with those individuals who are most similar to us. The more we have in common regarding the ways in which we take in information, process information, and structure our outside world, the easier it is to communicate. In fact, enduring, close relationships are generally those between people who share traits and characteristics of personality and temperament as well as values. Our attitudes and perceptions edit the messages we hear from others. We have the greatest misunderstandings and risk of conflict with those who differ from us.

In this chapter we review key principles of communication as a process and identify communication skills necessary for effective negotiation. Our focus is on interpersonal complexities in communication.

Principles of effective communication are divided into four general categories: (1) listening, (2) speaking, (3) **filtering,** and (4) **watching.** The first two are important regardless of who is on the other side of the communication process. The latter two are particularly important when the one with whom we are communicating is the least like us.

THE COMMUNICATION PROCESS

The process of communication may be analyzed in steps. A message flows through the following steps or subprocesses: the **source,**

encoding, the **channel, decoding,** and the **receiver** (Berlo 1960). The *source* is the person originating the message. That person *encodes* it—structures it according to his or her understanding. The *channel* is the medium through which the message is sent—the spoken word, the written word on paper or electronic medium, and body language. *Decoding* is the receiver's interpretation and understanding of the message. Much purported communication stops there. In order to ensure that communication has, in fact, occurred, one more step is needed—**feedback.**

If the receiver re-sends the message in confirmation of what was understood and that feedback coincides with what was intended, we can be fairly certain that communication has occurred. However, if the original sender, or source, does not *hear* the feedback, no one will know whether communication occurred. Listening, therefore, is critical to communication.

Noise can occur at any step, even in feedback. We tend to encode messages according to our own way of taking in information and subject to our own perspectives and biases. Sometimes we use shortcuts and codes familiar to us that are not familiar to others. Our personalities, our culture, our language, and our attitudes can all create noise and present barriers to communication. Sometimes we see and hear what we want to see and hear, despite the clarity of the message!

Communication is difficult! The more people involved in the process, the greater the complexities and opportunities for noise. Some channels are richer than others. Direct, face-to-face communication is the richest. It provides the greatest sources of information as well as the greatest opportunities for immediate feedback. Verbal and body language are available in face-to-face interaction. Negotiation is best conducted face to face. In telephone communication, verbal tone and immediate feedback are available but body language is not. Written communication must be undertaken with special care to avoid unintended offense or unintended meaning.

There are rules we can follow that will help us do our best. We can become aware of ourselves and our ways of encoding and decoding. We can learn to listen. We can learn to speak effectively as well as request and give feedback. We can filter our messages in ways that aid the other's understanding. We can observe. Finally, as we continue to follow those rules we can learn more about perception. We address the additional complexities of perception in later chapters.

Hot Tip!
Practice listening and speaking rules on topics about which you are passionate.

RULES FOR EFFECTIVE LISTENING IN NEGOTIATION

Good negotiators, like good communicators generally are active listeners. Most of us, absent training and practice, are relatively poor listeners. Extroverts usually have particular difficulty in developing listening skills. Quietly listening, on the other hand, comes naturally to introverts. All negotiators should follow the rules set forth in the following box.

> ✓ Talk less and listen more.
>
> ✓ Seek new information.
>
> ✓ Do not stop listening before the other person finishes because you think you know what he or she is going to say.
>
> ✓ Do not stop listening in order to remember what you want to say next.
>
> ✓ Do not assume that you know what the other person means.
>
> ✓ Do not interrupt.
>
> ✓ If you do not understand, say so.
>
> ✓ Show interest. Lean forward, nod, or smile.

RULES FOR EFFECTIVE SPEAKING IN NEGOTIATION

Later, in other chapters, we address more particular or tactical statements used in negotiation. The following rules should be adopted as general guidelines permeating all of your negotiation messages:

✓ Do not answer a question if you are not prepared.

✓ Do not answer a question that was not asked, unless you are *sure* that it will aid the process of mutual understanding.

✓ Do not be afraid to answer a question with a question.

✓ Do not answer a question if the timing does not suit your strategy, but promise to answer it later.

✓ Do not ask a question that will trigger the reciprocal question back to you if you are not ready or prepared to answer it.

✓ After you ask a question, *stop*, close your mouth, and open your ears so that the person can answer and you can hear!

✓ Occasionally ask a question to which you already know the answer in order to test the other's veracity.

✓ Restate or summarize what you understood the other person to say.

✓ State your understanding and appreciation for the other's position.

✓ Do not be offensive or rude.

✓ Until you are ready to agree, use conditional statements and hypotheticals.

✓ Do not say things to show off.

✓ Do not be afraid of appearing stupid.

✓ Do not be afraid to be silent.

> **"Speech is silver; silence is golden."**
>
> *German Proverb*

If you are surprised by the rule, Do not be afraid of appearing stupid, bear in mind that it is not the same as *being* stupid! Many times we fail to seek clarification because of this fear. It is unlikely that your counterpart will presume you stupid for seeking information. However, if that does happen, it will give you an advantage. We discuss underestimating your counterpart further in other chapters.

FILTERING

The principle of filtering is premised on knowing who you are and what type of personality the person has with whom you are dealing. To be effective in the communication process, one must be aware of his or her own internal editing, recognize clues, and relate transmissions to the personalities involved. We are largely unaware of our automatic editing. Our natural tendency is to assume that others are like us. We project our characteristics onto others. Our reactions to others depend in large part on how we perceive them. While perception is addressed at greater length elsewhere in this book, our focus here is on practicing filtering techniques.

Filtering removes the debris of our automatic editing and allows for effective transfer of intended meaning. There are two basic rules for filtering:

1. Know your prejudices, biases, and tendencies, and allow for them.
2. Listen and speak to the other in his or her language.

It is the failure of the filtering process that accounts for much tension, anger, destructive conflict, and many breakdowns of the negotiation process. The way to improve your filtering skills and, therefore, your communication and negotiation skills is to recognize how you interact, how you react to your opposites, and how your opposites react to you.

Usually the hardest part of that quest is acknowledging how others perceive you. For example, to your opposite you may be perceived as argumentative or even abrasive when you think you are merely getting to the point and getting to resolution. To your opposite you may be perceived as scattered or wishy-washy when you think you are being open to alternatives and trying to accommodate.

In order to improve your filtering skills, make a note of your interpretation of and reaction to the characteristics and behaviors of the various personalities and temperaments described in other chapters. Next, make a list of the effort you must make in negotiations with your opposites. Remember, the more you are able to use your nonpreferences, the fewer blind spots you will have in negotiation. Some examples are provided to get you started. Following the practice examples is a general filtering approach to use in resolving conflict caused by personality differences during negotiations.

EXAMPLES OF FILTERING SKILL BUILDING

Choose the examples that apply to your personality characteristics, and practice.

- I am an introvert. I get angry when someone states the obvious or repeats what has already been said. I need to be patient when negotiating with people who do this, because they are not intending to annoy me. They are different from me.
- I am an intuitive. I am impatient with details and I cannot stand it when someone cannot see the big picture. I need to be patient when negotiating with a sensor, because details are important to him or her. In order to get through to a sensor, I must present details.
- I am a sensor. I can anger people when I interrupt to insert or correct facts. When negotiating with an intuitive, I must remember that we have to discuss more than details. We must discuss goals and broad issues.

- I am an intuitive. When dealing with a sensor, I must be aware that he or she wants specific questions and specific answers.
- I am a sensor. When dealing with an intuitive, I must be aware that he or she looks for the meaning of things. I must appreciate the intuitive's need to think of concepts and to be relational.
- I am a sensor. I must replace the word "you" with "I." Rather than saying "Your numbers are wrong," I must say, "I looked at it differently."
- I am a judger. I know when I am right. I think about things before I make up my mind. I have no tolerance for disagreement or alternatives. If something is worth doing, it is worth doing right. I need to recognize that my way is not the only way. When negotiating with perceivers, I must allow them to have their own views. I must realize that they speak of their ideas and perceptions. Not everything they say represents their judgment or final view.
- I am a perceiver. I can see all sides to an issue. When I voice alternatives with a judger, I create anger. I must make it known that I am contemplating out loud, and I must increase the importance of resolving issues expeditiously when I negotiate with a judger.
- I am a judger. When dealing with a perceiver, I must make an effort to collect and consider new and additional information that may affect my ultimate decision.
- I am a perceiver. I must make a conscious effort to come to closure on issues.

WHEN CONFLICT ARISES IN NEGOTIATION

- Privately consider whether the dispute is due in whole or in part to temperament and personality differences or is a conflict on a substantive matter or issue.
- If the problem is only one of personality/communication differences, relate to the other person on his or her terms and in his or her language.
- If conflict persists despite the filtering attempts, determine and agree on what is in dispute.
- Then proceed with negotiation on that issue (or proceed with understanding that there was not a real dispute).
- If conflict escalates at any time, call *time out.*

Remember that the minimal features of conflict include values, meanings, attributions, communication and, most importantly, interdependence. Also remember that interpersonal skills will make you look like a genius, and genius is often perseverance in disguise!

WATCHING

Watching is paying attention to nonverbal clues—body language. **Kinesics** is the term used to refer to the study of nonverbal communication in human interaction. Our emotions and motives are frequently displayed in our nonverbal behavior. Motives in this regard are our expectancies of pleasantness or unpleasantness. The activation of expectancies moves us into action—behaviors. Feelings, or emotions, also move us to actions. Smiling, frowning, and crying are obvious examples. Some of these physical actions are automatic. That is, often we do not consciously decide to take the action or we are unaware of the action.

It is often possible to obtain information from observing body language. It is also important to recognize what your body language may be signaling to the other person—your counterpart. You may need to guard against unintended communication. Some words of caution are in order, however. There are cultural differences in body movement and comportment, and people do have habits and idiosyncrasies that may not have the meanings typically applicable to those behaviors. In addition, individuals knowledgeable in kinesics may purposely attempt to convey a message through body language. A person can control many actions and expressions that would otherwise convey their emotions; however, it is usually not possible to control for all of the available clues. Nevertheless, in a case of purposive body language, the conclusion you draw from the behavior may not be appropriate to the situation.

Therefore, in order not to be misled, the primary things to watch for in the behavior of others are two: (1) body language that conflicts with the verbal message being conveyed and (2) changes in behavior relative to the situation or the person being observed. In watching the behavior of others, your overall guide should be to listen to your inner feelings. Your subconscious reading of the nonverbal clues will usually be accurate. With those words of caution and suggested use in mind, certain elements of body language, along with their *typical* meaning, are provided in the next section. Drawings depicting some of this language are also presented.

BODY LANGUAGE

Anxiety and/or anger can be shown by tone of voice, tension in the facial muscles, clenched teeth, clasping objects, dilated pupils, general body activity rather than stillness, stiff posture, perspiration, short glances, or averted stares.

Facial expressions convey pleasure, anxiety, and relief and are generally easier to control than gross body movements. However, look for the inappropriate smile while explaining a problem. For example, a verbal message explaining a problem and requesting help may be accompanied by a subconsciously generated smile that indicates no real concern for resolution.

Eyebrows can signal surprise or puzzlement. The mouth can signal pleasure or displeasure.

While a single head nod indicates permission for the other to continue talking, multiple head nods indicate a desire to speak. It may also provide a flag that the person is no longer listening to you and, rather, being focused on what he or she wants to say.

A person looks more at people he or she likes than at those he or she dislikes. However, intense staring can be used to intimidate and can be aggressive.

Bright light behind an individual can create power for them. If you are seated in front of the desk of someone whose back is to a bright window, the physical arrangement creates a power imbalance in favor of the person behind the desk.

Height differences create power differentials. The unaided difference in height of the individuals creates a differential. The physical arrangement, such as variation in chair height, can create such differential. The drawings in Exhibit 6-1 demonstrate effects of vertical space differentials.

Shifty eyes usually do not indicate dishonesty. Usually, they indicate submissiveness or unwillingness to address an issue. Looking off to the left while telling a story, however, may indicate deception. Remember that creativity comes from the right side of the brain—the same side that controls the left side of the body!

Rapid or excessive eye blinking may indicate that the person is uncomfortable, exaggerating, tense, lying, or very alert.

Rubbing eyes often indicates that the person is not accepting what has been explained or presented. This can be a clue to the need for more explanation or persuasion.

Using the hands to substantially cover the face may indicate nonacceptance or a reaction to behavior interpreted as aggressive.

EXHIBIT 6-1

Vertical Space Illustrations.

Man has height power   Height power neutralized   Woman has height power

Placing the hands over the mouth while speaking may indicate fear of acceptance, or it may indicate deception in what is being said.

A significant change in activity, such as substantial reduction in general body movement or an obvious attempt to make and hold eye contact after generally not having had significant eye contact, may indicate deception. It may also be an intimidation ploy.

Body movements that are inconsistent with the spoken word may indicate deception. For example, shaking your head "No" while saying "Yes" is likely to indicate either deception or noncommitment.

Stroking the chin or placing the knuckles under the chin indicates interest. The chin resting in the palm indicates boredom. While touching the bridge of the nose is a sign of concentration, stroking the nose may be a sign of exaggeration or lying. (It may also be a response to an itch!)

When a man brings his hands to his chest, it usually indicates openness and sincerity. When a woman brings her hands to her chest, it usually indicates shock.

The wringing or twisting of hands indicates substantial frustration. Steepling the fingers conveys confidence. The meaning of other arm and hand positions varies with the direction to which the palm faces relative to the other person. The drawings in Exhibits 6-2, 6-3, and 6-4 provide examples.

EXHIBIT 6-2

Hand Gesturing Illustrations.

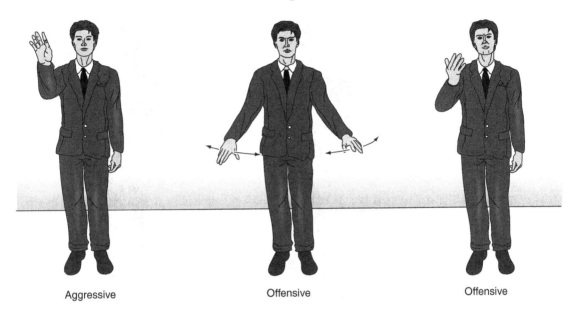

Aggressive   Offensive   Offensive

EXHIBIT 6-3

Hand Gesturing Illustrations.

Open and friendly   Open and friendly

EXHIBIT 6-4

Hand Gesturing Illustrations

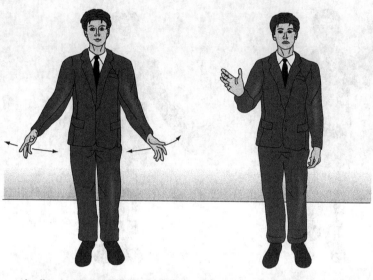

Inoffensive, indicating emphasis   Indicating power

Sitting on the edge of the chair indicates interest in the conversation. Leaning back or putting one's hands on the back of one's head indicates either confidence or dominance. It may be aggressive behavior.

Crossed arms or crossed legs with a closed body position indicate a closed or defensive attitude. Drawings presented in Exhibits 6-5 and 6-6 depict samples of body demeanor.

ELECTRONIC COMMUNICATION

Electronic communication is becoming more important in negotiations. It is prudent to be aware of what has developed in expressing emotion through electronic forms. The use of all capital letters expresses shouting. Other symbols are used to express various other emotions as set forth here:

Colon followed by a close parenthesis is a smile. :-)
A colon followed by a forward parenthesis is a frown. :-(
;) is a wink.
<g> is a grin.

<u>**EXHIBIT 6-5**</u>

Open Body Demeanor Illustrations

Open and relaxed

<u>**EXHIBIT 6-6**</u>

Closed Body Demeanor Illustrations

Closed and withdrawn   Closed and bored   Closed and pensive

;-@ is a yell.
;-D is shock.
;-e is disappointment.

REFLECTION AND PRACTICE

Have you experienced a negotiation during which communication seemed relatively easy and requirements were clear? Try to identify briefly what contributed to the effectiveness of the communication.

Have you experienced a negotiation during which communication was very difficult or, perhaps, so ineffective that negotiations broke down with no resolution whatsoever? Try to identify briefly what contributed to the difficulties.

If any portion of your answers to the preceding two questions relates to your counterpart's personality, temperament, behavior, or demeanor, identify whether or not those factors are similar or dissimilar to your personality, temperament, negotiating behavior, or demeanor.

Go to a place with which you have little familiarity. Do not talk. Listen and pay special attention to nonverbal behaviors. After making your observations, identify how the behaviors affected your interpretations and conclusions regarding what you saw.

Listen to a friend or associate for two minutes with no talking on your part. Then try to provide a verbatim account of what was said. Do this again with someone else. Do it again, but increase the time to four minutes. Do this exercise while you are watching a television program. Watch the program for two minutes and then try to provide an account of what was said.

Performance Checklist

✓ Communication is the process of effectively conveying intended meaning. Communication is critical for negotiation success. Communication is complex. Key steps include encoding, decoding, and feedback. Noise can occur during any steps in the process.

✓ Much noise can be eliminated by understanding ourselves and our opposites and by following rules for speaking and listening and watching body language.

✓ Filtering techniques will assist us in negotiation communication.

✓ When conflict arises in negotiation, one should assess whether it is substantive or due to temperament and/or other communication failure, apply filtering techniques to determine the precise substantive matter in dispute, or call time-out prior to escalation.

✓ Written negotiation is most vulnerable to unintended communication.

Key Terms, Phrases, and Concepts

Communication

Filtering

Watching

Source

Encoding

Channel

Decoding

Receiver

Feedback

Kinesics

Review Questions

Mark each of questions 1 through 3 as True (T) or False (F) and answer questions 4 through 10.

T F 1. People typically look more at people they like than they do at people they dislike.

T F 2. Multiple head nods by the person to whom you are speaking likely indicates that he or she has stopped listening.

T F 3. Shifty eyes may indicate submissiveness.

4. What are the minimal features of conflict?

5. What are the two most important things to remember about body language?

6. Name the four general categories of principles for effective communication.

7. Why would it be true that we are able to communicate best with those who are most similar to us?

8. Explain the importance of feedback in the negotiation process.

9. What one thing can you do to increase your communication effectiveness in negotiation?

10. Critically evaluate your typical body movements during interactions with others. What messages might you be sending through your habits?

Case 6.1

Jack asked, "How is the Southwestern project coming along?" Ms. Lee said, "I need to talk to you about that." "I don't want to hear any excuses, just get this project done," Jack yelled to Wei Lee. Ms. Lee said, "Fine. I quit. Do it yourself." Ms. Lee is the senior project manager and is in charge of completing a customized training program for the firm's largest client. Jack was hired from the outside just two months ago as vice president of training. Ms. Lee believes that her credentials are more appropriate and impressive than are Jack's. Ms. Lee expected the job. She has no alternatives lined up. Jack has already earned a reputation for being harsh in a place where people formerly enjoyed working. The particular project in question includes extensive material/course manual preparation as well as classroom sessions. Before the interruption, Ms. Lee was attempting to communicate to Jack that the client had requested a significant variation from what was originally contracted. The good news that Ms. Lee had to share was that the client had agreed to double the fee.

Case Discussion Questions

1. How many rules for effective listening and speaking has Jack broken?

2. How well has Wei handled this conflict? Can you suggest any alternative actions that would have been consistent with good practices?

3. If you learned that Jack dislikes female professionals, what additional insight does that provide regarding communication difficulties between him and Ms. Lee? What might you suggest to Jack?

Chapter 7

A Note on Cultural and Gender Differences

PERFORMANCE COMPETENCIES FOR THIS CHAPTER

- To understand what culture is
- To appreciate cultural differences in negotiation
- To consider potential gender differences in negotiation

"If civilization is to survive, we must cultivate the science of human relationships—the ability of all peoples, of all kinds, to live together, in the same world at peace."

Franklin D. Roosevelt

WHAT IS CULTURE?

Culture consists of all of the beliefs, behaviors, and products common to members of a particular group. It includes values, customs, language, rules, tools, technologies, goods, laws, institutions, and organizations. A national culture is the set of values, beliefs, attitudes, and behavioral expectations—or **norms**—shared by the majority of individuals residing in the country.

Culture shapes the way individuals think, the way they view the world, and the way they interact. Most individuals are unaware of the magnitude to which the dominant culture in which they were raised affects them.

Each of us learns norms of behavior that intersect all phases of our lives. The culture may prescribe acceptable roles by gender as well as acceptable behavior by gender. The culture may also prescribe many things by race, ethnicity, and other human characteristics.

We can think in terms of national culture and many subcultures thereof. There exist subcultures by ethnicity or national heritage, such as Amish settlements or American Indian reservations, for example. Subcultures may exist by geographic region as well. Institutions and organizations possess cultures of their own that are subcultures of the country culture.

> "A corporation's culture is what determines how people behave when they are not being watched."
>
> *Thomas Tierney, former CEO, Bain & Company (The Economist, July 27, 2002)*

The culture with which an individual has the most significant contact is likely to be the culture that most affects that individual's values, beliefs, attitudes, and behaviors. Similarly, the dimension of individual similarity determines the strength of the culture. That is, the less diversity existing within a country or smaller social group, the stronger the culture. A strong culture places pressure on diversity and creates conflict with diversity.

What is written down in institutional structure, laws and regulations, and history is referred to as the *formal* culture. However, culture goes beyond that to what is termed the *informal* culture. Even though the informal culture may be more difficult to understand, it significantly affects behavioral norms and expectations.

WAYS TO CLASSIFY COUNTRY CULTURES

Many dimensions differentiate cultures at all levels.[1] Some key dimensions are noted here due to their relationship to interpersonal interaction. Those dimensions are **time orientation, formality, power distance, individualism versus collectivism,** and **context.**

Time orientation is a dimension that describes the relative focus on time. The American culture tends to perceive time as important and scarce. Such view leads to impatience as well as to valuing punctuality. Eastern cultures tend toward the opposite.

Formality refers here to pomp and ceremony, tradition, and formal rules. Relative to other cultures, the American culture is rather devoid of such formalities. Latin Americans enjoy pomp and ceremony—and formality generally. Middle Eastern, Eastern, and southern European cultures favor relatively more formality as compared to the American culture.

The dimension of *power distance* refers to the degree of social status stratification embedded in the culture. This dimension may be viewed as high- or low-power distance acceptance. Countries with low-power distance include the United States, Great Britain, Canada, Austria, Finland, Norway, Ireland, Germany, Sweden, Denmark, and Israel (Hofstede 1980). Countries with high-power distance include Mexico, South Korea, Japan, India, Pakistan, Thailand, Argentina, Brazil, Chile, France, Spain, Italy, Belgium, and South Africa (Hofstede 1980).

The *context* dimension refers to the extent to which the context, situation, and individuals involved may affect behavior and meaning in interaction. In a **low-context culture** such as the United States, a person is expected to say what he or she means and expects the meaning to be consistent across situations (Wilson 1992). Low-context cultures include the North American, German, Swiss, Scandinavian, and British. In a **high-context culture,** context is central to meaning—nonverbal and subtle cues are critical in communication (Borisoff and Victor 1989). High-context cultures include the Chinese, Korean, Japanese, Vietnamese, Arabian, Greek, and to a lesser extent Spanish and Italian.

[1] One of the most often cited approaches for differentiating cultures is that used by Geert Hofstede (1980). Hofstede's study was limited to one large organization, and the data are now old. The material in this chapter borrows two dimensions and other findings from Hofstede's work—power distance and individualism versus collectivism—but presents more recent thinking on cultural differences as well.

The dimension of *individualism versus collectivism* refers to the expectation and preference for individual effort, benefit, and recognition versus collective effort, benefit, and recognition. Country cultures that are relatively collectivist include Japan, Denmark, and Singapore (Hofstede 1980). Country cultures that are higher in individualism include Greece, Germany, Hungary, Egypt, Hong Kong, and North American countries (Hofstede 1980). Some researchers consider low-context cultures to be individualistic and high-context cultures to be collectivist (Wilmot and Hocker 2001, 35).

RELATIONSHIP OF CULTURAL DIMENSIONS TO PERSONALITY

If what is discussed in the preceding section sounds like some of the personality traits discussed elsewhere, it should. Culture affects development of personality characteristics by placing value on certain behaviors. For example, a **cultural emphasis** on time scarcity is consistent with producing Type A personalities. Capitalistic economies may foster development of the Type A characteristic.

Some research has reported that low-context cultures generate many internal locus of control individuals, while high-context cultures generate external locus of control individuals (Triandis 1980). That is consistent with the high-context person emphasizing private goals and control in negotiation while the low-context person emphasizes interdependence and group benefit, as noted in the next section.

Other research reports that low-context cultures stress linear logic, while high-context cultures stress integrative thinking (Gudykunst and Ting-Toomey 1988). In high-context cultures, members rely heavily on inferred meaning while low-context people strive hard to find a literal meaning (Borisoff and Victor 1989, 141). This is consistent with reports that more than 70 percent of Americans are sensors (Kroeger and Theusen 1988).

We should also expect cultural differences in the need for personal and social power. Some research has found that individuals from high-context cultures are more willing to use social power to accomplish goals, at least for the group (Ralston, Gustafson, Cheung, and Terpstra 1993; and Ralston, Gustafson, Terpstra, Holt, Cheung, and Ribbens 1993).

CULTURAL DIFFERENCES AND THEIR EFFECT IN NEGOTIATION

Cross-cultural differences in communication and negotiation are at the forefront of interest today. Key problems include **semantics, connotation, tone,** and expectations. As to *semantics*, be aware that some words do not translate between languages. As to *connotations*, be aware that words may mean different things in different languages and in different settings. As to *tone*, be aware that in some cultures a personal and informal style is preferred while in others a more formal style is expected. These expectations relate to the general degree of formality in the culture.

Those countries high on the formality dimension identified earlier are where a more formal approach is expected. Choosing the wrong style can be embarrassing and insulting. In many cultures it is customary to have personal, social discussion prior to and in conjunction with business meetings. Such behavior is expected as part of the formality. Negotiators from less formal cultures, as well as from more time-oriented cultures (such as Americans), are well advised to allow time for necessary formalities. They are also well advised to allow their counterparts from other cultures to be less punctual or time focused, and they should allow the other party time to come to decision or agreement. Harmonizers and action seekers, as described in another chapter, are likely to adapt to these cultural differences more readily than will controllers and pragmatists.

> **HOT TIP!**
> Cultural sensitivity will enhance your negotiation performance.

Individual spatial boundaries differ among cultures. When in doubt, maintain a respectable distance and refrain from personal contact. However, let your counterpart take the lead in initial greetings and in spacial distance. Take your cues from your counterpart.

Gift giving, style of dress, and the use of alcohol vary among cultures. It is best to inquire ahead of time when possible. Be prepared for all options and follow the examples of your counterparts when you are unaware of the rules.

In many collectivist and high-context cultures, self-interest is not valued. Self-expression that does not further the needs of the group may be met with disapproval. In high-context cultures, aggressive and direct confrontation may be considered rude or ignorant (Borisoff and Victor 1989). Individuals from individualistic cultures, particularly Western cultures, will find that in negotiating with a counterpart from a high-context culture, particularly Asian cultures, what must be stressed is harmony and common, or group, good.

Negotiators from individualistic cultures typically balance the advantages and disadvantages of relationships with the perceived individual benefit to them. Negotiators from collectivist cultures are typically willing to commit for the benefit of their group, even if the action is not most advantageous personally. Negotiators from collectivist cultures are more likely to criticize themselves than are those from individualistic cultures, because collectivists place higher value on the group than on themselves (Heine, Takata, and Lehman 2000).

Based on the research cited earlier, it is likely that many negotiators from high-context cultures will use an intuitive approach or exemplify the harmonizer temperament. It appears more likely that many negotiators from low-context cultures will use a sensing approach to information and exemplify the pragmatist or action seeker temperaments.

Face saving is important in all cultures; however, it may be exemplified differently by culture. It is widely recognized that face saving is often paramount in Asian cultures. In those cultures, offensive, directive, or power-over negotiation may be perceived as loss of face and bring an end to negotiations.

It is also widely recognized that being wrong is perceived as losing face in Arabian cultures. Value is placed on expertise and supporting evidence. The nature of face saving in cultures such as these presents a greater challenge in using collaborative negotiation than in other cultures. The solution must in no way be interpretable as inconsistent with the party's position.

In all high-context cultures, face saving is very important. Saving face includes receiving personal respect and having one's values and beliefs respected. Such values and beliefs include the belief that interpersonal relations are important and that a strong group best guarantees individual benefits (Triandis 1980). It is good practice to be respectful in all negotiations, even in individualistic cultures.

In learning cultural sensitivity, you should also recognize that the issues discussed in this vein are not relevant only when negotiating across national boundaries. In view of the cultural diversity in the United States (as well as other countries), these issues and differences may surface within home borders. Wherever they occur, cultural differences can result in communication failures, unnecessary conflict, and failure to come to agreement.

CONSIDERING GENDER DIFFERENCES IN NEGOTIATION

While practicing your communication skills in your quest to become a more effective negotiator, you may consider research regarding style differences between men and women. There is renewed interest in gender differences in communication and negotiation.

Some research has concluded that men as a group are more likely to use conversation to emphasize status, knowledge, and/or control, while women as a group are more likely to use conversation to create understanding and connection between the parties (Tannen 1991, 1993). It has also been reported that even when actual behaviors appear identical, the genders may conceptualize differently (Wilmot and Hocker 2001). Wilmot and Hocker state that men are more likely to see the self as independent, while women tend to see the self in relationship with others. Effective negotiation requires a view toward interdependence rather than power over others. It also requires mutual empathy. According to the research, it may be that women come to the negotiation task more likely to possess the more effective perspective and approach.

Studies also have indicated that in male-female interactions, males tend to dominate the conversation (Wilmot and Hocker 2001). Furthermore, studies show that females may be more willing to trust but are unforgiving of trust violations (Wilmot and Hocker 2001).

Gender differences, in situations where they truly exist, may relate to culturalization. That is, in some cultures (such as the United States), men may perceive an accommodating approach to be weak while women may perceive a direct approach as aggressive or insulting. Variations in culture create variations in what are presumed to be gender-typed behavior and roles.

Craver (2002) compared negotiation performance of male and female law students over sixteen years in a law school negotiation course. His data suggest that gender does not significantly influence negotiation results. While what is known about gender differences may be little, one thing is certain: Those males who underestimate their female counterparts do so at their peril!

Performance Checklist

✓ Culture is a set of laws, institutions, technologies, goods, values, customs, beliefs, language, attitudes, behavioral expectations, and norms shared by the majority of individuals in a country. Many subcultures exist around ethnicity, heritage, and geography and in institutions, organizations, and groups.

✓ Key dimensions of culture relevant to negotiation include time orientation, formality, power distance, individualism versus collectivism, and context. Certain cultural dimensions may influence the development of certain personality characteristics, such as Type A, locus of control orientation, and sensing versus intuiting. Cultural differences should be recognized and observed in negotiation, particularly as they impact style of interaction.

✓ Some research suggests a gender difference in negotiation communication style as well.

Key Terms, Phrases, and Concepts

Culture

Norms

Time Orientation

Formality

Power Distance

Individualism versus Collectivism

Context

High-Context Culture versus Low-Context Culture

Cultural Emphasis

Cross-Cultural Differences in Communication and Negotiation

Semantics

Connotation

Tone

Review Questions

Mark each of questions 1 through 4 as True (T) or False (F) and answer questions 5 through 10.

T F 1. People in collectivist cultures such as China and Israel may perform better in groups than alone.

T F 2. Culture includes values, customs, language, technology, and more.

T F 3. Culture does not impact a person's way of thinking.

T F 4. Countries tend to have their own unique culture of business.

5. List at least six things that differ by culture with examples of specific cultures.

For questions 6 through 10, identify a country you might be in if the statement were true in your particular situation.

6. Personal questions are not asked in business situations. Privacy of others is highly respected.

7. It is August and most people are on vacation while the conduct of business slows to a crawl.

8. Time is observed in "ishes." Meetings regularly begin a half hour behind the appointed time.

9. Cold calls are considered offensive. Formal introductions are expected.

10. Hugs are not given in public.

Case 7.1

It was reported on June 11, 1997, by *NBC Nightly News* that according to a study completed, women are genetically predisposed to developing interpersonal skills such as perceiving the attitudes and needs of others.

Case Discussion Questions

1. Which personality dimensions relate to emotional intelligence, such as sensitivity to the needs of others mentioned in the case?

2. Does culture affect development of certain personality characteristics by gender? If so, how?

3. Do you think that this phenomenon has changed over time? In which countries do you think the conclusion reported in the case is true today?

Chapter 8

Interests and Goals
in Negotiation

"Do not let what
you cannot do
interfere with what
you can do."

John Wooden

PERFORMANCE COMPETENCIES FOR THIS CHAPTER

- To understand the major types of interests and goals relevant in negotiation
- To learn how to identify and rank goals in negotiation
- To understand that goals change in negotiation
- To learn how goals affect your negotiation strategy

With this chapter, we begin the first step toward commencing actual negotiations. Once you have assessed and diagnosed the conflict and identified a potential overall goal to manage or resolve the conflict through negotiation, you are ready to begin preparation for the interaction. You should arrive at this step with some understanding of your personality, style, and temperament along with the ability to observe rules for effective communication and cultural differences.

This chapter describes general types of interests and goals involved in any negotiation and that exist on all sides of a conflict. We discuss how to come to *GRIP*—how to identify and rank your interests and goals as well as the interests and goals of the other party or parties. We also explain how interests and goals affect negotiation strategy and how they may change during negotiation. Additional complexities in recognizing and understanding interests and goals are addressed in a separate chapter.

TYPES OF GOALS

You should identify four types of goals in order to come to *GRIP* with the negotiation challenge. The letter *G* stands for the substantive gain you desire. The letter *R* stands for the relationship interests and goals you desire or that may be intertwined in the substantive issues. The letter *I* stands for *you* in the problem or transaction—your self-esteem and face-saving needs and goals. The letter *P* stands for the process—your goal regarding the nature and style of the process to be used. Each type of goal is addressed in the following sections.

GAIN ASPIRATIONS

When a conflict is presented, external things are typically sought by the parties. It is helpful to think of these as **gain aspirations**—the substantive and tangible things sought. Examples of *G* goals might be to complete a project by a specified date, to complete two projects within the same time period, to work half days, to get a promotion or raise, to receive a specified amount of money, to be with a particular person, to sell a particular asset with a certain net cash flow, to generate a certain number of dollars in profits, or to motivate someone to work more hours or with more efficiency.

Your external, or *G* goals, are likely to be the easiest to identify. You should also attempt to identify *G* goals held by the other party or parties to the conflict. It is common, particularly if you tend to hold a negative view toward conflict, to assume that *G* goals of others conflict with your own. That may, indeed, be true. However, the view that *G* goals are incompatible is typically a false perception. You may be surprised how often the exercise of hypothesizing potential alternative goals on both sides leads to common ground that meets the most valued goals of all parties. More often than not, people do not want the same things. At a minimum, you can anticipate that individuals will value and rank things differently. We introduce empathy and finding common ground later in this chapter and then discuss them further in a later chapter.

RELATIONSHIP GOALS

Relationship goals or relational goals are the ones that go to the type of relationship sought or sought to be maintained. These goals describe the nature and value you desire for the particular relationship and the particular person or persons involved, respectively, in the conflict. For example, you may desire to build a new friendship or business relationship or to continue an existing one undamaged. You may desire not to hurt the other's feelings, because you value that person. You may desire the other person to feel your fondness for him or her. You may desire the other person's commitment to your project or to the organization. You may desire your boss to like you and to like working with you. To distinguish *R* goals from *G* goals, note that staying employed may be a *G* goal, while the nature and quality of the relationship would be the *R* goal. You may see from these examples that relational goals reflect on all of the individuals in the conflict.

You will likely find it more difficult to identify relational goals—both yours and the others—than to identify *G* goals. Often relationship goals masquerade as *G* goals. The complexities of perception that are addressed in the next chapter present greater difficulties in understanding relationship goals, as well.

I GOALS

HOT TIP!
I goals also often masquerade as *G* goals.

When considering ***I* goals,** you are finding yourself in the conflict. Ask "Who am I and where am I in this conflict?" Your self-image, your self-esteem, your ego needs, and your fears will be present to some extent in every conflict. These goals can be closely related to relationship goals. For example, let us hypothesize that you have prepared an extensive analysis and recommendation that you want adopted by your peers or your boss. While there may certainly be a *G* goal of attaining the tangible results anticipated in your recommendation, there is also likely to be an *I* goal of being viewed as smart or effective. There may be an *I* goal of not wanting to be viewed as incompetent or deficient in any way. Sometimes we allow *I* goals to overshadow *G* goals to our later regret.

Identifying your fears will assist you in identifying your *I* goals. What are you afraid of? Do you fear looking stupid? Do you fear losing? Do you fear getting hurt, either emotionally or tangibly? Fears and, therefore, *I* goals may also relate to types of power. We discuss power and fear at greater length in other chapters of this book.

Other examples of *I* goals include wanting to be viewed as the peacemaker or problem solver, or wanting to be viewed as fair, or not wanting to be treated unfairly, or wanting to be respected and to be treated with respect. As noted in previous chapters, face-saving is important in all cultures and rises to a level that permeates the entire negotiation process in some cultures.

I goals tend to make us inflexible and either avoidant or competitive. The resulting competitive behavior is often to attack the other's person—to attack his or her self-esteem. Such behavior is reactive and will cause a spiral of increasingly negative conflict. In identifying *I* goals, the challenge is to control your own ego and use the *I* goals of the other toward constructive ends. Recognize that others need to feel respected and justified.

In a later chapter, we explain how to own up to and express your feelings in nonoffensive ways. In another chapter, we also explain how to incorporate the other's *I* goals into persuasive arguments. To underscore the importance of *I* goals, note that they are used in effecting resolution of even the most extreme conflict situations. Face-saving is a primary tool used by hostage negotiators.[1]

PROCESS GOALS

Process goals describe how you want the interaction to proceed. Process includes the approach discussed in an earlier chapter (constructive/destructive), the style discussed in an earlier chapter (integrative/distributive), the manner of communication, procedures, and the voice or participation expected and permitted by all parties.

---

[1] See, for example, Rogan and Hammer (1994).

Selection of the appropriate process will be affected by the personalities involved, G goals, R goals, I goals, and the context. You should ask yourself what process will work most effectively to manage or resolve this particular conflict. As is further explained in another chapter, sometimes the process is the first thing requiring negotiation.

The process is important to the interaction in many ways. Process is sometimes more important than the actual tangible outcome. A process perceived as unfair by one party can cause dissatisfaction with an otherwise acceptable outcome. Procedural justice studies consistently demonstrate that people are more dissatisfied by what is perceived to be an unfair process than they are with less than optimal results derived in what is perceived to be a fair process.[2]

The more parties involved, the greater will be the complexity and number of process choices. For example, in a work team, will everyone receive an equal vote? In a multiparty transaction to be negotiated, does each party get equal time or equal review? Process is critical even in negotiations between two parties, regardless of how simple the substance. If one party leaves the negotiation table feeling like he or she was not permitted to fairly present his or her position or feeling pushed into an agreement, the agreement may not hold. That party may break the agreement, upon which a new conflict will arise.

The process may accentuate preexisting power differentials or may tend to disperse power. Empowering others can be effective in generating creativity as well as in developing support and agreement. These concepts are addressed further in chapter 10. The process may be directive or competitive. The process may be cooperative and collaborative.

If you hold the ultimate authority along with the responsibility for outcome, you have adequate information, and time is short, you might choose a directive process. Sometimes cooperative processes initiated run out of time and call for a directive termination. An example might be a president's declaration of war. Alternatively, in a context where face-saving is of paramount importance, you should place high importance on ensuring a cooperative process viewed as fair by all parties. A good rule of thumb is to design and use collaborative processes except and only when clear reasons exist not to do so.

---

[2] See, for example, LaTour (1978); Lind (1992, 1994); Lind, Kulik, Ambrose, and De Vera Park (1993); Thibaut and Walker (1975); Tyler and Lind (1992); and Walker, LaTour, Lind, and Thibaut (1974).

EVALUATING AND RANKING GOALS

Once you have identified what you believe to be all interests and goals involved in the conflict, you must begin to evaluate and rank them. Look at them critically. Take a systems approach, as explained elsewhere in this book. Look at interrelationships among goals. Look at subsidiary goals and interactive repercussions of attaining goals.

It is necessary to assess the relative value and importance of the goals. Some types of goals may not exist in some conflicts. For example, when you are bartering with someone whom you never expect to see again, relationship goals will be virtually nonexistent!

This step involves assessing which goals may be incompatible or, perhaps, the same thing by different names. It may also disclose that some goals are relatively unimportant. It will help you determine what you truly want and help you to find common ground and trade-offs. It will help you begin to think creatively toward resolution. Once you have evaluated and ranked your goals, you may begin to develop a coordinated plan.

Exercise 8.1

As practice in identifying interests and goals, think of your two most recent negotiation interactions. For each one, separately, go back to the conflict that triggered the need to negotiate and come to GRIP using the preceding material.

EVALUATION

If you found that you negotiated the wrong thing or used an inappropriate process, you have perhaps learned something about evaluating and ranking goals. If you are pleased with your approach and the result obtained, that is great! You may have found that the goals changed during negotiation. Alternatively, you may want to reconsider the approach used and the results you obtained. The phenomena of changing goals and hindsight are discussed in the next section.

CHANGING GOALS

Goals may change during and after negotiation. Part of the change phenomenon involves our perceptions and our resolution of psychological discomfort, which are addressed in the next chapter. Goals also change and new goals arise in response to new information during the interaction. Our original goals may prove to be unattainable. Our perception of the other party's goals may have been

KEY POINT
One thing is
constant—
change.

incorrect. Other assumptions and information used in setting your goals may have been incorrect. We address more specifically how to deal with changing goals in later chapters. The following subsections are intended to introduce you to the changing nature of goals.

PROSPECTIVE GOALS

Prospective goals are the ones we hold going into the negotiation. They represent specific intentions that we want to accomplish and that can be communicated.

Exercise 8.2

Identify the prospective goals from the two interactions in exercise 8.1. Also identify any new goals that arose during the interaction and how any of your prospective goals changed during the interaction.

Now evaluate those changes relative to the outcome of the negotiation. Did *I* goals arise and cause face-saving to dominate your other goals? Did face-saving on either side cause deterioration in the interaction? Did *I* goals arise on either side due to the process used? Did unanticipated *G* or *R* goals arise? Did negotiation fail to produce an agreement? What interests and goals are primarily responsible for the failure?

EVALUATION

If much of the foregoing occurred in your negotiation and no agreement was reached, you might look toward more preparation, more analysis of your *GRIP*, and more focus on process next time. If, on the other hand, unanticipated goals arose that accomplished as much or more than you originally sought, one of three things is likely true: (1) you adapted very well and did very well; (2) you set your goals too low; or (3) your view has changed. We further address setting goals and adapting to new information in a later chapter. Reason 3 is discussed in the next subsection.

RETROSPECTIVE GOALS

Retrospective goals are the most complex. People have a need to make sense of their behavior and decisions. Sometimes we adjust our perspective retroactively to make ourselves feel better. We may tell ourselves that what we did not get was not important after all or that what we got is much better.

KEY POINT
We are all
Monday morning
quarterbacks!

The phenomenon of developing retrospective goals may help in future interactions. For example, suppose you determine retrospectively that process was much more important than you thought it was prospectively. In your next negotiation with that person or in a similar context, you can increase the relative value of your *P* goals.

Developing retrospective goals may also serve little function other than rationalization and internal face-saving. Care should be taken to keep this phenomenon from creating retaliatory goals for the next interaction as well. Further explanation of this psychological process is presented in another chapter of this book.

GOALS AND YOUR NEGOTIATION STRATEGY

Identifying and ranking your goals and the goals of your counterparts—what we designate here as coming to *GRIP*—are necessary in order to develop your overall plan or negotiation strategy. Coming to *GRIP* is a key ingredient in preparation, as noted in chapter 14. You need to come to *GRIP* before making your decision to avoid, manage, or resolve the conflict. Coming to *GRIP* enables you to choose whether or not to negotiate at all. If, for example, your *R* goals in a particular case are much more important than your *G* goals, you might choose not to negotiate the *G* matters at all. You may focus negotiation efforts on *R* goals. As an example, consider an occasion when your best friend did something you dislike very much and you reacted in conflict. If it is something unusual and not likely to recur, your primary focus may be on mending hurt feelings.

Furthermore, you need your *GRIP* to know what you want. Before you decide *how* to get there, you must have a pretty good idea where you want to go! Coming to *GRIP* is a prerequisite to finding common ground necessary for a successful outcome in negotiation. Identifying interests and goals requires some understanding of perception and power, which are addressed in the next two chapters.

After identifying your goals, you should clarify them in a manner that can be communicated to and understood by your counterpart. Clarity will be required to assert your interest and goals. You should search for common goals—common ground, which is the basis for collaborating and persuading as addressed in other chapters.

DEVELOPING YOUR GRIP

Thinking of what you want and what your counterpart wants in terms of types of goals discussed in this chapter will help you succeed in negotiation. As noted already, identifying your counterpart's goals requires empathy and will likely require more thought than that necessary in identifying your own goals. Once you understand the concepts presented here, the only way to master the skill is to practice. Cases 8.1 through 8.3 at the end of this chapter may be used as role-playing dramatizations as you practice developing your *GRIP* and your empathy simultaneously.

Performance Checklist

✓ There are four types of goals to be identified in every negotiation. These are gain aspirations (*G* goals), relationship goals (*R* goals), ego issues (*I* goals), and process choices (*P* goals).

✓ It is helpful to identify and rank these goals from the perspective of each party in the conflict.

✓ Goals may change during and after negotiation. Sometimes negotiation should be interrupted to evaluate and address new information or a shift in goals. An individual may adjust his or her goals retrospectively to make sense of the negotiation outcome. Retrospection can, however, assist one to improve future negotiation performance.

✓ The step of identifying and ranking goals enables you to come to *GRIP* with your negotiation challenge. It provides information necessary for the choice and development of appropriate strategies. It also facilitates finding common ground that is critical to collaborating for mutual satisfaction.

Key Terms, Phrases, and Concepts

Gain Aspirations

Relationship Goals

I Goals

Process Goals

Prospective Goals

Retrospective Goals

Review Questions

Mark each of questions 1 through 4 as True (T) or False (F) and answer questions 5 through 10.

T F 1. The substantive, tangible things I want are *G* goals.

T F 2. My ego in the transaction or issue generates *I* goals.

T F 3. The relationships between or among individuals who are negotiating generate *R* goals.

T F 4. The way I plan or anticipate the negotiation to unfold comprises *P* goals.

5. Which of the two types of goals are easily confused?

6. Which two types of goals are most difficult to identify?

7. What might you do to improve your skill in identifying the interests and goals of others?

8. What care must you take regarding retrospective goals?

9 and 10. Fill in the blank: I must come to *GRIP* before I decide whether to _____ , _____ , or resolve a conflict.

Case 8.1

BUYING A CLASSIC CAR

Assume that one party has always wanted a particular make, model, and color of car. Now that party is prepared to purchase it and has found the car of his or her dreams offered for sale by the owner. As each party (the buyer and the owner), come to *GRIP* with the negotiation challenge they decide what type of strategy is appropriate for each. (You should fill in the car details that are fondest to your heart!)

Case Discussion Questions

1. What are the interests and goals of each party?

2. Is there anything that either or both parties may want to avoid?

3. How may either or both parties collaborate for mutual success?

Case 8.2

NEW BUSINESS RELATIONSHIP SCENARIO

One party's work organization, based in Washington, D.C., has recently begun a project in Wichita, Kansas. The project will require fifteen to twenty employees to travel to Kansas and spend, on average, three weeks in residence there. It is expected that the project will span a period of nine months to completion. This first party has located an apartment complex nearby the location where the project work will be done. The apartment complex has traditionally required minimum lease terms of one year but does have a few vacancies. The organization desires to have its people in this apartment complex rather than in hotels.

Case Discussion Questions

1. How would you identify and rank the interests and goals of each party?

2. What common ground can you find between the parties?

3. What strategy would you use as the organization's representative? What strategy would you use as the apartment complex representative?

Case 8.3

PRENUPTIAL AGREEMENT

Two romantic partners have decided to tie the knot. One has spent a great number of years in a very financially lucrative career and has substantial net worth and positive cash flow. The other has spent an equal number of years working hard as a dedicated teacher and has paltry savings and little extra regular cash flow. Both desire to agree on how living expenses will be shared, how parenting duties will be divided (if that should arise), and how things will be divided and organized upon the unlikely event that they separate or one experiences an untimely death. Analyze how each party comes to *GRIP* with the negotiation challenge and what each party's overall strategy might be.

Case Discussion Questions

1. Can you identify any critical differences in the goals of the parties? Are there any real incompatibilities?

2. What strategy do you suggest each party use in the negotiation?

3. How directive might either party be, if at all?

Chapter 9

Understanding the Importance of Perception in Negotiation

PERFORMANCE COMPETENCIES FOR THIS CHAPTER

- To understand basic psychological principles of perception
- To learn how individual differences affect perception
- To recognize that there are differences between self and others' perceptions
- To learn how perception affects attitude, goals, and decisions in negotiation

"It's not what we don't know that gives us trouble; it's what we know that ain't so."

Will Rogers

121

Preceding chapters discussed how individual differences may affect your approach to conflict and negotiation as well as your negotiation style, temperament, and communication. We also noted how cultural differences may affect those aspects of negotiation. Prior chapters provided general guidelines for identifying potential goals in the process of preparing for negotiation. Perception affects all that has been discussed thus far.

Each of us continually perceives and makes judgments about others. Each of us makes decisions based upon our perceptions. How do we know our perceptions are correct?

Each of us is continually being perceived by others. Each of us has an individual perception of ourselves that is affected not only by our personality characteristics but also by what we perceive to be others' perceptions and opinions of us and how we would *like* to be perceived by others.

Individuals possess distinctly opposite preferences for taking in information and dealing with the world, and these differences affect perception. Furthermore, all of these factors affect behavior. It is no wonder that communication is difficult! This chapter explains how the complexities of perception affect every aspect of negotiation interaction.

EVERYONE DOES NOT SEE THE SAME THINGS

What did you see when you first looked at the preceding figure? Did you see the same thing the second or third time you looked at it? Ask someone else to look at it. Did he or she see the same thing or things that you saw?

There are many ways to analyze and explain individual differences in perception. Many theories of perception exist. Many are complex. Approaches to understanding perceptual differences include those that range from field dependence versus field independence to eye movement and memory association and too many in between to name here. More than one theory may explain differences in viewing the figure.

The point is merely that differences do occur. Fortunately, it is not so difficult to understand the principle sources of perceptual variations most common in negotiation. In fact, we may take another look at some of the same individual differences discussed in an earlier chapter for explanations of some perceptual differences.

We will use certain additional psychological theories that focus largely on automatic or unconscious cognitive processing.

THE COMPLEXITY OF PERCEPTION

Perception may be understood as the process of selecting, organizing, and interpreting stimuli. In perceiving, we create what are called **cognitive structures.** Cognitive structures may be thought of as mental maps for assigning meaning to our existence and interactions. You may also think of cognitive structures as file drawers for organizing and maintaining information.

    We perceive the world and everything and everyone in it—inanimate objects, animals, and human beings. Perception affects our attitudes, beliefs, goals, and decisions. We set goals and take actions based upon what we believe to be true. Perception is impacted by our view of the world, our cultural and other learned expectations, our biases and prejudices, our learning and cognitive styles, and other personality characteristics. Any or all of these factors can distort perception.

    Person perception is the most complex perception. With all of the factors that impact perception generally, an additional ingredient impacts person perception. We attribute psychological processes to other human beings. We do this in two general ways. We usually perceive people as causal agents. Our perception of others often leads us to infer intentions and attitudes of others. We are also prone to expect what we experience with others to be repeated in their future behavior. We make judgments regarding the purpose of others' behavior, assessing blame and culpability. We assess the validity of what others say and do. This process provides fertile soil for distorting information.

    Perhaps the most important concept to bear in mind in understanding person perception is that we tend to assume that others' cognitive structures are like ours. This is the other general way in which we attribute psychological processes to other human beings. This tendency can also render errors in our perception. We typically presume and infer that others possess the same attributes and characteristics as we possess. We perceive emotional states in others, and we often project our characteristics onto others. The attributional and judgment processes are further explained later in this chapter.

    Given what has already been presented in earlier chapters about individual differences affecting interaction, it should be understood

KEY POINT
Perception affects all that we do.

that perception—or misperception—may create conflict. Or, misperception can masquerade as real conflict in the mind of one party while totally escaping recognition in the mind of the other. In a later chapter, we expand our discussion regarding selective perception as it relates to persuasion.

THE EFFECT OF PERSONALITY DIFFERENCES AND CULTURAL EXPECTATIONS ON PERCEPTION

KEY POINT
Extroverts perceive differently than introverts.

As noted in prior chapters, there are many facets of personality that affect how individuals behave and interact. It is helpful to revisit extroversion/introversion and sensing/intuiting relative to perception.

Extroversion and introversion may be considered as the framework for an individual's cognitive structures. If you think of cognitive structures as file drawers, the framework represents the file cabinet. Our sensing and intuiting preferences also affect those structures. An introverted attitude and the intuiting preference are abstracting and internal in nature. An extroverted attitude is concrete and external. The extrovert and the sensor seek to build pragmatic and practical frameworks. The introvert and the intuitor build conceptual and theoretical frameworks.

In perceiving people and things, we seek to develop mental pictures consistent with our cognitive structures. Therefore, the extrovert and the introvert will seek, see, and select different **stimuli** and organize those stimuli differently. The sensor will seek validity in things that can be verified by physical senses. The intuitor will seek the unusual and creative and will see validity in things consistent with his or her conceptual structures.

The sensor tends to organize perceptual stimuli according to experience. The intuitor performs a conceptual process in organizing stimuli. The filtering exercises presented elsewhere in this book demonstrate stimuli selection differences between sensors and intuitors. This preference difference often also affects assumptions and judgments about others, as noted in the section on attribution later in this chapter.

Exercise 9.1

EXERCISE IN PERCEPTUAL DIFFERENCES BY PERSONALITY CHARACTERISTICS

- Pair up with someone who is a strong opposite of you in either or both of the preferences of extroversion/introversion and sensing/intuitive. Try to complete a task together without speaking a word aloud or communicating in any way. You may organize an office or a cabinet. You may draw an object, such as a flower or a building. You must alternate actions. For example, one of you makes a stroke in the drawing followed by the other making a stroke and so forth.

- Try the experiment again with another person whose preferences are like yours.

In exercise 9.1, you may have found the other person's perception of organization to be different from yours. You may have found the other person's mental picture of the object drawn to be different from yours. It is likely that in doing the experiment, you found difficulties in completing the task with your opposite. You may have felt a struggle. A difference in approach exemplifies perceptual differences. It is likely that working with the person whose cognitive structures are more like yours felt more comfortable.

Since learning and expectations affect our cognitive structures, cultural differences can also affect our perceptions. For example, as noted previously, high-context cultures value and expect cooperation and collectivism. Thus, someone with an Asian cultural filter may perceive direct confrontation as inappropriate and offensive behavior.

ATTRIBUTION THEORY

The focus of **general attribution theory** is on the cognitive processes at work in assessing validity of information perceived.[1] Attribution theory provides a model that assists in understanding how people's inferences about the causes of a communicator's statements affect acceptance of or agreement with those statements as well as how inferences affect attitudes toward others. Thus, the following model is used in explaining the role of perception in attitude formation. It also will serve as a base for improving your persuasive abilities as addressed later in this book.

---

[1] Much research on the general attribution theory investigates persuasion and other social influence. (See Eagly and Chaiken 1993.) Theoretical approaches to understanding interpersonal perception utilized in this chapter include Heider (1958); Jones and Davis (1965); and Kelley (1973).

THE ROLE OF PERCEPTION IN ATTITUDE FORMATION

People evaluate the validity of messages for the purpose of acquiring valid attitudes; and, in evaluating validity, people infer cause and motive to the message. We seek to decide whether to accept communication and we seek to decide the causes for the communication. Our perception of the cause affects our acceptance of the message or our assessment of reality. Contextual cues such as the communicator's personal circumstances and the intended recipients of the message are taken into account in inferring cause and motive. We generally engage in these cognitive processes quite unconsciously. Whether we are aware of it or not, our perceptual processes result in our finding reasons, or causes, for the verbal or behavioral message.

The reason for the message may be attributed to external reality, which is referred to as **entity or environmental attribution;** to the situation; or to the personal characteristics of the communicator, which is referred to as **actor attribution.** We may simplify matters here solely by distinguishing between external and internal causes. That is, the situation and the environment are both external to the person. If external causes are not attributed to the words or behavior, the message is attributed to a cause internal to the communicator/actor.

In selecting the cause, or making the attribution, we assess **consensus, consistency, and distinctiveness.** We evaluate whether or not an individual's behavior is consistent with our prior experiences with *that* individual in similar situations—consistency. We also evaluate whether or not an individual's behavior agrees with that of *others* in similar circumstances—consensus. And, we evaluate whether or not the individual's behavior is distinctively different from prior experience with *that* individual generally—distinctiveness.

If we find low consistency—the behavior is not very similar to how *this* person behaves in other contexts—then we attribute cause to external sources. If we find high consensus—the person acted very much like others do in similar circumstances—then we attribute cause to external sources. If, on the other hand, we find high consistency (this person behaves similarly in other contexts) and low consensus (most people do not behave the same way), we look to the third factor—distinctiveness. We attribute cause to the person when we find low distinctiveness. Finding low distinctiveness is viewing the behavior as typical of this person. If, on the other hand, the behavior is unusual or seems not to fit our expectations for this

Exhibit 9-1

Decision Tree

Consistency? → No → External causes

→ Yes → Consensus? → Yes → External causes

→ No → Distinctive? → No → Internal causes

→ Yes → Particular
external causes
and internal causes

person, we find the behavior highly distinctive. Finding high distinctiveness may lead us to attribute cause of the behavior to particular others, events, or circumstances or to a combination of such external factors and internal causes. The decision tree in Exhibit 9.1 depicts the process.

The repercussion of our attribution affects not only our acceptance of the communication but also our attitude toward the person perceived. The actor-communicator is not held responsible for the positive or negative effects of behavior attributed to external causes. He or she *is* held responsible for behavior attributed to internal causes.

In drawing our conclusions and forming attitudes, we perceive patterns and relate experiences contained in our cognitive structures. We also, of course, use our way of understanding. We relate our prior perceptions from similar circumstances as well as our prior experiences with others who have traits and behaviors similar to those of the person we are currently perceiving.

Our biases, stereotypes, and prejudices are activated quite automatically in this process. If we hold an opinion regarding some group or class of people, we are likely to perceive an individual from that group to be consonant with that opinion. We are affected by past experience—accurate or not. We infer traits and attitudes from behaviors.

We tend to attach a high level of validity or reality to messages we perceive as having both high consistency *and* high consensus. We also tend to make a consistent error in our attributions. We tend to ignore external causes and emphasize internal causes in attributing motives and traits to others. This is especially true when the effects of others' behavior are negative to us. This over-attribution occurs in ascribing traits to others and in attributing what are essentially facets of the circumstances or situation to others rather than accurately identifying what may be the true existence of traits. Psychologists refer to this phenomenon as the **fundamental attributional error** or bias. This error also occurs quite automatically unless contrary information is clearly available and/or we make a concentrated effort to correct our initial biased perception.[2]

The fundamental attributional error often exemplifies itself as a negative assessment of or a negative attitude toward the other person. That is, when we perceive that something negative has happened to someone else, we attribute the cause to who that person is or something that person did. We blame others for their predicaments. Alternatively, we may fail to believe what someone says, due to our attribution of internal motives on that person's part or to that person's particular way of being. We may also inappropriately blame the person for something bad that happens to us.

Studies suggest that those with an intuitive preference are significantly less prone to the fundamental attributional error (Hicks 1985). This difference is consistent with sensors taking in information from experience as compared to intuitors taking in information conceptually. Prior experience triggers the fundamental error.

How Attribution Appears in Negotiation

It may help to pause and consider the application of attribution in a negotiation setting. For example, let us assume that you receive an invoice for a printing and advertising project. The amount due is significantly greater than you expected based upon the estimate provided before work started. Let us also assume that this is the third business arrangement with the person and in each of the prior experiences the bill was larger than the estimate. Also assume that your general experience is that other contractors abide closely to their estimates. In considering a negotiation, do you tend to feel like the cause of the conflict is the other person? Do you feel like the bill is probably overstated?

If you follow the decision tree diagram (Exhibit 9.1), you will find that it, too, points to an internal attribution. If you committed the typical attributional error, you may also hold an attitude about the other person's motives or possibly his or her credibility. You may, for example, think that the estimate was intentionally low to

[2] See, for example, Gilbert (1989); Gilbert and Jones (1986); and Ross and Fletcher (1985).

obtain the contract. You may think that the bill has been intentionally overstated. You may take things personally by thinking the person thinks you will not challenge the bill. It is possible that you will resist evidence to the contrary, depending upon the strength of your attitude. The reality, on the other hand, may be that certain changes occurred—external factors—that caused a legitimately higher amount to be due.

If we alter our hypothetical example slightly, we can see an example of the fundamental error in another way. If we assume that this project was our first experience with this person, we would have nothing from which to find high consistency. Our attribution tree would predict an external attribution. However, we are likely to commit the fundamental error and form the same negative attitudes as described in our first version.

SELF-SERVING BIAS

While we typically attribute the cause of others' messages and behaviors to internal sources, we are kinder to ourselves! Psychologists refer to this phenomenon as the **self-serving bias.** When we find ourselves saying or doing something less than positive, we attribute the cause to external factors. Maybe the Devil made you do it!

We tend to attribute others' success to external causes and others' failures to internal ones. But, we tend to take credit for our own success and point to others for our failures. It may be that individuals with an extremely high locus of control are less prone to attribute their own failures to external causes. Nevertheless, even internals indulge in the self-serving bias. Once aware of this phenomenon, we can try to check it or minimize its impact on our attitudes and decisions.

ME, MYSELF, AND I

There are two components to self-other perception. One is that we may perceive ourselves differently than we are perceived by others. That is, either we are projecting a different personality than we believe we are projecting, or we are misperceived by others. A misperception by others may be the result of our behavior or faulty perception on their part. The other component is our accuracy in

knowing how we are perceived by others. The difference between self and others' perceptions of an individual is one of the key factors affecting interaction.

George Herbert Mead's (1934) theory of **symbolic interaction** provides a useful perspective in understanding aspects of perception. *Me* is the part of you acting according to what you believe is expected.[3] It is you playing various roles in life. It is based on your perception of expectations for you. *Myself* is you in a third-person tense within a social context. It is how you think others see you. The *I* represents you as a unique individual with your unique interpretations, goals, and desires in the first-person tense separate and apart from the expectations of others.

We have a private self and a social self—*I* and *me*. We may consciously or unconsciously project an image of ourselves that differs from who we are privately. Attempts to influence others' impressions are motivated by our desire to make our public self congruent with our desired self or with what we think we should be. We try to match *me* and *myself*. We may also be trying to change some aspect of ourselves. What we think others attribute to us implicitly or explicitly plays a role in forming our sense of our own perceptions, motives, intentions, and identity.

We see others through our lenses and we think they wear the same lenses. There is an effect of self-perception reciprocal to the preceding one. Our perception of others is colored by our self-perception (Bem 1967, 1972). Exhibit 9.2 depicts the dynamic interaction of these phenomena.

RECOGNIZING PERCEPTUAL DIFFERENCES IN NEGOTIATION

SELF-OTHER PERCEPTION

Exercise 9.2

This exercise will provide you with insight on how others perceive you. It will be particularly useful in situations in which you find differences in self-other results.

Ask an acquaintance to share with you his or her perception of each aspect of personality discussed previously in this book. Do the same for that person. Try the experiment again with others. See if

---

[3] At times, individuals may seek to project a false *me* for some particular purpose or for manipulation. Nevertheless, the perception principles discussed here apply.

<u>**EXHIBIT 9-2**</u>
Dynamic Interaction of Perception and Self-perception

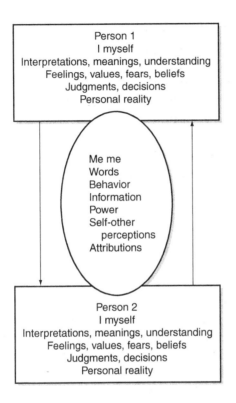

Person 1
I myself
Interpretations, meanings, understanding
Feelings, values, fears, beliefs
Judgments, decisions
Personal reality

Me me
Words
Behavior
Information
Power
Self-other
   perceptions
Attributions

Person 2
I myself
Interpretations, meanings, understanding
Feelings, values, fears, beliefs
Judgments, decisions
Personal reality

there are differences in self-other perceptions. Also see if the differences are affected by how close you are to each person with whom you do this exercise.

Exercise 9.3

Another activity that will be fun and will provide evidence of self-other perceptual differences may be conducted like a game in almost any social setting. It is recommended that the game be played with five to twenty people. Each person takes a turn at making three statements about himself or herself. Two of the statements are to be true, and the third is to be fabricated. The statements should describe things that are unlikely to be known by the other participants. The task for the others in each case is to decide which statement they believe to be untrue. After the game is finished, it may prove enlightening to consider what influenced others' perceptions of you.

GETTING TO KNOW *YOUR* PERCEPTION PROCESS

Exercise 9.4

- Observe for five minutes in a place you know very well. Use all of your senses, but be inanimate. Write a short description of what you saw. Observe without thinking of meanings.
- Observe again for five minutes in the same place, but this time pretend that you are here for the first time from another planet. Write a short description of your observations. Again, observe without thinking of meanings.
- Are your observations different in each case? Why or why not?

This exercise should demonstrate the role of experience, prior learning, context, and frame of reference.

THE ROLE OF PERCEPTION IN GOALS AND DECISIONS

Since perception affects all that we see, perhaps it is already clear that it affects our goals and decisions. We have already explained how perception affects attitudes toward ourselves and others. We also need to recognize that others may have difficulty perceiving what we think is clear. Furthermore, our perceptions and goals can become distorted. Distortion may cause us to set inappropriate or unrealistic goals. It may also interfere with our ability to see common ground. Our attitudes toward others may be distorted. Distorted goals as well as distorted judgments about others may cause us to make decisions that are not in our best interest.

We can take another look at our earlier example of the invoice conflict. You will recall that the phenomenon of attribution may have caused one party to believe that the invoice was overstated. That attitude or belief may lead to a goal of adjusting the invoice to the level of the original estimate. It may even lead to a refusal to negotiate. Such a goal or decision may be inappropriate or unrealistic.

Performance Checklist

✓ Everyone continually perceives the world and everything and everyone in it. Perception affects all that a person thinks and does. We infer attitudes and make judgments about people and things through perception. We attribute psychological processes and emotions to others. We also attribute intentions and causes for communication and behavior to others. We are prone to the fundamental attributional error of attributing the cause of others' communication and behavior to them personally. We do this particularly when the effects are negative in our view. Those with an intuitive preference may be less prone to the error. We are kinder in our self-attributions than we are in our attribution to others.

✓ Perception is an individual process affected by our cognitive style and other personality characteristics as well as by our prior experiences, biases, and prejudices. We tend to assume that others perceive as we do. We try to make sense of our world through perception.

✓ We may perceive ourselves differently than others perceive us. We all have a me, myself, and I that may be affected by perception differences.

✓ Perception affects not only attitude toward ourselves and others but our goals and decisions as well. In negotiation we should expect goals, communication, and decisions to be affected by perception and reality.

Key Terms, Phrases, and Concepts

Perception

Cognitive Structures

Stimuli

General Attribution Theory

Entity or Environmental Attribution

Actor Attribution

Consensus, Consistency, and Distinctiveness

Fundamental Attributional Error

Self-serving Bias

Symbolic Interaction—Me, Myself, and I

Review Questions

Mark each of questions 1 through 5 as True (T) or False (F) and answer questions 6 through 10.

T F 1. We each possess mental maps that we use to assign meaning to and make sense of what we perceive.

T F 2. Another name for mental maps is cognitive structures.

T F 3. One of the major difficulties in negotiation that is presented by perception is that we think others are like us.

T F 4. Perceived conflict may be mere differences in perceptions, or misperception.

T F 5. Extroversion and introversion preferences are frameworks for a person's cognitive structures.

6. Name two personality preferences other than extroversion and introversion that affect cognitive structures.

7. Explain the difference between an individual's cognitive framework and his or her cognitive structures.

8. Describe the extrovert's process of selecting stimuli and building frameworks.

9. Describe the introvert's process of selecting stimuli and building frameworks. Distinguish the extrovert and introvert processes.

10. Explain the role of sensing and intuiting in the perception process. Be sure to include the key perceptual difference between individuals with a sensing preference and those with an intuiting preference.

Case 9.1

Tony Taxpayer's return has come up for audit by the Internal Revenue Service (IRS). He took some deductions this year for an office in his home. Amelio Auditor at the IRS has disallowed that deduction and invited Tony to come to the office to discuss that item as well as a few other items on the return. Tony's profession is tax consulting, and he listed his occupation on his return as attorney. Tony has taken several deductions this year that might be considered aggressive; however, Tony believes that he has done no wrong. In fact, he thinks he is being singled out due to his profession. He is short on money and is worried about paying any additional assessment the IRS may make. Therefore, he is planning on giving up the office deduction in order to close the audit as quickly as possible. Amelio has never seen a home office deduction that was proper except for his own during his pre-IRS days as an independent consultant.

Case Discussion Questions

1. Apply general attribution theory to analyze and explain each party's attitudes and conclusions.
    Hint: Use consensus, consistency, distinctiveness, and the fundamental error.

2. Explain how perception affected each party's negotiation goals.

3. Apply the theory of symbolic interactionism to each party in the case by identifying where you see each party's "me, myself, and I."

Chapter 10

Effects of Power in Negotiation

"Power is the
ultimate
aphrodisiac."

Henry A. Kissinger

PERFORMANCE COMPETENCIES FOR THIS CHAPTER

- To learn the major types of power involved in negotiation
- To distinguish between real and perceived power in negotiation
- To practice assessing power
- To learn constructive ways of using power
- To learn about psychological games in negotiation
- To learn the personal impact of power and games in negotiation

Your **personal power** is the most critical component in negotiating. That power comes from understanding yourself and using all of the interpersonal skills discussed throughout this book. There are factors that arise in the negotiation process that are usually referred to as sources or types of power. It is important not to be intimidated by these factors.

Generally, the existence or extent of the power will depend upon the counterpart's perception of it and acquiescence to it. That is if, rather than being intimidated or subdued by your counterpart's power or strength, you *appear* unaware of the power, your counterpart's power will actually weaken. Your refusal to recognize or be adversely affected by the power may actually trigger a loss of confidence in the other side.

Conversely, if you are the one with power, you need to be aware of the other side's potential ability to dissipate your strength and play to your needs. In this chapter we identify the major types of power that affect negotiation and that you must assess during the preparation and execution phases of the process. Your goal is to identify the sources and types of power on both sides of the negotiation table, use your powers, and react appropriately to powers held by your counterpart. To that end, we first discuss specific types of power and then proceed to discuss reality versus perception, ways to use power, and the psychological games often played during negotiation.

TYPES OF POWER

Many authors have addressed power in various terms. French and Raven's (1968) work on the identification of the powers of legitimacy, expertise, reward, coercion, and referent power is, perhaps, the most widely cited. Those five types and six additional types—situation, identification, time, popularity, persistence, and patience—are addressed here. Specific tactics related to the use of some of these powers are presented in chapter 15.

THE POWER OF LEGITIMACY

The **power of legitimacy** is that power derived from real, perceived, or imagined authority. It is usually formal in nature. The power comes in several forms. Television broadcasts, particularly news programs and documentaries, are examples of this power. The printed word is another form and one that is often present in negotiations. We are all conditioned to believe the truth of the written word and other formal publications. Typically, people tend not to question the written word. Preprinted forms, signs, and newspapers are examples of printed words that often warrant challenge.

For example, if someone tells you that his or her preprinted legal contract cannot be amended, you do not have to accept that. It may be certain that the person making such statement has no authority to amend it, but it is not true that you must sign it as is! The person with the actual power to make the amendment decision may not even be aware of your request if you simply acquiesce to the stated power of legitimacy.

POSITION POWER

Title or position carries a form of legitimacy power often referred to as **position power.** This category includes positions, professional licenses and certifications, and degrees of education. When your counterpart is clearly aware that you know of his or her position power, it would be disrespectful to openly pretend it does not exist or to denigrate it. Disrespect or rudeness always sets a negative tone, which is not conducive to a win-win result. Nevertheless, in situations in which legitimate position power exists and is known, you must guard against letting the apparent imbalance of power diminish your goals and your confidence.

Plan your style of communication with the counterpart's position and self-perception in mind so as not to create offense and conflict. Recognize that your knowledge of your counterpart's expectations and needs, like all other knowledge used in the process, increases your power. Place this knowledge of the counterpart's ego needs into *your* arsenal of personal power to control the situation and persuade the other side to the result you seek.

You should use the power of legitimacy when it is advantageous to you. You should question the power of legitimacy when it appears as a roadblock to your goals. When it is real, you should respect it.

EXPERTISE POWER

Expertise power may be real or apparent expertise about the particular matter under negotiation. Sound preparation, as addressed in a separate chapter, will guard you against being subjected to faked expertise power. The one who has real expertise power is at an advantage. It is nearly impossible to avoid ultimately deferring to expert information and support. Note also that sharing any information generally creates a bond between the two parties. Withholding information can intimidate the other side.

REWARD POWER

Reward power can also be real or imagined. If you think that someone can affect you, that person has power over you. Reward power is of varying levels. It can relate to emotions or tangible things. For example, if someone knows that it is important to you to be recognized—even with a warm greeting or a birthday card—that person can affect your emotions and, therefore, your behavior by withholding that recognition. The authority to promote is another example of reward power.

Since negotiation is about fulfilling needs on both sides, reward power is implicit in every negotiation. People will not negotiate unless they are convinced that the other side has the ability to help them or hurt them. At least, people *should* not be negotiating unless there is potential for mutual gain! Therefore, it is important to manage this power.

Preparation in identifying the needs of both sides is the key step to managing this power. When you specify exactly what you will and will not do very early in the process, you diminish your power. Reward power is part of your bargaining arsenal. When someone has or when you perceive that someone has the power to reward you, you need to guard against being diverted from your goal. It is also possible to utilize knowledge of your counterpart's perception of reward power to make him or her feel as though he or she has controlled the outcome. This power can be used to make both sides feel successful.

COERCIVE POWER

Coercive power is the power to do something unpleasant or unwanted to another person. It is a power that is used in a competitive negotiation style. It may be the power to punish or embarrass. If the punishment or embarrassment to which you might be subjected is unacceptable to you, you should not negotiate with the person who holds such coercive power. If, on the other hand, the repercussion is something within a tolerable range and one you are willing to risk suffering, then plan your interaction accordingly. You will have to disregard the other's coercive power in order to attempt to neutralize it. Keep in mind that there is a natural tendency to imagine worse consequences than the other side can actually cause.

REFERENT POWER

The easiest way to understand **referent power** in the context of negotiation is to relate it to charisma. You will recall that charisma was discussed in another chapter. It is referent power that sells a great volume of merchandise. People buy particular brands of sport shoes because they subconsciously identify with the famous athlete who wears the brand and they want to be like him or her. Referent power is the power you have when another person wants to be like you, to be close to you, or to be liked by you.

Referent power is closely associated with your personality and your personal style. It is not present in all negotiations; however, do not neglect to look for it. An example of the existence of referent power may be in negotiating a venture capital transaction. If you are the experienced business person intending to fund the venture and the counterpart is relatively inexperienced in business, that counterpart may want to be just like you one day. You can use that power in bringing about mutual gain.

SITUATION POWER

Situation power is understood by the fact that the facts and circumstances you face may on occasion simply be to your disadvantage. In such situations especially, you must determine in your preparation stage whether there exists an acceptable alternative to a negotiated agreement. In these situations especially, you must be prepared to either accept what you set as your bottom line or walk away.

As an example, suppose that you become aware of an error on your tax return. In negotiating with the Internal Revenue Service, you must recognize that the balance of power in the situation is not to your benefit!

IDENTIFICATION POWER

Identification power is the power to relate to the other person. It is different from referent power discussed earlier. When you convey understanding, empathy, cooperation, and respect, as well as a willingness to create a mutual solution, you create the power of identification. Identification power is one of the primary forces in persuasion. We address persuasion in depth in a later chapter.

TIME

Time pressure of a deadline bearing down can present enormous power. If you are the one facing time pressure, recognize that you are at a disadvantage. Early and extensive planning are the best antidotes to negative time pressure. Individuals with Type A personality characteristics likely are most susceptible to negative effects from being subjected to this power.

POPULARITY POWER

Popularity power is sometimes referred to as the power of competition or needs. A good example is the fact that people will not loan you money as long as they think you need it and have no options! When you are perceived as needy or desperate, the value of all that you possess declines in the minds of others. If a bank is one of several from which you may borrow money, that bank will be anxious to make you a loan.

If you tell someone of an idea and report to them that the other three people you told love it, that person will likely hear your idea with a receptive mind. The converse, of course, is also true. If you tell someone that your idea was rejected and/or that it is probably not very good, you diminish the value of the idea before you even present it!

PERSISTENCE POWER

Quiet but resolved tenacity is a powerful tool in negotiation. A proposal rejected once is not necessarily dead! Using the **persistence power** is not continually repeating the same words. It is to resist giving up. It is to find different ways to explain and support your proposal. It is to find additional mutual benefits in your proposal.

PATIENCE

Patience is often ignored as a power, but it can be the greatest power of all. It applies throughout the negotiation process. Patience in

"Patience and
gentleness is
power."

Leigh Hunt

allowing your counterpart to consider proposals and to answer questions was noted in a prior chapter relative to effective communication skills. Patience is also helpful when analyzing your options and preparing for negotiation. Individuals with Type A personality characteristics will likely find this power somewhat difficult to use.

REAL VERSUS PERCEIVED POWER

You should challenge your perceptions as you identify and analyze power in negotiation. Some powers will indeed be real. You must consider whether the effects of real powers over you are positive or negative and to what degree. Often we imagine greater negative potential repercussions than really exist, as is noted in the description of certain powers in the preceding sections.

Sometimes we also perceive power that does not exist at all. Most powers must be allowed or enabled to produce any effect. Examples of enabling power were also noted in some of the preceding sections. The negative effects of power, particularly misperceived power, are fodder for psychological games. Those games are addressed in a separate section later in this chapter.

It is also necessary to guard against underestimating your power and overestimating the power of your counterpart. Information and knowledge that come from sound preparation are keys to finding power and overcoming misperceptions of power.

RECOGNIZING AVAILABLE POWER

You can practice assessing your perception of and reaction to power regularly. Some simple examples from everyday life are provided here to get you started.

Examples in Obtaining Professional Services

A common phenomenon is to allow professionals to substitute their opinions and judgments for our own in areas outside of their expertise. Those who are the licensed professionals in these situations should guard against substituting their needs and preferences for those of their clients or patients. The powers of legitimacy and expertise run afoul at times in these relationships. At first glance, the following examples may seem trivial; however, they are examples of ignoring and giving up clearly available power. Reflect on the examples to assist you in identifying other situations in which you may be failing to use your power.

Your Dentist or Doctor

Suppose you are having a crown replaced on one of your front teeth. The reason you are replacing the crown is that it has become yellowed over the years. The dentist tells you that the new material that will comprise the new crown will never change color. You, therefore, decide you would like to whiten your teeth prior to the procedure. The dentist tells you that you do not need to whiten your teeth. Furthermore, he tells you that it does not make sense to whiten your teeth and that you should match the new crown to your existing color. His reasoning is that as you age your teeth will yellow. Even if the crown is slightly darker than you currently want, over time all will match. It quickly becomes clear in your conversation that he is not going to sell you the whitening treatment. You know that you are paying a lot of money for your new crown. You know what you want. What do you do? Do you swallow your frustration and accept his opinion? Who is in charge here? Whose smile are we dealing with? Whose preference for color is most important here? Who says that it makes more sense to plan for old age rather than making yourself happy now? You have the power here to get what you want. What would happen if you were to tell the dentist that you will be very unhappy with him in the event that you do not like the color of your teeth and new crown? The last thing he wants is your unhappiness with him!

Example in Obtaining Travel Services

Suppose you learn in March that you must make a trip in June. The trip is absolutely necessary for business; and, since it will occur during a busy travel season, you make your reservations immediately. You inquire about the lowest possible fares. You are told that those tickets would be nonrefundable; however, you cannot accommodate any of the schedules for those low fares. You end up with a regular rate. The airline issues no paper tickets. You receive a confirmation in the mail within a couple of weeks and file it. A short time before the trip, a business conflict arises that necessitates cancellation of your trip. You call to request a refund. The airline representative advises you that your ticket is nonrefundable. You examine the confirmation slip and find no words to that effect. How do you respond? Is your first impulse to accept the situation? What powers are being used by the airline? (The powers of legitimacy, coercion, and situation power are being used by the airline representatives.) What powers are available to you? Can you identify the powers of legitimacy and persistence for your use?

Example in Obtaining Home Repair Services

Suppose you call your neighbor's handyman to have a light fixture in your home changed. You ask the price. He responds that it probably will not be much. He further advises you that when he does those types of things and runs into no problems, the charge is usually $25.00. He arrives in your home and changes the fixture. At one point, he gets parts from his truck to make a substitution for a piece missing from your fixture. He finishes the job in fifteen minutes. You ask how much to pay him. He asks you if $45.00 sounds okay because, after all, he had to fix that part for you. Do you just pay? What is the balance of power in the situation? Does he have any power at this point? As soon as he finished the job, he lost his power. If you think $45.00 is not fair, you have the power to negotiate.

Example in Obtaining Retail Goods

Assume you need a new refrigerator. Your old one gave up the ghost this morning, so you need one today. Before you enter the store, you decide that $700.00 is your limit. You are in luck because the store is having a sale today. You find a model marked on sale for $749.99. The salesperson approaches and asks if she should write up the sale. When you do not answer immediately, the salesperson walks away. At that moment, what is the balance of power? Is the salesperson using the power of reverse psychology? Do you consider that you may have power in the fact that the store has enough stock to find it necessary to run a sale? Does the store hold the power of legitimacy? Do you assume that the price is not negotiable? Rather than falling prey to the power of time pressure to get your new refrigerator home, consider using the power of time to your benefit. Perhaps the salesperson is paid on commission and needs more sales today for her next paycheck.

Example of Apparent Helplessness

This final example is provided to emphasize the point that you almost always have some power—regardless of the situation or initial perception. Consider the actions of the prisoner in the following scenario.[1]

[1] This story is adapted from the scenario depicted in Cohen 1980, 54.

Imagine a prisoner in solitary confinement. The prisoner is dressed; but he has no belt, no shoe laces, and nothing that he could use in any manner to hurt himself or to threaten others. He smells the smoke from the guard's cigarette. He can see the guard through the tiny porthole of his cell. He respectfully and politely asks the guard for a cigarette. The guard shrugs off the request without comment and continues strolling back and forth. The guard has perceived the prisoner as helpless. The prisoner, however, has different thoughts. The prisoner summons the guard again and politely says that if he is not given a cigarette within the next thirty seconds he will bang his head against the concrete wall until he is bloody and unconscious, and, furthermore, when he awakes he will tell the officials that the guard beat him. The prisoner even admits to the guard that the story will likely not be believed but that there will certainly be an investigation and a lot of inconvenience for the guard. The prisoner also promises to be very good, if only he could have one cigarette. Do you think that the guard gave the prisoner a cigarette?

THE MANNER OF USING POWER

In addition to recognizing various types of power, it is necessary to understand the effects of how power is used. Power may be used toward constructive or destructive ends. The manner in which it is used will, in large measure, determine its effect. Power may be used over others in aggressive ways to pressure, intimidate, or manipulate. Power may also be given to others or shared with others. Using power in the first way is sometimes referred to as a *power-over technique* (Dahl 1957). Giving and sharing power are sometimes referred to as *power-to techniques* (Dahl 1957).

> **HOT TIP!**
> Do not just give in, but *do* give *to*.

Since most individuals do not enjoy being subjected to threatening or aggressive displays of power, power-over techniques are generally divisive and result in destructive ends. They fall into the competitive style of negotiation discussed elsewhere in this book. While most types of power may be used in a power-over manner, the ones particularly conducive to the technique are position, expertise, coercive, reward, and situation.

In some negotiation contexts, the parties hold very different types and degrees of power. It is always the case that if there is nothing potentially to gain from negotiation, a nonnegotiated alternative is likely the best outcome. If the party holding the balance of power nevertheless has something to negotiate, restraint of power is an effective technique. It is important to understand that when a person perceives himself or herself with no power and no options, that person has nothing to lose. When one has nothing to lose, one might do anything. Behavior under those circumstances is hard to predict. The party who thought he or she held all the power may be sadly surprised at the outcome!

Individuals with a high need for personal power are likely to be susceptible to the power-over technique. Such individuals should exercise special care in tempering their impulses.

An often-cited approach to analyzing power is to divide it into three categories—designated, distributive, and integrative (Dahl 1957). This approach is helpful in understanding power-to techniques. Power may be designated to one of the parties by the parties or by the nature of the issues or context. The powers of position and expertise are prime examples of designated power.

Power may be distributed or given to a party. A power-to technique may be used to accomplish a more even power balance for the purpose of increasing the other party's interest and motivation to find mutual resolution. Typically, the most effective technique is to integrate, or share, power. This technique is collaborative in nature and generates constructive, mutually satisfying ends. The act of restraining power often has the effect of integrating power. Individuals with a high need for social power are likely to find the power integration technique quite comfortable.

PSYCHOLOGICAL GAMES

Another way to employ power-over tactics, albeit in a subtle rather than aggressive way, is to engage in psychological games. In this section, we describe certain psychological games in general that may appear at any stage of the negotiation process. Psychological maneuvers and stratagems are organized, intentional patterns of behavior designed to manipulate the other person. A maneuver is a brief or limited action, while a stratagem is more prolonged and pervasive. Specific tactics used to play these games are addressed more fully in another chapter.

The two major categories of interpersonal, psychological games are *con games* and *head games*. The desired outcome of the con game is tangible. The desired outcome of the head game is emotional, which may be used for the purpose of later gaining tangible value. Psychological games are generally consistent with a competitive style of negotiation.

In playing these games, negotiators use disingenuous comments or displays of attitude. The ulterior motive may be to induce a concession or to create an illusion of greater power than exists. These games can disadvantage the other side if they succeed in making the recipient believe that he or she is in the weaker position or, of course, if the recipient makes an unnecessary or unpaid-for concession.

The best defense to a false statement made to exaggerate power is to stop yourself from accepting it without critical internal evaluation and to look for and ask for information that might support or fail to support the illusion. Examples of statements or conduct made to induce a concession include false flattery, feigned weakness, or feigned anger. You must guard against acting on sympathy, guilt, or fear in response to weakness or anger—feigned or real.

Real anger is a loss of control and usually results in making a mistake such as premature disclosure of information. In trying to distinguish between feigned and real anger, watch for signs of loss in control as well as nonverbal signals that confirm or contradict the emotion displayed. An appropriate response to anger may be to show personal offense or embarrassment. You may also ignore it.

> "Let us never negotiate out of fear, but let us never fear to negotiate."
>
> *John F. Kennedy*

Another maneuver often used is for the negotiator to defer to a higher authority. The best rule is to negotiate only with the person who has the ultimate authority or with the person who holds authority on the other side equivalent to the authority you hold. If you find yourself in a position—perhaps after negotiations have commenced—of negotiating with someone who claims lack of authority, do not agree to anything final. Terminate the proceedings until the appropriate individual appears. Your termination of discussions will quickly disclose whether or not the play was a bluff.

Another ploy often used is to begin discussion of a distasteful issue in order to weaken your emotional strength. This psychological game is intended to divert attention from the major issue or issues to be negotiated or the issues on which you may have the stronger position or power.

Bluffing is a maneuver used by some negotiators. Consider this carefully. Bluffing is lying. The other ploys we have discussed are also considered by many to be lying. Good negotiators do not have to lie. Lying is unethical as well as risky conduct. Credibility is important in negotiation. You will have greater success in changing the other side's opinion if you have established your integrity and credibility. As you will see in studying the principles of persuasion later in this book, credibility is extremely important in successful negotiation.

> "It takes a lifetime to build a reputation, and only a short time to lose it all."
>
> *Anne Mulcahy, Chairman and CEO, Xerox Fortune, November 18, 2002*

Regardless of where you personally draw the line, you must be prepared for such ploys from the other side. Everyone does poorly in determining when they are being bluffed. The best protection is sound preparation, as is discussed throughout this book. It is useful to know that the one who bluffs typically has the weaker hand and the weaker interpersonal skills. It is also useful to know that those who do successfully bluff never do so unless it is absolutely necessary, they are willing to carry out their bluff if called, and they do not ever expose it after they have succeeded!

Sometimes reverse psychology is used in the negotiation process. We tend to want what we think we cannot have! The psychological term for this phenomenon is *reactance* (Brehm 1966). Properly done, this maneuver may be effective on an extremely negative counterpart who has moved into a win-lose attitude. Rather than being competitive in nature, it may be used to neutralize the other side's competitive stance. Such a competitive, negative counterpart will want what he or she thinks you do not want! This maneuver is dangerous and should always be attempted with hypothetical statements such as "what if."

When real anxiety and frustration occur in the negotiating process, reactions may be anger, aggression, flight, distorted thinking, and various defense mechanisms. When you lose your personal control, you may play psychological games on yourself! Examples include rationalizing your position, ignoring the existence of a conflict, or projecting the unacceptable position or motive onto the other side.

Performance Checklist

✓ Your personal power is the most critical component in negotiating. There are at least twelve specific sources or types of power that arise in negotiation: legitimacy, position, expertise, reward, coercive, referent, situation, identification, time, popularity, persistence, and patience.

✓ Power may be real or perceived.

✓ Power may be designated, distributive, or integrative. Distributing and integrating power are power-to techniques that use power constructively and are consistent with the collaborative style of negotiation.

✓ Power is used to play psychological games. Games and power-over techniques are aggressive and competitive and typically generate destructive outcome.

✓ Most power requires enabling by the person it would affect in order to have any effect. We often permit others to have power over us. The recipient of a con game or head game may counteract such efforts by maintaining self-control and guarding against misperceptions.

Key Terms, Phrases, and Concepts

Personal Power

Power of Legitimacy

Position Power

Expertise Power

Reward Power

Coercive Power

Referent Power

Situation Power

Identification Power

Popularity Power

Persistence Power

Review Questions

Mark each of questions 1 through 3 as True (T) or False (F) and answer questions 4 through 10.

T F 1. You should avoid negotiating with someone who holds coercive power over you.

T F 2. Reward power may have a tangible or emotional foundation.

T F 3. A person is the most powerless when he or she is perceived as having the most need.

4. Which two names are used to describe the type of power described in question 3?

5. Which type of power is present in an organizational gatekeeper who controls the distribution of reports and proposals?

6. Explain the differences between and among legitimate power, position power, and expertise power.

7. Explain the difference between referent power and identification power.

8. Identify at least six things that might serve as identification power between you and another negotiator.

9. Describe at least one way in which you may constructively use the power you have in your current daily organizational role.

10. Try to assess the ulterior motive underlying the flattery you most recently received. Did you lose the head game?

Case 10.1

Sophia and Isaam are colleagues and peers in the same organization. Sophia is vice president and general counsel; Isaam is vice president of finance. They have been friends for many years and, in fact, completed their MBAs together. They are currently participating in completing due diligence relative to a potential acquisition. Sophia is the project team manager for the acquisition audit/investigation. Sophia and Isaam differ in their perceptions of certain key matters discovered and, therefore, disagree on whether or not to proceed with the acquisition. Sophia maintains that understanding and disposition of the matters require legal expertise. They are about to discuss their findings and recommendations with the CEO who is very excited about going forward with this transaction and generally disdains being told of problems when it means he cannot do what he wants to do.

Case Discussion Questions

1. Which powers are held by Sophia, Isaam, and the CEO? Which, if any, of the powers you identified are merely perceived, or imaginary?

2. How would you describe the relative balance of these powers?

3. Do you have any suggestions for Sophia that may lessen or eliminate the conflict between her and Isaam?

Chapter 11

Asserting Yourself

- To assess your current level of assertion
- To understand the difference in passivity, aggression, and assertion
- To recognize aggression and its impact on negotiation
- To learn the dynamics of anger and anger management
- To learn assertive behavior and its impact on negotiation

> "If you have a
> point to make,
> don't try to be
> subtle or clever."
>
> *Winston Churchill*

In negotiation, if you are to obtain what you desire, you must communicate your desires. The manner in which your needs and desires are expressed significantly impacts success in attaining your goals. In this chapter, we build on the principles of effective negotiation communication outlined earlier in this book by examining the impact of passive, assertive, and aggressive behavior. We examine the role of fear and anger in negotiation behavior. Mastering the material in this chapter will provide the foundation for developing your persuasion skills addressed in the next chapter. We begin with an opportunity to assess your current behavioral patterns.

ASSERTION ASSESSMENT

Complete the **assertive ACT survey** in exhibit 11.1 prior to reading the rest of the material in this chapter.

EXHIBIT 11-1

Your Assertive ACT Survey

The questions that follow will assist you in determining the extent to which you act assertively. Three responses are required for each statement. All questions should be answered one column at a time. First, rate the matters for each of the fifty statements in column A for the level of anxiety or discomfort it causes you. Next, cover column A so that you cannot see your answers and rate the matters for each of the fifty statements in column C for the caliber. This column is to record how important the matter is or how much it counts for you. Finally, cover your answers for columns A and C and proceed to rate in column T the frequency with which you take the action indicated for all fifty statements. (If you have *never* found yourself in the situation described, you may skip the statement.)

For columns A (Anxiety) and C (Caliber), use the following scale:

1 = none, 2 = little, 3 = a medium amount, 4 = much, 5 = a great amount

For column T (Taking the Action), use the following scale:

1 = never, 2 = once in a while, 3 = more often than not, 4 = almost always, 5 = always

A	C	T	
____	____	____	1. I refuse to loan my things to others.
____	____	____	2. I ask for an increase in compensation at work.
____	____	____	3. I return defective products.
____	____	____	4. I decline an invitation for an activity I do not like.
____	____	____	5. I decline an invitation when accepting would interfere with something else I want to do.

A	C	T	
___	___	___	6. I return food at a restaurant that is not to my liking.
___	___	___	7. I ask for clarification when I do not understand.
___	___	___	8. I ask for repayment of loans I have made when they are due.
___	___	___	9. I ask for a refund when I am overcharged.
___	___	___	10. I ask for or apply for promotions.
___	___	___	11. I tell someone inoffensively that they cut in line.
___	___	___	12. I say my feelings are hurt when they are.
___	___	___	13. I express my opinions when they differ from others' opinions.
___	___	___	14. I ask for service assistance or other help when I need it.
___	___	___	15. I make requests of others to do things for me.
___	___	___	16. I initiate meetings.
___	___	___	17. I invite other people to do things with me.
___	___	___	18. I am the first to speak to business associates.
___	___	___	19. I speak to strangers.
___	___	___	20. I tell people how I feel when they do something I do not like.
___	___	___	21. I give compliments to people.
___	___	___	22. I tell people when I notice something different about their appearance.
___	___	___	23. I initiate collection efforts for money owed to me.
___	___	___	24. When I do not know something, I say so.
___	___	___	25. I express my feelings to people who bother me.
___	___	___	26. When individuals invite themselves to join me and I do not want them to, I express my true feelings.
___	___	___	27. I tell people when I think they have been unfair.
___	___	___	28. I tell people bad news that they need to know.
___	___	___	29. When I am unable or unwilling to have a conversation with someone, I say so.
___	___	___	30. I tell someone that I was not listening to him or her.
___	___	___	31. I ask for a change of duties, position, or job transfer at work when I want one.
___	___	___	32. I admit when I do not know how to do something.
___	___	___	33. I admit when I make a mistake.
___	___	___	34. I tell someone when his or her data are wrong.
___	___	___	35. I tell someone when he or she has made an error.
___	___	___	36. I say "no" when I want to say "no."

A	C	T	
_____	_____	_____	37. I decline high-pressure efforts to get me to do something that I do not want to do.
_____	_____	_____	38. I resist sales pressure for things I do not want.
_____	_____	_____	39. I resist peer pressure to spend money I cannot afford to spend.
_____	_____	_____	40. I resist solicitations for money I cannot afford to give.
_____	_____	_____	41. I say that I am angry when I am angry.
_____	_____	_____	42. I say things that accurately state what I feel.
_____	_____	_____	43. I say things that accurately state what I think or mean.
_____	_____	_____	44. When I make an error and when I hurt or offend someone, I apologize.
_____	_____	_____	45. When someone provides constructive criticism of me, I seek more information.
_____	_____	_____	46. I look people in the eyes when I talk to them.
_____	_____	_____	47. I say what I am afraid of.
_____	_____	_____	48. I inquire about others' feelings.
_____	_____	_____	49. I find it easy to tell others that I like them.
_____	_____	_____	50. I find it easy to receive compliments.

Scoring Your Assertive ACT Survey

Total column A _____   Total column C _____   Total column T _____

[If your C score is less than 150, the results are unclear. Skip to the note at the end of this section.]

Compute the percentage your T score is of your A score. _____ percent

Examples: T score of 120 divided by A score of 160 = 75 percent

T score of 200 divided by A score of 160 = 125 percent

Generally, the closer the relationship between A, C, and T, the more assertive you are.

T scores of 90 percent and above = very assertive.

T scores of 75–89 percent = fairly assertive.

T scores below 75 percent = not assertive.

A and C scores are expected to be within fifty points of each other:

If your C score is more than fifty points greater than your A score, *but* your T score is 85 percent or higher, *good work!* Keep doing what you do!

If your A score is more than fifty points greater than your C score, *and* your T score is 75 percent or higher, investigate your underlying fears while you continue to work on your assertive behavior.

Your low C score may make the results on this survey unclear. If more than three statements were left unanswered, for example, your score is unreliable. You may want to try a free-form assessment by thinking about how you act with regard to the things in life about which you care the most.

Source: Survey adapted in part from E. D. Gambrill and C. A. Richey, *Behavior Therapy* (1975; repr., 6 DeJanasz-Dowd-Schneider, *Interpersonal Skills in Organizations*, chapter 5, McGraw-Hill, 2001), 550–61.

Passivity, Aggression, and Assertion Defined

Failing to try to make your opinions and desires known is **passive behavior.** Failing to address conflict is passive behavior. Passive behavior is keeping your feelings to yourself. Avoiding interpersonal conflict and avoiding negotiation may be passive behaviors. Bear in mind, as noted in previous chapters, that an avoiding approach to interpersonal conflict is sometimes appropriate. However, an avoidance approach does not *have* to be synonymous with passivity. It is possible to be assertive even in those situations in which you have chosen not to engage the conflict or not to negotiate, as explained later in this chapter.

Aggression comes in two styles—passive and hostile. **Passive-aggressive behavior,** like plain passive behavior, is failing to specifically address or make known your opinions and desires. With passive-aggressive behavior, however, rather than simply keeping one's feelings to oneself, one acts out. Fears, frustration, and anger are expressed in *indirect* actions such as sarcasm and other signals intended to be subtle expressions of conflict, dislike, disrespect, or disapproval. Being *avoidably* or habitually late for meetings and appointments, for example, is passive-aggressive behavior.

Hostile-aggressive behavior is *not* so subtle. It is striking out with *direct* impolite or belittling comments. It is directing comments to the *person* of the other rather than to the substance of the matters at hand. Hostile-aggressive behavior may range from mild to severe. Hostile-aggressive behavior is competitive, but one need not be aggressive when using a competitive negotiation style or tactic, as is explained later in this chapter.

Passive-Aggressive Behavior and Its Impact on Negotiation

Passive-aggressive behavior is, at best, noise in the communication channel. It impedes understanding necessary to find common ground and resolution. It may be perceived, consciously or unconsciously, as insulting. At its worst, passive aggression leads to hostile aggression and a continuing negative interaction spiral. Aggression, even in the passive form, may inhibit our cognitive abilities because we are somewhat angry and misdirected in our thinking.

In some sense, we expect the other person to read our minds when we engage in passive-aggressive behavior! Have you ever said aloud or to yourself following an interaction, "He certainly must have known that I didn't want to do that"? If you don't express yourself or ask for what you want, you will likely not get it.

We often engage in passive-aggressive behavior unconsciously. We acquire habits of using such behavior. Passive aggressiveness may be expressed not only through words but through body language and physical arrangements as well. Leaning back and placing your feet on the top of the desk while talking with someone is likely to be perceived as passive aggressive behavior. Leaning back and placing your hands behind your head, likewise, may be perceived as passive aggression. Both of these gestures can convey lack of respect or offensive domination.

HOSTILE-AGGRESSIVE BEHAVIOR AND ITS IMPACT ON NEGOTIATION

> "Strong and bitter words indicate a weak cause."
>
> *Victor Hugo*

Aggression is an attack. While passive aggression may miss the mark or go *consciously* unnoticed by the target, hostile aggression will be received! When you feel attacked, how do you respond? Our instincts can cause us to want to strike back or seek revenge. Except in an emergency situation (for example, when you physically remove another person from danger), not much that is positive or constructive can come from aggression.

When negotiation becomes hostile, the parties no longer communicate. Thus, at best, hostile aggression will lead to no agreement. At worst, it will lead to a bad agreement or, perhaps, physical violence. Where there is hostile aggression, there is a dominance of anger. Anger causes our intellectual and creative abilities—the very abilities we need to negotiate—to shut down.

THE IMPETUS FOR PASSIVE AND AGGRESSIVE BEHAVIOR

Interestingly, all three behaviors we have discussed—passive, passive-aggressive, and hostile-aggressive—have a common source—fear. From fear comes anger. Individuals respond in their own way to fear and anger. While specific fears differ from individual to individual and from situation to situation, the root of fear invokes our self-esteem in some way. Therefore, to understand why we act in a manner that is passive, passive-aggressive, or hostile-aggressive, we must understand the dynamics of anger and investigate our fears and self-esteem.

THE DYNAMICS OF ANGER

Anger creates distress and physiological changes. It reduces cognitive functioning. It increases blood pressure. One notable physical sign of anger is enlarged eye pupils. Redness in the face caused by the rush of blood may also be noticeable. Unresolved anger may lead to inward or outward aggression.

Anger is not mere frustration. Anger is debilitating. Anger is wishing that someone or some thing were different. Anger leads to aggression—passive or hostile. Anger is a loss of control—in effect, temporary insanity! The anger is in control, not you. When you are out of control, you cannot think clearly or rationally. You will have poor judgment and make poor decisions. Anger begets anger. It is *not possible* to change the other person through anger. Quite the contrary; your anger will entrench the other person's position and/or create anger on that person's part. Once that occurs, two people who are temporarily insane are attempting to negotiate!

You cannot effect a productive change while under the influence of anger. You must regain self-control before you can change yourself, the situation, or the other party's opinion. To get control, you must examine the underlying fear that is causing your anger.

"You cannot make a crab walk straight."

Aristophanes

FEAR

The root of all anger is fear. Fear makes us feel vulnerable. It triggers our fight-or-flight instincts. We may respond to fear by holding in or striking out. We may instinctively want revenge when we feel slighted.

Fears involved in negotiation may include those of not getting what you want, not winning, not being liked, not being respected, not being accepted, not being understood, not knowing enough, not being competent, or not being seen in the light you prefer. You may also fear losing, appearing stupid, being manipulated, being overpowered, or that resources are scarce. Try to identify other fears you have had in preparation for or during your negotiation experiences. Did the fear assist your negotiation in any way?

Fear may lead you to be passive, to avoid, or to disengage. A pervasive or regular pattern of passive behavior is likely to be related to unacknowledged fears. Even when you behave passively, your fear can lead to anger turned inward. When fear does give way to anger, you may express the anger in passive-aggressive or hostile-aggressive behavior. All three behaviors damage your negotiating ability.

Fear leads to competitive thinking and, thus, impedes successful negotiation. Now see if you can identify a common theme in these fears. The common theme is *you*—your self-esteem!

SELF-ESTEEM

Our **self-esteem** is our personal sense of value and worth. Individual beliefs and values affect self-esteem. Our perception of how others view us also affects our self-esteem. Our fears are our worries that our self-esteem will be damaged. We fear that we will not be as good as we think we are or want to be. We fear that others will think less of us. We then protect ourselves by holding in our fears and/or succumbing to anger. In either case, the behavior is one of powerlessness; and a feeling of powerlessness exasperates the fear and anger!

The next section of this chapter provides tools for **anger management** that will also help you to identify and conquer your fears and build your self-esteem. Following that, we discuss assertive behavior. Identifying your fears, managing your anger, and building your self-esteem will help you to behave assertively. Assertive behavior is critical to negotiation success. You will find that there is a dynamic interaction between self-esteem and assertion. If your ACT score was low on the survey in Exhibit 11-1, it may reflect a need to increase your self-esteem. Practicing one will assist you in developing the other.

ANGER MANAGEMENT TOOLS

In order to better control and manage your anger, you will have to identify your fears and confront them by determining whether there is something real to fear or whether there is a misconception at the root of the fear. If the fear is not realistic, your anger should subside. You may ask yourself what you are gaining from the anger. Try to engage in alternative, open thinking. If the fear *is* realistic, investigate what you may do to get rid of it. What can you do to take yourself out of harm's way? What are your options? What are your needs?

If you are one who is typically quick to anger or whose anger escalates quickly, you may find it useful to regularly practice the techniques in the list provided in Box 11-1. It may also be insightful, while you are *not* angry, to talk with someone who regularly sets you off. Be open, using the assertion techniques in this chapter, to discussing each others' perceptions and feelings.

As mentioned earlier in this chapter, many of your fears likely relate to your self-esteem. You may follow the steps provided later in Box 11-2 for increasing your self-esteem. You should also find it useful to practice the assertion-building tools presented later in this chapter in Box 11-3.

> **"Even a paranoid has some real enemies."**
>
> *Henry A. Kissinger*

ANGER MANAGEMENT TECHNIQUES

Box 11-1   Anger Management

- Check your perceptions. Check your approach. Challenge your thinking.
- Recognize your anger.
- When you feel anger, stop! Hold your breath for ten seconds. Try to postpone your anger.
- It's okay to say, "I am angry. I need a moment."
- When you are angry, think about things that make you smile.
- Identify what you are afraid of. Determine whether or not the fear is realistic.
- Determine what you can do to get rid of the fear. Do it!
- Ask yourself how important the fear is relative to other values and goals. If today were your last day on earth, would what you fear matter?
- If you are angry about something past that you cannot change, change your perception and understanding. Release the anger. Forgive.

- Think creatively in alternative terms. For example, when that car darts in front of you on the road and slows you down, consider whether that event may be keeping you from a ticket or an accident up the road!

- Challenge your thinking more! When someone is late, are you angry because you fear that person does not value your time or value you? When the deal will not close, are you angry because you fear you will run out of time? When things do not go in the order you prefer, are you angry because you fear you will not get what you want? Recognize your value and worth. Recognize that you have options. Speak your concerns and desires. Do not get mad!

- When someone is angry with you, acknowledge the anger rather than responding in anger.

- Before you lose control with someone else and as a last resort, scream into a pillow.

- Catch yourself in your rage. Silently tell yourself, "Good job for catching yourself!" Tell yourself that you slipped but are now in control.

- Build your listening skills.

- Build your internal locus of control. Decide what you can do and what you cannot.

- Build your self-esteem.

- Build your assertion skills.

- Maintain a journal on your daily encounters with your anger and fear, detailing how you felt and how you handled them.

- Smile and laugh more. It is not possible to be both angry and happy or to think love and anger at the same moment.

- Fall in love with a pet. As you care for that pet, observe the pet's forgiving and loving attitude and demeanor. (Note that although this is a highly recommended and effective technique, you must first ensure that you can trust yourself not to vent your anger on the pet.)

Box 11-2   Increasing Self-Esteem

1. When you or someone else says something negative to you as a person, cancel it. Tell yourself that it is not true. Differentiate between actions and the person.

2. Focus on all of the things about yourself that you like. Tell yourself that you like yourself. You may say, "I am a competent person," and "I am a nice person."

3. Identify your accomplishments every day and congratulate yourself on them.

4. Visualize yourself the way you want to be.

5. Search for positive adjectives that describe you.

6. Resolve to fix the things about your behavior that you do not like, but do not confuse them with being a lesser or bad person.

7. And, yes, care for a pet! That creature's love for you will make you feel better about yourself!

Box 11-3 Assertiveness Training Steps

- Greet people. Be the first to speak.

- Give compliments to others.

- Use *I* language regularly to express your perceptions and feelings and desires.

- Express your feelings when they happen.

- Ask others to explain their reasoning, but do this using *I* statements such as "I would like to hear the reasoning for that."

- Speak up when you do not agree.

- Make eye contact.

The foregoing may sound simple. Try an experiment that will demonstrate how powerful these steps can be. Think of something that makes you angry. It may be something or someone who regularly makes you angry. It may be a recent experience that is fresh in your mind. Try to feel the anger. Now that you are angry, take a look at the photograph in Exhibit 11-2.

Are you still angry? All of the preceding advice should help. The power of a pet just may be the best help!

Remember that controlling your anger will make you a better negotiator.

EXHIBIT 11-2

Dr. Cocoa

INCREASING YOUR SELF-ESTEEM

Your unconscious mind absorbs your thoughts and words, as well as the words of others, as though they are true. When those thoughts and words are negative toward you, your self-esteem may be negatively affected. Your self-esteem affects your confidence, or lack thereof, and affects your negotiation performance.

The more you are with persons who make you feel good about yourself, the better it will be for your positive self-esteem. If you find yourself regularly with people who make you feel inadequate or negative about yourself in some ways and you cannot choose to be away from them, you should assertively confront them with your feelings and desires. You may also follow the items listed in Box 11-2 to increase your self-esteem.

ASSERTIVE BEHAVIOR AND ITS IMPACT ON YOU AND NEGOTIATION

Assertive language and assertive behavior reflect your feelings and desires. Being assertive is to own your feelings and desires and to express them in nonoffensive ways. Being assertive is to attack the issues rather than the people. Assertion is speaking up and voicing your opinions when you disagree.

The most useful way to identify and practice assertive behavior is to watch for and use *I* statements in specifying and clarifying matters in conflict. To be assertive, a statement should also comply with five criteria. It should (1) specify the particular behavior or issue to which you want to speak; (2) contain your feelings about the behavior or issue; (3) explain the effect on you of the particular behavior or issue; (4) empathize with the other person's view; and (5) offer, or indicate openness to, a solution. Because assertive language is comprised of *I* statements and is specific, it forces us to think before we speak, to focus our thoughts, and to refrain from insulting the other person. Thus, it also helps in anger control. Further, because when we are assertive we are taking care of ourselves, it helps increase self-esteem as well as helping to resolve internal conflict.

Assertive behavior fosters communication and resolution in negotiation. Assertive behavior fosters cooperation and collaboration. However, it may also be utilized when you choose to avoid—or not negotiate—a conflict. Rather than avoiding with nothing more, you may assertively explain your position and decision to not engage. Similarly, using assertive language, a competitive negotiation (such as purchasing a car, for example) may be spared destructive negative escalation. These concepts relative to avoidant and competitive systems are addressed further in another chapter.

The steps listed in Box 11-3 can be used to practice your assertion every day. It is often helpful to maintain a journal on your assertion-building progress.

Performance Checklist

✓ Your assertive ACT survey score provides you with information for improving your negotiation effectiveness.

✓ Communication behavior may be passive, passively aggressive, aggressive, or assertive. Passive behavior is keeping your feelings and desires to yourself. Passive-aggressive behavior is expressing yourself in indirect ways that are unlikely to be understood by others. Aggressive behavior is direct and offensive. Assertiveness is expressing one's feelings and desires in a manner that accepts responsibility. It is to own one's feelings and to craft communication with *I* statements that focus on issues rather than individuals.

✓ Passive, passive-aggressive, and aggressive behaviors are noise in the communication channel at best. At worst, they beget anger and precipitate a negative, destructive spiral of interaction.

✓ Fear and anger, particularly as they relate to self-esteem, are at the root of these ineffective behaviors. Anger is a loss of control. Fear and anger impede the very cognitive abilities critical to negotiation success. Anger-management and self-esteem-building exercises are helpful in beginning to develop assertive negotiation behavior.

✓ Negotiation requires communication of desires. Assertive communication is the foundation for persuasive argument and negotiation success.

Key Terms, Phrases, and Concepts

Assertive ACT Survey

Passive Behavior

Passive-Aggressive Behavior

Hostile-Aggressive Behavior

Self-Esteem

Anger Management

Review Questions

Mark each of questions 1 through 7 as True (T) or False (F) and answer questions 8 through 10.

T F 1. Assertion is mild aggression.

T F 2. Aggressive behavior is acceptable in negotiation as long as it is not hostile-aggressive behavior.

T F 3. Anger creates physiological changes.

T F 4. The root of all anger is fear.

T F 5. Some people think best when they are angry.

T F 6. The root of low self-esteem is fear.

T F 7. The cause for low assertion may be low self-esteem.

8. Name five things you can do to increase your assertiveness in negotiation.

9. Identify two anger-management techniques that you will begin utilizing.

10. Analyze your behavior for passive-aggressive characteristics that you may begin to work to change.

Case 11.1

Dulce has been with her organization for three years and has received outstanding performance evaluations. Farai came on board one full year later than did Dulce. Based upon what Farai has said, Dulce believes that Farai is earning the same amount of salary as she does although he is at a lower rank. Dulce has been fuming about Farai's salary. It appears objectively clear to everyone that Dulce has superior educational and experiential credentials. Rumor has it that Farai is not performing very well, although rumor also has it that Farai and the vice president have become pretty chummy.

Dick, the vice president, has come into Dulce's office and says the following: "I wanted to be sure that you were told before the information is generally disseminated. We are promoting Farai to director of the division. You know that you are invaluable in the work you do. We cannot afford to lose you to administrative matters that Farai will be performing. I hope that you will give Farai your full support. Thank you."

Dulce responded, "Oh, if you had offered it to me, I would have declined. I don't want administrative work."

Case Discussion Questions

1. Is Dulce's behavior merely passive (unassertive) or passive-aggressive? Why or how?

2. What effect is Dulce's behavior having on Dick? What effect is Dulce's behavior having on her and her working relationships?

3. If you were Dulce, what would you want? Create a script for Dulce that is assertive communication designed for effective negotiation.

Chapter 12

Principles of Persuasion

PERFORMANCE COMPETENCIES FOR THIS CHAPTER

- To recognize the difficulties of persuasion
- To learn the fundamental keys of persuasion
- To learn when persuasion is unlikely
- To learn the role of diplomacy in persuasion
- To practice your persuasion skills

"Many can argue;
not many
converse."

Louisa May Alcott

Principles of getting along with people generally apply to the negotiating process. One such principle is that people like to make their own decisions and judgments. In persuasion, we must deal with others' perceptions and inferences as well as convince them of the validity of our arguments. Therefore, in persuading people, your job is to lead them with information demonstrating that the result you want is beneficial, or not harmful, to them. You have a better chance at persuasion when you can show that a proposal is good for both (all) sides.

Persuasion is difficult until you have the keys. However, what is understood about cognitive processing suggests that persuasion is *im*possible at times. Previously in this book, we discussed coming to *GRIP* with your overall strategy and goals, including the process of assessing relative powers. In this chapter, we build on that material and utilize additional psychological theories to show you how to use your *ACES* and cross the *CREEK* to persuasion. We also discuss principles that will help you identify when you and others may not be persuaded. Just as with the other skills necessary for successful negotiation, you may have to practice persuasion techniques. Practice exercises are provided in this chapter.

SOCIAL JUDGMENT THEORY

As stated in a prior chapter, people search for validity in perceiving and assessing information. We also know that individuals perceive through their individual lenses and automatically infer reasons for or causes of verbal and behavioral communication. With knowledge of perception and attribution as a base, we may explore further cognitive processes involved in persuasion. Since attitudes, opinions, and beliefs are all dynamically interrelated—any one can affect another—what we discuss here applies to all three. The word **attitude** describes a positive or negative or good versus bad feeling about something or someone. The word *opinion* describes a position on something or someone. *Beliefs* are what one knows to be true. When the word *attitude* is used in this chapter, however, the principles apply equally to opinions and beliefs.

Social judgment theory emphasizes the effects of prior attitudes on perceptions of others' attitudes and on the related influence of persuasive communication (Eagly and Chaiken 1993). The focus is on distortions in perceiving attitudes of others. The theory explains certain phenomena that occur prior to processing persuasive or argument-based communication. The research helps us understand attitude change (Petty and Cacioppo 1981, 1986).

In contrast to the unconscious cognitive phenomena discussed in chapter 9, at the core of social judgment theory are the assumptions that people know their attitudes and are able to determine what attitudinal changes they are willing to accept or reject. Each message is compared to the individual's current attitude. If the message is close to the existing attitude, change may occur; but, if the message is too far off, the individual will reject the message and leave attitude unchanged. To understand the theory, it helps to conceptualize attitude in segments and from two perspectives. People have a **latitude of commitment** in which their attitudes or beliefs are firm. People also have a **latitude of noncommitment** or indifference, in which they hold no attitude or opinion or hold attitudes to which they are only lightly committed. People perceive persuasive messages in a range of similarity and dissimilarity. That perception creates a **latitude of acceptance** and a **latitude of rejection.** The next section addresses where resistance is likely and how such resistance may or may not be overcome.

LATITUDES OF COMMITMENT, NONCOMMITMENT, ACCEPTANCE, AND REJECTION

The latitude of commitment is where change or persuasion is least likely to be successful. That is because we are referring to firmly held positions, attitudes, opinions, or beliefs. Some portion of the latitude of commitment will clearly constitute the person's latitude of rejection. That is, statements that are squarely inconsistent with attitudes and beliefs in the latitude of commitment will be rejected. Some portion of the latitude of commitment will, however, be within the person's latitude of acceptance! That is, attitudes perceived to be substantially the same as or consistent with committed attitudes *will* be accepted.

Attitude will change only when the persuasive message is perceived to be within the latitude of acceptance or the latitude of noncommitment or indifference. The persuasive impact is greatest in the latitude of noncommitment (Hovland, Harvey, and Sherif 1957; Peterson and Koulack 1969). It is easiest to persuade one who holds no prior opinion or attitude on the matter.

Research has also confirmed the existence of a **disconfirmation bias** in the evaluation of messages or arguments (Edwards and Smith 1996). That is, arguments incompatible with prior beliefs are scrutinized longer, subjected to more extensive refutational analyses, and judged to be weaker than arguments compatible with prior beliefs. Furthermore, it has been established that people are *unable* to evaluate communication or evidence independently of prior beliefs (Edwards and Smith 1996).[1]

We tend to accept at face value arguments that sound to us to be compatible with our prior beliefs. We tend to scrutinize arguments we perceive to be incompatible with our prior beliefs. We even try to undermine evidence that is contrary to our beliefs. This bias has been found in both inductive and deductive reasoning (Edwards and Smith 1996). There is an automatic activation in memory of material relevant to the arguments we hear as incompatible with our beliefs. We typically report more information in the process of evaluating an incompatible argument than we report when evaluating a compatible argument.

Unconscious cognitive phenomena also affect persuasion. The automatic errors and biases discussed previously in this book occur in evaluating persuasive messages. Furthermore, we experience discomfort when presented with conflicting information. The additional unconscious cognitive processes involved in persuasion are addressed in the next section.

COGNITIVE DISSONANCE

People perceive attitudinally similar statements as more similar than they are in reality, and vice versa (Sherif and Sherif 1967; Sherif, Sherif, and Nebergall 1965). This is similar to the principle referred to as *false consensus bias,* which is the tendency to believe that others share our attitudes and behaviors (Ross, Green, and House 1977). This is also somewhat similar to the phenomenon of **cognitive dissonance.** This research provides insight to additional unconscious processes involved in persuasion.

"*Cognitive dissonance* is a state of tension that occurs whenever an individual simultaneously holds two cognitions that are psychologically inconsistent. The existence of dissonance, being psychologically uncomfortable, will motivate the person to try to reduce the dissonance and achieve consonance. . . . The strength of the pressure to reduce the dissonance is a function of the magnitude of the dissonance" (Festinger 1957, 2, 3, 18). Dissonance, or psychological discomfort, may arise when an individual tries to entertain one or more thoughts that are inconsistent with an existing attitude

---

[1] See also Batson (1975); Cacioppo and Berntson (1994); Chapman and Chapman (1959); Darley and Gross (1983); Ditto and Lopez (1992); Geller and Pitz (1968); Koehler (1993); Kunda (1990); Lord, Ross, and Lepper (1979); Nisbett and Ross (1980); Ross and Lepper (1980); and Sherif and Hovland (1961).

or belief or are inconsistent with each other. It can also arise when an individual behaves in a way that is inconsistent with one or more thoughts or an existing attitude or belief. Since human beings do not like mental discomfort that comes with dissonance, they try to eliminate or minimize it.

Attempts to reduce dissonance occur unconsciously and make attempts at persuasion more difficult. Cognitive dissonance may help in understanding why attempts to persuade within another's latitude of rejection are likely to fail. The only way to eliminate dissonance is to change one or more relevant elements—thoughts or behaviors. The relative value or importance of an element may be changed. One or more elements may be rejected. One or more elements may be added. Forgetting is another way individuals reduce dissonance or effect change. Our perception may play tricks on us while we undertake attempts to reduce dissonance.

Cognitive dissonance can cause us to engage in selective perception. We attempt to avoid information that may increase discomfort. We experience a drive toward mental harmony and balance. Thus, in addition to what we already know about different personalities perceiving differently, when one seeks to eliminate dissonance, one distorts perceptions. Dissonance is not limited to logical inconsistencies, and reduction steps need not be logical to others. The dissonance and balance are in the mind of the perceiver. Examples will help you understand the effects of dissonance in persuasion.

The harmful effects of tobacco are well-voiced, yet individuals continue to smoke and chew tobacco. Their behavior is inconsistent with research and warnings. A person may hold a strong belief that smoking is not harmful. Let us consider such belief to be in that person's latitude of commitment. A warning that smoking is harmful is, then, in his or her latitude of rejection. Considering the warning about tobacco creates cognitive dissonance.

The warning will be subjected to great scrutiny and attacked with counterarguments. Dissonance-reduction efforts may include reducing the value of the research or rejecting it altogether. Another rejection technique may be to accept the research as to others but to add the belief that the negative effects do not apply personally. Such a person is likely to quit using tobacco only if he or she becomes persuaded that the belief about personal effects is in error. That may be a tough persuasion exercise since it is in the person's latitude of rejection and subject to dissonance-reduction distortion in perception! Nevertheless, understanding the psychological processes will enable us to focus persuasive efforts where they are likely to be the most successful.

As another example, let us say that you have been working sixty hours per week during the last eight months. You are understaffed, but you are meeting all deadlines. You believe that you are a stellar employee. Your boss gives you a less-than-stellar performance review. You are likely to perceive the review as incompatible with being a great employee. You may engage in the false consensus bias by perceiving the review as not so bad. If your boss shows you some of your errors along with the negative repercussions caused, you may engage in the disconfirmation bias. You may refute or minimize the allegations and errors. You may be unable to see the errors. You may even add the thought that the boss is out to get you! That would be one way to reduce dissonance. It counteracts the imbalance created by the poor review.

You may substitute something you do or consume that others say is harmful and analyze your own cognitive processes to more fully understand these concepts. Dissonance and reduction efforts will be increased proportionally with the importance of the matters causing discomfort. The greatest reduction efforts are seen when the self-concept or ego is involved.

NEGATIVITY BIAS

That human beings are subject to a **negativity bias** is well established in the research.[2] Negative information weighs more heavily than positive information in forming evaluations (Ito, Larsen, Smith, and Cacioppo 1998; Skowronski and Carlston 1989; and Peeters and Czapinski 1990). Evaluations of others are less favorable than a mere averaging when a negative is introduced (Anderson 1965). This phenomenon underscores the importance of searching for common ground and information that will be perceived as positive and beneficial when attempting to persuade.

In constructing persuasive arguments, it is a good idea to lead with the information most beneficial to the other party. Starting with the least beneficial item or effect or starting with negative aspects is likely to cast a negative cloud over the person's perception. Good news, bad news is an appropriate approach!

---

[2] See, for example, Ito, Cacioppo, and Lang (1998); Ito, Larsen, Smith, and Cacioppo (1998); Kanouse and Hansen (1972); and Peeters and Czapinski (1990).

PREPARING YOUR ARGUMENTS TO PERSUADE

Understanding the psychological processes discussed thus far should help you understand that there is a big difference between mere argument and communication that persuades. There are some rather simple, practical steps you can follow that will allow you to maneuver through the psychological complexities in a way most likely to be successful.

You must find and advance a benefit for the other party while admitting the benefits to you. You must arm yourself with sound support for your argued positions. You must communicate in an empathic way that connects the parties. You must be credible. And, finally, you must advance a reason for the other to agree. The sections that follow address this work in more detail.

GOING FOR ACES

Yes, persuasion can be difficult, but it is possible! There are keys that will help you overcome the psychological difficulties noted. In going for **ACES**,[3] we are talking about finding a reason for the other to agree. It is the focus of your appeal. As others search for validity in what you propose, they need at least one reason for attaching validity. For each argument you advance, you need only one *ACE*; however, the more *ACES* you have, the more likely will be your success. If you focus your arguments toward one of the four *ACES*, you are likely to persuade.

The *ACES* are appropriateness (*A*), consistency (*C*), effectiveness (*E*), and things special to the person or circumstances involved (*S*). Arguing appropriateness is arguing that it is the right thing to do. If what is proposed is consistent with the other person's perspective of what is right, it should fall within that person's latitude of acceptance. Consistency arguments appeal to a person's sense of justice and fairness. They also provide the comfort of psychological balance.

Effectiveness is found in an outcome desired and in solutions that bring about the best result for all parties. A special appeal may be used where, despite extreme effort on both sides, circumstances do not permit the most desired outcome. Your proposal may be the next best alternative, albeit only partially effective.

---

[3] Credit for the *ACE* approach is given to Reardon (1991). What is proposed here is a slight variation from Reardon's model.

It must be remembered that your appeal must be perceived as an *ACE* from the perspective of the *other*. Personality and cultural differences may affect what the other person values as an *ACE*. If you believe that something is appropriate but your counterpart holds a different value system, your appeal may be rejected. Usually, however, appeals to appropriateness hinge on professional, ethical, or legal standards generally observed.

You may appeal on the grounds of consistency where, for example, you are asking the other to return a reciprocal action on your part. You may also use consistency where your proposal would rectify a prior error or injustice.

Effectiveness is often the most successful appeal. Everyone wants their problems solved! Determining the focus of your appeal is just one part of the work to be done. You must build your case, as is explained in the following sections.

CROSSING THE CREEK

You may think of crossing over to persuasion as crossing the **creek,** because the acronym may help you remember the tools you need. The *C* is for common ground. The *R* is for reinforcement. The *E* is emotional connection with the one you seek to persuade. The second "*E*" is for empathy. And, finally, the most persuasive key is keeping your credibility (*K*), which derives in part from your *ACES* but primarily from your personal integrity.[4] Credibility and common ground are essential. That is, the other party must see the benefit to them and must believe you. Empathy assists in finding common ground. The more reinforcement and emotional connection you can use, the more likely you will succeed in persuading. Each tool is addressed in the sub-sections below.

COMMON GROUND (C)

In an earlier chapter, we discussed identifying your interests and goals as well as trying your best to identify the interests and goals of the other party. If you want to accomplish your goals, that is, persuade the other to do as you desire, you must find mutuality. This is finding common ground. This is also consistent with maintaining

---

[4] Conger (1998) is acknowledged as advising establishing credibility, framing goals for common ground, reinforcing your position with logic, and connecting emotionally.

an open mind and using a collaborative approach, as discussed in previous chapters.

You find common ground where both parties want the same outcome. You also find common ground by looking for things you can do for or provide to the other. Structuring arguments consistent with the other's frame of reference or perspective is also part of finding common ground. Doing so creates a greater likelihood that your argument will fall into the other's latitude of acceptance. It will also tend to minimize cognitive dissonance for the other, thereby increasing the likelihood of persuasion.

In a prior chapter, we discussed the conflict inherent in asking for a raise. We can use that simple scenario to illustrate finding common ground. Note that as the complexity of a matter for negotiation increases, so does the potential area for common ground increase. In our scenario, you must ask yourself if your boss and the organization likely want you to remain with the organization. In assessing the views of others, remember to check your fears and perceptions. If you believe your continued employment is not strongly desired, you may have difficulty finding common ground! Alternatively, if your boss believes your intention is not to stay with the organization in the long run, there will be little, if any, common ground. In such cases, you will have to persuade a change of opinion prior to thinking about asking for a raise.

If, as is often the case, both parties very much desire continued employment, you have strong common ground. Along with that common desire is likely to be a desire by each that the other be happy and satisfied. There may be additional common ground. Is there a project or deadline approaching that both parties desire to complete or meet? Perhaps your boss desires a promotion and the best chance of her success is for you to move into her position.

REINFORCE WITH SUPPORTING FACTS AND DATA (R)

Reinforcing is to support your positions with those things that lead to your conclusions. You may use logic and reasoning; however, those processes are prevalent in your attempts to find validity as you go for *ACES*. Here, the focus is on what may be viewed as hard data—or external evidence—to support validity.

In our raise request example, your request may be supported with market salary survey data. Perhaps you can reinforce your request with evidence that you have taken on additional responsibilities or have completed additional education or certifications

> "Men are apt to mistake the strength of their feeling for the strength of their argument."
>
> *William Ewart Gladstone*

relevant to your job. Perhaps you can tie your request to a performance bonus system by demonstrating your contribution to the organization's financial success.

Just because you see the logic in your position or feel passionately about what you propose, it does not follow that the other person will simply agree! Your chances of persuasion increase with every ounce of support you offer. As noted in a previous chapter, people infer causes for the statements and behaviors of others. In negotiation, the other person will presume that you have a personal interest in the outcome of what you propose. In fact, it is common to be suspicious of others' self-interests.

To demonstrate, assume that instead of asking for a raise you are proposing a new line of business. The fundamental attributional error would suggest that your boss may tend to think your interest is solely for personal benefit. Reinforcing your proposal with external data will tend to diminish that perception.

Providing support will help to counteract the fundamental attributional error and unconscious biases and prejudices. Providing external support will increase the likelihood of acceptance. If your arguments are perceived as highly consistent and in consensus with what others in similar circumstances would argue, they are likely to be attributed to external reality.[5] People attach a high level of validity to such messages. It is important, again, to remember potential cultural and personality differences. Some people prefer general and conceptual reinforcement while others prefer detail, for example.

> "When Bishop Berkeley said, 'there was no matter,' and proved it—twas no matter what he said."
>
> *George Gordon Byron, Don Juan*

EMOTIONAL CONNECTION (*E*)

As the one doing the persuasion, you should be enthusiastic and involved; and you will likely have no problem doing so. What helps to persuade is to make a connection to the emotions of the *other*! Resist the automatic tendency to think that the other person is just like you. Filtering techniques described elsewhere in this book will help you connect with the other party.

It is harder to make this emotional connection with those about whom you know little. As is noted in the chapter on preparation for negotiation, you should seek information about the person you hope to persuade as well as seeking information about the substantive

---

[5] As explained in chapter 9, high consistency and high consensus together tend toward attribution for the cause of the statement to be made to external reality.

issues and problems to be addressed. In cases in which you know little about the person and are unable to connect with his or her particular emotions, you will have to focus greater attention on finding *ACES*.

In our raise request example, perhaps you and your boss have followed the same career path and you are perceived as following in his or her footsteps. Perhaps the two of you share common visions of future developments for the organization.

Referent power and identification power, discussed in another chapter, are two sources for emotional connection. There are usually other sources of emotional connection. Most people have pet peeves, pet causes, and soft spots in their belief systems. Whether it is love for a special dog or child, or love for orderliness, or something else, tap into it!

EMPATHY (*E*)

You have, hopefully, learned much about empathy in understanding individual differences discussed throughout this book. Being empathetic is to acknowledge and respect those differences. It is also to acknowledge and respect the other person's values, needs, goals, and positions with the same deference you give to your own. Trying to put yourself into the other person's shoes will create empathy. When you are able to place yourself in others' shoes and recognize what they hold important, you stand a greater chance of recognizing how your proposal relates to their prior attitudes. Working on being empathetic also often opens one's eyes to common ground that would otherwise be missed.

Personality differences may affect the ability to empathize. Those with an intuitive preference may find empathizing easier than do sensors. The difference is due to the conceptual framework used by intuitives versus the concrete and experiential perspective relied on by sensors. Empathy enhances credibility—the last and biggest part of the *CREEK*.

AND THE KEY: KEEPING YOUR CREDIBILITY (*K*)

It will always come down to *you*! You are the deciding factor in the persuasion effort. It is you who is presenting the reasoning and support. It is you who is tapping into the emotions of the other. Since the common human error is to make attributions to the person, you want to be viewed in the best possible light. If you are not trusted or believed, you will not persuade. Since your self-interest in what you propose is presumed, your credibility is key to believing your common ground and reinforcement.

Your credibility comes from your expertise, your knowledge of the problem and related issues, your composure, your approach, the confidence you portray, and your reputation. The first two sources derive from your preparation, which is addressed in a separate chapter. The rest is you as a person, including your ethics.

Persuasion is not manipulation or coercion. It is presenting arguments and support and then letting the other decide. That having been said, it is possible to use persuasion techniques to manipulate. However, manipulation involves the added tactics of withholding information, misrepresenting, deception, or lying. Such conduct not only is unethical but may be actionable as fraudulent. Negotiated agreements entered into through manipulation or fraud usually end up in another dispute. Most assuredly, you will never successfully persuade a person again after having tricked him or her previously. In our raise request example, if your organization receives a job reference inquiry about you at the same time you are arguing your intention to stay with the organization long term, your credibility is gone!

Credibility is, of course, related to trust. There are varying types and degrees of trust. Trust based on deterrence, knowledge, and identification is relevant to persuasive communication in negotiation.[6]

When deterrence-based trust is used to gain acceptance of your argument or agreement with your proposal, the acceptance or agreement is motivated by fear of consequences. The use of coercive power discussed in another chapter is an example of using deterrence-based trust. Acceptance gained in this manner is usually temporary and often evokes retaliation.

Knowledge-based trust and identification-based trust may be used to enhance your credibility. Knowledge-based trust is not expertise power that was described in an earlier chapter. Knowledge-based trust may stem from one's reputation for integrity. It should be noted, however, that it is not limited to honesty and integrity. It is, rather, confidence in what the other person will and will not do. It comes from familiarity and prior experience with the person. The concept also helps to explain why credibility is so hard to recover once lost. We build a knowledge base about others.

> **"A liar is not believed even though he tell [sic] the truth."**
>
> *Marcus Tullius Cicero*

[6] These concepts of trust are drawn from Shapiro, Sheppard, and Cheraskin (1992) and Lewicki and Bunker (1996).

Identification-based trust is the strongest and stems from understanding, respect, empathy, and a connection between the parties.

In negotiation, trust runs in both directions. As stated in previous chapters, similarities in personality characteristics and perception generally make communication more effective. Interestingly, individuals who are untrustworthy typically trust no one!

Some people do use manipulation and deceptive tactics in negotiation. While you maintain your credibility, you may also test the credibility of others. When you are the one being persuaded, you may regularly ask yourself whether the other person is the only one gaining something. If so, there is a good chance that you are being manipulated. You should also verify the accuracy of evidence provided to you; and do not ignore your feelings about the interaction. If something does not feel right, at least postpone to undertake additional preparation.

Pushing will damage your credibility. Be assertive rather than aggressive, as discussed in the previous chapter. Allow the other person time to evaluate and decide. Being defensive will damage your credibility. It is worth repeating here that people like to make their own decisions. Your empathy, confidence, and composure will assist you in perfecting a diplomatic approach.

"The liar's punishment is not in the least that he is not believed, but that he cannot believe anyone else."

George Bernard Shaw

"Use soft words in hard arguments."

H. G. Bohn 1855

WHEN PERSUASION IS UNLIKELY

As already stated, arguments that fall within the other's latitude of rejection are likely to be rejected. There are certain cues to indicate that such is the state of affairs. If the other person repeats our argument inaccurately or with a different meaning, the person may be engaging in selective perception caused by cognitive dissonance. Such a frame of mind may also be indicated by persistent retorts that what you are arguing is not true.

You may attempt to reframe your arguments using the steps described in this chapter. You may also seek different or additional common ground. You may ask why the person is not convinced. If you are able to determine particular prior opinions or beliefs held by the person that are incompatible with your argument, you may find the source of the person's cognitive dissonance. If so, you may be able to focus persuasive argument toward those matters or the relative importance of issues that appear inconsistent.

If all of these attempts fail, it is likely that the other person cannot and will not be convinced. You should consider a postponement to prepare a different resolution. You should check *your* perceptions and *your* emotional hot spots in reevaluating your arguments and alternatives. Perhaps you are experiencing selective perception. Perhaps the other's counterargument falls within *your* latitude of rejection.

When you have done all that you can to communicate clearly and effectively, you have utilized *ACES* and principles for crossing the *CREEK* to no avail, and you have exhausted all creative alternatives to argue, you may want to terminate negotiation and select a nonnegotiated alternative. Doing so should be considered success!

DIPLOMACY

The art or skill of diplomacy will aid the reception of all that you say. What you say in negotiation is no exception to that rule.

> "Diplomacy . . . the act of restraining power." *Henry A. Kissinger*
>
> "Iron hand in a velvet glove." *Charles V*
>
> "A diplomat is a person who can tell you to go to hell in such a way that you actually look forward to the trip." *Caskie Stinnett*

The quotations in the box above fully define diplomacy. You may try a few simple scenarios to practice diplomacy.

Scenario 1

Assume that someone who reports to you has done something wrong that you, in fact, consider rather stupid. How may you restrain your power and, therefore, be diplomatic?

Scenario 2

How may you diplomatically tell someone that there is spinach between the person's front teeth?

Scenario 3

When your hair stylist asks how you like your hair and you feel that you would like to place a bag over your head, how may you respond diplomatically?

ROLE-PLAYING EXERCISES AND PROBLEMS

Exercises 12.1 through 12.6 should help you practice applying principles of persuasion. In each scenario, find your *ACES* and cross the *CREEK*.

Exercise 12.1

Survivor

This exercise is most fun when played with a group of seven or more people so that all roles are filled. If you are imaginative, however, you may try it with only two people. One person may play the role of persuader. The other, of course, is the recipient of the persuasive argument—the captain in our scenario.

If this exercise is used in a group, appoint a leader to play the captain. Divide the remaining people into small teams of three to six members.

You have been shipwrecked on a deserted island. There is enough food to last for a couple of weeks. The water source is sanitary. There seems to be a volcano on the island. It is not currently erupting. There is one raft available. The captain can take only one team. Each team is to try to persuade the captain to take them. The captain will decide which team is taken to civilization and safety.

Exercise 12.2

Billy Goats

It will be fun to modify the children's story about Billy Goats Gruff to practice persuasion. There is a mean troll who lives at the base of the bridge over the creek. She enjoys eating billy goats. You may recall from the story that the troll was tricked into not eating two little billy goats only to be later beaten by the big brother billy goat. The troll has decided that she will never go hungry again!

This exercise can be played either one on one or in teams. When played in teams, the teams should develop their persuasive argument together and send a representative to talk with the troll.

You are to persuade the troll to let you cross the creek. You should prepare backup arguments and responses. The troll is expected to argue back.

Exercise 12.3

Rearrange the Furniture

You moved into your house two years ago. Time was very short when you arrived. The furniture has been exactly where the movers placed it ever since moving day. You are not particularly happy with the layout. You cannot move the large pieces by yourself. It is a sunny day, approximately seventy degrees outside, and you and your spouse both have the day off work. Persuade your spouse to help you rearrange the family room.

Exercise 12.4

Buy the House

You have been renting a lovely house for ten months. You love it. You love the neighborhood and the schools, restaurants, and shopping. When you signed the lease, you inquired about the possibility of buying. The landlord was firm in wanting to keep this house in the long term. You recently noticed that one of his other houses in the neighborhood just went up for sale. Persuade the landlord to allow you to purchase the house you are renting.

Exercise 12.5

Out Spot, Out

You find a sweater while shopping. It is exactly the sweater you have been wanting for years—just like one you previously had that was lost in your last move. It is the perfect color and size for you. It has a small spot and a very slight snag. You are pretty sure that the spot will come out, although you would not guarantee it to anyone. You also think that your sister can hide the snag. It also has a very expensive price tag on it. Persuade the store personnel to reduce the sweater by 15 percent or the best you can do.

Exercise 12.6

Your Turn

Now think of something you recently tried to persuade someone to do but failed. Prepare a new persuasive argument that you believe would have worked.

Performance Checklist

✓ Argument alone is unlikely to persuade. In persuading others, it is necessary to lead them with information demonstrating that the result is beneficial for all parties. At times, persuasion is not possible. People like to make their own decisions. People search for validity when perceiving information and are unable to evaluate persuasive arguments independent of their prior beliefs. Furthermore, all of the complexities of perception are involved in assessing persuasive arguments.

Chapter 12

✓ The keys to persuasion are to focus appeals on *ACES* (appropriateness, consistency, effectiveness, and special things) to cross the *CREEK* to persuasion with common ground, reinforcement using external data, emotional connection, empathy, and credibility. The most valuable key is credibility, which is related to trust.

✓ Each individual has a latitude of acceptance and a latitude of rejection. If the argument is too inconsistent with prior beliefs, the argument will be rejected. If the argument is not incompatible with prior beliefs, it may be accepted. The greatest likelihood of acceptance will attach to arguments regarding matters on which the person holds no prior opinion. Consideration of arguments incompatible with prior beliefs causes cognitive dissonance and may trigger selective processing along with efforts to refute the argument. Selective processing includes the false consensus bias, disconfirmation bias, and negativity bias.

✓ Diplomacy facilitates effective negotiation.

✓ Becoming more persuasive in negotiation requires practice.

Key Terms, Phrases, and Concepts

Attitude

Social Judgment Theory

Latitudes of Commitment, Noncommitment, Acceptance, and Rejection

Disconfirmation Bias

Cognitive Dissonance

Negativity Bias

ACES

CREEK

Review Questions

Mark each of questions 1 through 4 as True (T) or False (F) and answer questions 5 through 10.

T F 1. Social judgment theory holds that people search for valid or correct attitudes.

T F 2. Sometimes attempts to persuade are futile or doomed to failure.

T F 3. Appropriateness, consistency, and effectiveness are the best ways to ground one's arguments.

T F 4. Credibility is the single most important ingredient to persuasion.

5. Explain the latitude of indifference.

6. Explain how cognitive dissonance affects persuasive message processing.

7. Explain the difference between a belief and an attitude.

8. Why is it true that sometimes the most skilled negotiator will not succeed in persuasion?

9. Why do soft words make a hard argument more susceptible to acceptance?

10. Identify the steps in crossing the *CREEK* to persuasion.

Case 12.1

Your investment firm stands to gain a substantial amount of business if the country's tax laws are amended to promote self-directed retirement savings in the private sector. You must make three persuasive presentations. One presentation will be made to a group of individuals who are all between the ages of forty and fifty-five. Another will be to a group of individuals who are all under thirty years of age. The final one is to lawmakers. In each case, you seek to convince the group to agree to endorse your proposed change.

Case Discussion Questions

1. How will you assess the prior attitudes of each group? What effects will prior attitudes have on their perceptions of your argument? What may you learn about each group's attitude here by applying the theory of attribution?

2. How different are the *ACE* arguments that you would use for each group? How many *ACES* can you find for each group?

3. Can you use knowledge-based trust to enhance your credibility here? What information do you need and how will you use this trust?

Chapter 13

Rules of Negotiation and Common Mistakes

"The successful man will profit from his mistake and try again in a different way."

Dale Carnegie

PERFORMANCE COMPETENCIES FOR THIS CHAPTER

- To learn guiding principles for conducting negotiations
- To learn the most common mistakes made in negotiation
- To recognize the framework for negotiation strategies

In books on negotiation, emphasis is often placed on rules with a view that there is a script for or a single right way to conduct a successful negotiation. Nothing could be more misleading. However, there are, indeed, guiding principles that should overlay your personal strategies. In this chapter, we present general principles or rules that should be observed in all negotiations. We also describe mistakes commonly made. With awareness of such mistakes, you will be better prepared to avoid them.

RULES

Rule 1: Do not think of negotiation as a game.
Some view negotiation as a game. Although game theory is useful in understanding how to develop successful strategies, the process itself is not a game in a sense of being an amusement or a competition. To be sure, many individuals engage in games during the negotiation process. To enter into the process in a purely competitive game spirit is to adopt a win-lose approach. Games are played by prescribed rules and usually include referees and judges. Such is not the atmosphere of negotiation and influence. When you use a win-lose approach in negotiation, you risk losing all. Even if you walk away from the table thinking you have won, you will likely lose in the long run. If your counterpart cannot comply with the agreement, the promises will not be performed and the anticipated result will not come to fruition. Experts in negotiation do not enter into it as a game. Experts are adept in the art of human interaction, compromise, and accommodation.

KEY POINT
Games have losers.

Rule 2: Be prepared.
Preparing for the process includes gaining a working knowledge of the principles contained in other chapters of this book, gathering and analyzing information, and selecting and developing a strategy specific to a particular negotiation to be undertaken. Preparation is addressed in detail in the next chapter.

Rule 3: Know relevant aspects of your own personality and behavioral tendencies as well as your needs, goals, and power.
These items are addressed in several other chapters of this book.

Rule 4: Perceive and assess relevant aspects of your counterpart's personality, needs, power, and behavior.
These items are addressed in other chapters of this book.

Rule 5: Practice the rules of effective listening, speaking, filtering, and watching.
Several chapters of this book provide information for following this rule.

Rule 6: Never lose control of yourself.
The information in one other chapter is particularly helpful in following this rule.

Rule 7: Always look for common ground and common goals.
Chapters of this book address this principle.

Rule 8: Know when to continue and know when to walk away.
Your thorough preparation as described in the next chapter should prepare you to follow this rule. To borrow a few words of sound advice from Kenny Rogers, "**Know when to hold 'em, and know when to fold 'em.**" Be aware, however, that this rule is not intended to imply that negotiation is gambling. However, there is a chance at times that your goals will not be attainable through negotiation. Sometimes an issue or an entire deal is dead. Sometimes you cannot change the other person's perception. Sometimes your nonnegotiated options are your best options. Continuation out of sheer stubbornness or because so much time has already been expended will be fruitless or harmful. Such stubbornness can result in your agreeing to something not beneficial to you. No deal is better than a bad deal. There are always alternatives to a negotiated agreement.

Even worse is the situation in which you get what you want or the best possible resolution but fail either to recognize it or accept it! If you have adequately prepared for the process, you will have appropriately established your goals. Many individuals tend to think that if their offer is accepted, it must have been too pessimistic. Succeeding in attaining your goal is not a good reason to discard it!

If, on the other hand, you learn at the table that your preassessments were incorrect or incomplete to an extent that would cause you to substantially revise your target, then stop or postpone. In such event, you are not prepared. Allow yourself time to properly analyze and prepare. Do not fall into the trap of thinking your target was wrong just because you succeed in getting it accepted! You should have reasons (other than success)

KEY POINT
Sometimes quitting is a success.

for discarding a preestablished target. If you have no sound reasons for rejecting your preestablished goal, the time to evaluate it is in reviewing your performance afterward. If you did set your goal too low, you will have learned something for the next negotiation. It is possible that you succeeded in establishing a mutually satisfactory target in view of all of the components. Again, to quote Kenny Rogers, "There'll be time enough for countin' when the dealin's done."

Rule 9: Maintain your personal integrity, and trust yourself.
You must decide when withholding the truth or exaggerating (puffing) is acceptable as honest or is dishonest. Remember that you must inspire trust and build and maintain credibility but not trust the other side too much!

If the other party's trust of you is damaged during negotiation, seek to repair it immediately. Accept responsibility for feelings and repercussions you have created. Acknowledge the other party's perspective and feelings. Apologize for your errors. Use persuasion techniques.

Rule 10: Never negotiate with someone who has no authority to commit.
Doing so will place you in a no-win situation. The violation of this rule is one of the reasons that buying an automobile is so difficult. Typically, the potential car buyer is not allowed to negotiate with the manager who has the authority to sign the deal.

Rule 11: Confirm the status of the negotiation.
At the end of each negotiation session, seek consensus on what was accomplished and what is in agreement. Also confirm what is still to be negotiated.

Rule 12: Put it in writing as soon as possible.
Some people are capable of letting you think you have a deal until there is adequate time pressure on you to come to their terms. Even a confirmation letter is a good idea. You should always try to be the one who prepares the writing, and you should honestly endeavor to address the entirety of the agreement. Sometimes the person preparing the writing intentionally leaves out a detail that is unsavory to him or her. In those situations, of course, you must renegotiate in a sense to incorporate the full and correct understanding into the written agreement.

COMMON MISTAKES

The most common mistakes made in negotiation are failing to observe the basic rules we have presented. Set out in Box 13.1 are specific errors frequently made in the process.

Box 13-1   Negotiation Mistakes

- It is a mistake to assume what the other side wants. It is common to assume the parties' respective goals are incompatible. The other party almost always has needs and assigns values different from yours.

- It is a mistake to overestimate your weaknesses and/or to underestimate the weaknesses of your counterpart.

- It is a mistake to hold to a fixed plan in the face of new or additional information.

- It is a mistake to set your goal too optimistically or too pessimistically. The most common mistake in this regard is aiming too pessimistically.

- It is a mistake to set goals or take positions without reasoning and support that can be (and are) communicated to the other side. The inability to defend or support your position will lead to disbelief; rejection; and, possibly, conflict. If you are unable to support your position, your position may not be realistic or reasonable.

- It is a mistake to make a counterproposal to an unreasonable or unsupported offer from the other side. You will be negotiating against yourself! The better course of action is to insist that the other side explain, support, or amend its offer. Remember, too, to consider the personality of your counterpart. The unsupported offer or position may be conceptualizing out loud.

- It is a mistake to let the other side know that you are under a time deadline. There will be times, however, when the other side is aware of your time pressure. In those situations, you must recognize that your position is weakened and control your impulse to feel compelled. Remember that you have alternatives. Whenever possible, do not negotiate when you are up against a time deadline. Guard your natural personality characteristics of creating time pressure on yourself!

Box 13-1: *continued*

- It is a mistake to *jump* at the first offer from the other side. This is not to say that you should not accept the offer—if it is right. However, if you jump at it, you may rob the other party of face. Your counterpart may be unhappy and may try to change the deal or not comply later. The best course of action is to hide your enthusiasm; take your time to evaluate it; accept it tentatively; and bring up some smaller, remaining issues to allow the other side the opportunity to get something in return. Such face-saving for your counterpart will ensure success on both sides.

- It is a mistake to focus on what the other party gets. The other party's gain is not your loss! Focus on your goals. What the other party gets is what gets you what you desire.

- It is a mistake to respond to something for which you are not prepared. Your alternatives are to defer the issue or suspend negotiations while you go prepare.

- Not saying no in an acceptable manner is the final common mistake. You should not be critical or offensive, and you should not shift blame. Be firm, but give explanations for your rejections. Be assertive and persuasive.

FREQUENTLY ASKED QUESTIONS

How honest should I be? Should I disclose my bottom line? Lying about your spread will serve to make things more difficult. It leaves less room for finding common ground. The strategic disclosure of information is not necessarily dishonest. Exactly how the second question should be answered depends upon the personality and style of both parties.

   If your counterpart is not candid or is competitive, restraint in early disclosures of what you are willing to do may be appropriate. Furthermore, it is likely that you should be negotiating the process to be used in such instances. Typically, however, if you are adequately prepared, there will be no harm in honest, open, and assertive negotiation. There is no reason to fear the truth in such situations. Remember that you have alternatives.

Performance Checklist

✓ There are twelve simple guiding principles that will assist negotiators. The essence of those principles may be stated as to know yourself, to prepare thoroughly, to communicate assertively and persuasively, to feel no loss for what the other side gains, to know when to quit, to confirm the outcome, to be honest, and to trust yourself.

✓ Common mistakes made in negotiation generally relate to some manner of violating those guiding principles or in failing to allow the other side to save face.

✓ Awareness of guiding principles and common mistakes should provide a framework for developing negotiation strategies.

Key Terms, Phrases, and Concepts

"Know when to hold 'em, and know when to fold 'em."

Review Questions

Mark each of questions 1 through 3 as True (T) or False (F) and answer questions 4 through 10.

T F 1. Negotiation is a game.

T F 2. The hardest part of negotiation may be preparation.

T F 3. Being a good listener is not very important to negotiation.

4. Why is preparation so important to your ability to walk away at the right time?

5. If your trust were to be damaged during negotiation, what would you do?

6. Why is it a mistake to assume what your counterpart wants?

7. Is there any way to overcome time pressure?

8. What should you do if your counterpart does not support his or her position?

9. How will you train yourself to not focus on what the other party gets?

10. Why is it important not to be overly enthusiastic in jumping at the first offer?

Case 13.1

Clint is Marilyn's supervisor. Marilyn is a dedicated part-time employee who is known for taking on responsibility. Clint joked with his colleague that he could trick Marilyn into completing a project for him so that he could take a long weekend. Clint told Marilyn that only she had the skills and conscientiousness to complete the project properly and on target and, further, that it would be a big favor to him if she would accept the challenge. Marilyn agreed to do the project; however, when she could not reach Clint over the weekend to obtain additional explanation that was critical to completing the project, she left it incomplete. Clint placed full responsibility for the failure squarely on Marilyn who now feels that her stellar record has a big blemish. Marilyn is lamenting all this after giving up her entire weekend with no extra pay, to boot.

Case Discussion Questions

1. Which rules of negotiation did Clint break?

2. Which rules of negotiation did Marilyn break?

3. Can Marilyn still recover from her mistakes here? If so, how?

Chapter 14

The Negotiation Process and Preparation

"Whatever happens
never happens by
itself."

Sally Rand

PERFORMANCE COMPETENCIES FOR THIS CHAPTER

- To learn key terms used in negotiation
- To understand strategic behavior in negotiation
- To identify the stages of negotiation
- To learn the preparation stage of negotiation

There are certain terms commonly used by negotiators. It is helpful to recognize such terms and understand their typical meanings. It is also helpful to view the negotiation process as evolving in phases, or stages. Furthermore, it is necessary to understand that negotiation is strategic. In this chapter, we review key terms as well as the principal stages of the negotiation process. We discuss strategic behavior. Primary attention is devoted in this chapter to learning the preparation stage of negotiation. As is explained here, there are significant preparatory steps necessary to effective negotiation in addition, or supplementary, to those steps already mentioned concerning knowing and understanding self and others.

NEGOTIATING TERMINOLOGY

In previous chapters, the terms *approach* and *style* were introduced. One's **approach to negotiation** and to conflict refers to one's view, or attitude, toward them. Approach may be discussed as positive, neutral, or negative. **Style** was previously introduced as one's approach to a particular interaction. Those terms are noted briefly in the following paragraphs, along with the remaining key terms used in negotiation—strategy, counterpart, gambits, and technique.

STRATEGY

Your **strategy** is your overall plan. Your strategy goes beyond whether you plan to manage or resolve the conflict as described in another chapter. It is your plan for when, how, and in what order you may use particular techniques and tactics. Your strategy includes the plan for where you begin and where you end. Your strategy will be influenced by the particular type of issue or transaction to be negotiated. Your strategy will also be influenced by your attitude, personal style, and temperament; your values, beliefs, interests, goals, and powers; and your knowledge of the other side's style, temperament, interests, goals, and powers.

It is useful to borrow from game theory to understand negotiation strategy. **Strategic behavior** arises when two or more individuals interact and each individual's decision turns on what that individual expects the other(s) to do. Action that will effect the best

KEY CONCEPT
Strategic behavior seeks the best mutual result.

mutual result is expected rationally. Self-interest is at the center of such behavior.

Self-interest, however, is not synonymous with competition. Furthermore, what an observer may perceive as objective, rational, or logical behavior may not coincide with the actor's evaluation of the situation and alternatives. Care must be taken to analyze behavior in context and to consider the complex, dynamic interrelationships.

An adaptation from the classic prisoners' dilemma illustrates strategic behavior and game theory in negotiation. The prisoners' dilemma has long been used as a recommended negotiation skill-building exercise. It is reconstructed in part in Exercise 14.1.[1]

Exercise 14.1

Two cohorts in crime are apprehended by the police. Each has two issues to face. Each has undoubtedly violated the terms of his parole agreement. Each will return to jail for two years for that violation. Both have been accused of and arrested for a burglary. The police do not have a good case on the burglary; they have no hard evidence required for a conviction. The police, of course, do not share that information with the prisoners. The police separate the cohorts, assuring that there is no communication whatsoever between them. The police offer each the same deal.

The deal offered by the police contains three parts:

1. If one confesses to the burglary and the other does not, the one who confesses will go free.
2. If only one confesses, the police will press for a ten-year prison sentence for the one who does not confess.
3. The police will request a reduced sentence, probably six years, if both prisoners confess to the burglary.

Assume that you are one of the prisoners. What do you do? You have a dilemma of whether to cooperate or compete. You also have a dilemma of anticipating what your partner will do. The potential outcomes are as follows:

- If you both keep quiet, you will both get only two years in prison for the parole violation.
- If you confess but your partner keeps quiet, you will go free. Thus, if you think that your partner will keep quiet, it is best for you to confess. But what if he has figured things the same way?

[1] This story was first told by economist A. W. Tucker in 1950 and is now believed to be in the general domain of knowledge.

- If you keep quiet and your partner confesses, you will get ten years in prison.
- If you both confess, you will both get approximately six years in prison.

Try to determine the optimum, cooperative solution that *best* satisfies the needs or wants of *both* parties. If both parties keep quiet, both parties are spared the worst harm. Each obtains the second-best individual solution and the best possible mutual solution. If one of them were to go for the best individual possibility, he would risk losing everything. Neither prisoner can extricate himself from his partner. These prisoners, as is the case with negotiation counterparts, have a mutual problem. As will be explained in another section, if you do not have mutuality, it is likely that you should not be negotiating!

STYLE

Your style, again, is your approach to the interaction. Negotiating styles include avoidance, adversarial/competitive, compromising, and cooperative/collaborative, as explained in chapter 4. If the prisoners in Exercise 14.1 each take a competitive approach, they each will lose their best opportunity. If, on the other hand, each prisoner uses a collaborative style, each will obtain the best mutual solution possible under the circumstances.

COUNTERPARTS

It is not uncommon for people to use the term *opponent* in speaking of negotiation. However, consistent with the concept of mutuality and game theory, it is helpful to think in terms of **counterparts** rather than opponents. The term **counterpart** will be used consistently in this material.

TACTICS

Tactics are maneuvers, the actions you take and the moves you make. Names commonly used to describe tactics used in negotiation include questions, forbearance, postponement, surprise, withdrawal, threats, anger, reversal, bracketing, flinching, deception, diversion, reluctance, feinting, ultimatums, association, equalizing, begging, bullying, laughing, extrapolation, exaggeration, extreme positions, patience, blocking, emotional appeal, counteroffers, concessions, squeezing, and silence. In chapter 15, we address each of these tactics specifically.

GAMBITS

The term **gambit** is borrowed from the game of chess and is commonly used in negotiation parlance. Sometimes the term is used to refer to any maneuver designed for gaining advantage. In this book, the term is used to refer to the opening move or tactic in each major phase of the negotiation process.

TECHNIQUE

The term **technique** merely refers to the manner in which you use alternative and/or multiple tactics and gambits. Technique is addressed in depth in another chapter.

STAGES OF THE NEGOTIATION PROCESS

It is useful to examine the negotiation process in five phases or stages. They are the preparation stage, the introductory stage, the initiation stage, the intensification stage, and the closing stage. As will become more evident in later chapters and in the practice problems, interaction will vacillate among stages three, four, and five during actual negotiations, as multiple issues are addressed. The remainder of this chapter is devoted to the **preparation stage.**

THE PREPARATION STAGE

"What I need is a list of specific unknown problems we will encounter."

Lykes Lines Shipping

In previous chapters, we discussed interests and goals as well as power and the effect of time pressure. What you learned in those chapters will help in the preparation and execution phases. Preparation, however, is probably the toughest part of the negotiation process. After diagnosing and analyzing the nature of the conflict or challenge, as explained in chapter 3, it is necessary to begin specific preparations toward executing your overall conflict strategy. Preparation requires research, careful thought and analysis, and creativity. It occurs prior to the commencement of the parties' designated negotiation meeting. It is possible to identify checklists of steps to follow during the preparation stage. This chapter provides such a list.

It is typical to feel like the other side has more information about you than you have about the other side. It is also typical to feel like the other side has more power and less time pressure. These natural feelings of inadequacy underscore the importance of preparation. The tasks in preparation are set forth in twenty steps:

1. Gather as much detail as possible about the transaction and component and related issues to be negotiated. This step includes brainstorming to identify components of the transaction. For example, in addition to dollar amount, components of the transaction may include payment terms, time, delivery or transportation charges, services and service charges, and warranties. There will be supplemental issues or components of most things that you negotiate. Avoid having tunnel vision. Remember the holistic approach of systems theory explained elsewhere in this book.

2. Determine what you want and need. This may sound simple, but you must distinguish between emotional and tangible needs. You must also decide how you will control your emotions. A previous chapter provides guidance for this step.

3. Rank your wants and needs in order of importance and identify which issues are interchangeable and/or related.

4. Assess how your counterpart perceives your needs and wants.

5. Try to determine what your counterpart needs and wants. In this step you should also consider how your counterpart may attain satisfaction. Try to identify your counterpart's alternatives to a negotiated agreement with you. Your analysis should include tangible needs as well as emotional needs such as the need of the other side to feel in control or to boost personal ego—face-saving needs.

6. Determine what you have that your counterpart will or may want, need, or accept, as well as what you may do that your counterpart does *not* want you to do. This step may serve to expand the pie as described in a prior chapter, making integration and collaboration easier. This step may also disclose power you possess that will increase your confidence, particularly in the event that your counterpart becomes competitive. Remember the diplomatic principle of restraining power, however.

7. Determine on what issues there can be or may already be agreement. Determine the extent of disagreement on each issue or component.

8. Assess all types of power that you have. Decide when and how you plan to use your powers.

9. Assess what power you think your counterpart has over you, as well as what power your counterpart thinks he or she has over you. Determine whether each power is real or merely perceived.

10. Assign a value to all components of the matter or matters to be negotiated, and assess whether there is potential for common ground on which you may structure a negotiation.

11. *Determine your options to a negotiated agreement.* This step is critically important! You must do this for several reasons. This step will determine whether or not there is adequate mutuality to negotiate at all. This step will give you the power *not* to accept a detrimental outcome in the negotiation process. This step is also likely to uncover additional alternatives not previously recognized.

KEY POINT
The acronym
OTNA should
remind you that
"sometimes you
ought not
negotiate"!

12. Determine alternative negotiated solutions that would be acceptable to you.

13. Reevaluate all of your positions identified in steps 2 through 12, and decide whether or not to negotiate.

14. Prepare reasons that can be communicated to your counterpart that will support all of your positions following the principles addressed in other chapters of this book. You must come up with reasons for your counterpart to agree with you.

15. Determine our overall parameters—three key positions on each issue and component. One position will be the best proposal for which you can provide reasonable support. This position is also likely to be your opening position. The second position to determine is that which represents the best you can reasonably expect to walk away with. This is your realistic target. The third position is the worst you would accept—your walk-away position. This third position is one that you have determined to be worse than one or more of your nonnegotiated alternatives.

16. Anticipate your counterpart's arguments to all of your proposals. Try to anticipate what his or her parameters are likely to be. Try to determine your counterpart's options to a negotiated agreement.

17. Prepare alternative approaches aimed at the potential style to be used by your counterpart observing the principles discussed elsewhere in this book.

18. Prepare an agenda and alternative agendas. These will be your guides to approaching the interaction.

19. Determine your strategy, including the amounts and timing of your negotiation positions.
20. Prepare to be flexible. This includes being prepared not to use your agenda. This includes being prepared for new information. Expect the unexpected!

An additional word of caution is in order. In following the steps we have outlined, be careful not to become rigid in your thinking. This advice is particularly relevant to individuals who possess the thinking preference in the Jung typology.

No matter how well you prepare, there will be additional information gathered once you begin your face-to-face meetings. You must remain open to new information and new ideas of resolution. You must know your overall goal well enough to be flexible in how you get there. If you stick to your plan in the face of new information and changing circumstances, your counterpart will benefit from your tunnel vision—or negotiations will break off without agreement.

Where and how you gather information will vary depending upon the nature of the transaction as well as the parties involved. You will have to adapt to the particular circumstances. Some potential sources are noted here. In gathering information, ask questions of everyone—secretaries, assistants, and those who have negotiated with this person in the past. Listen. Third parties, such as suppliers, competitors, and customers, can be sources of information. Publicly available financial data are a great source of information.

In certain situations, you will also be required to decide whether to negotiate solo or to have one or more people join you as a team. Team negotiation is addressed in a separate chapter. Teams can present benefits and detriments. Weak team members make you vulnerable to the other side's ability to create conflict or to gain information. An effective team member can be a great source of creative alternatives and communication assistance.

PRENEGOTIATION PREPARATION EVALUATION

As a final step and overall guide to preparing for negotiations, answer the following questions.

- Am I comfortable negotiating in this particular situation?
- Is it possible for negotiation to meet my needs?
- Is the expenditure of my time and energy worth the potential benefit I may gain?

If you cannot answer "yes" to these three questions, you should probably follow an alternative to negotiation or complete additional analysis and preparation.

Performance Checklist

✓ Your negotiation strategy is your overall plan for when, how, and in what order you may use particular techniques and tactics. Your strategy is influenced by your personality characteristics as well as by your interests, goals, and powers. Negotiation strategy may be understood in terms of game theory. Your negotiation style is your approach to the negotiation. Counterpart is an appropriate term for reference to the other party in negotiation. Tactics are particular moves made during negotiation. Gambit is another term for certain tactics. Technique is the manner of using particular tactics.

✓ Strategic behavior arises when two or more individuals interact based upon expectations of what the other will do. Actions that will produce the optimum mutual result are logically expected.

✓ Negotiation may be understood as evolving in phases—preparation, introduction, initiation, intensification, and closing.

✓ Preparation may be pursued in twenty steps that accomplish the following: identifying issues, gathering information, determining goals, assessing social or interpersonal aspects, identifying nonnegotiated alternatives, setting parameters on each issue, formulating persuasive arguments, formulating strategy designed for the particular audience, and remaining flexible. If preparation discloses that it is not possible for negotiation to provide a better outcome than a nonnegotiated alternative or that you are not comfortable with beginning the negotiation, you are not prepared to negotiate.

Key Terms, Phrases, and Concepts

Approach to Negotiation

Style

Strategy

Strategic Behavior

Counterparts

Tactics

Gambit

Technique

Preparation Stage

OTNA

Review Questions

Mark each of questions 1 through 5 as True (T) or False (F) and answer questions 6 through 10.

T F 1. To apply game theory to understand negotiation behavior is to see negotiation as a game.

T F 2. Self-interest drives strategic behavior.

T F 3. One's approach to negotiation may be viewed as synonymous with one's view and attitude generally.

T F 4. One's style is one's approach to a particular negotiation interaction.

T F 5. There are four major styles of negotiation.

6. Explain why identifying and analyzing interest, goals, and power are necessary in the preparation phase of negotiation.

7. Consider and discuss why deciding what you want may not be as easy as it sounds.

8. Do you think that using the term *counterpart* rather than *opponent* facilitates effective negotiation? If so, how?

9. What do you consider to be the most critical step in the preparation process?

10. Why is it necessary to determine three position points on each issue to be negotiated?

Case 14.1

You are under contract with your current employer for one year at a time. You have been offered a renewal contract that will commence three months from now; however, by the terms of the offer, you must accept it within the next ten days or it will be revoked. You are virtually certain that this will be the last year of work available for this employer, because it is experiencing financial difficulties. You have a great potential position pending with another employer. Although the organization's authorized representative has indicated that you are the top candidate, no formal offer is likely to materialize for at least thirty days.

Case Discussion Questions

1. What options does each of the parties have?

2. How should those options affect each party's negotiation strategy?

3. Play the role of each party in assessing the other's likely behavior or strategy for the negotiation.

Chapter 15

Alternative Styles, Strategies, and Techniques of Negotiation

PERFORMANCE COMPETENCIES FOR THIS CHAPTER

- To learn how to begin negotiations
- To learn specific tactics used throughout the negotiation process
- To recognize special issues in representative negotiating
- To understand the impact of deception and ethics in negotiation

"Thinking well is wise; planning well is wiser; doing well, wisest of all."

Persian proverb

The psychological and sociological principles explained in other chapters should make it understandable that identifiable patterns—actions and reactions—may develop in the course of negotiations. It is useful to discuss these patterns in terms of alternatives. The material in this chapter should provide insight into use of various alternatives identified.

Alternative tactics are grouped here by the stage of the negotiation process to which they are most often used and are referred to by names commonly used in negotiation parlance. Keep in mind, however, that various issues may be in different stages during the process. In addition, some issues thought to be resolved can resurface and require a second and different resolution. It is not over until it is over! You should not expect negotiations to proceed in a clear-cut, sequential manner.

There are no rules regarding when each tactic may be used. Feel free to use them in ways that suit your style and strategies. Personal use of tactics is more fully addressed in another chapter. It should become evident here that some tactics are clearly identifiable with particular styles of negotiation and temperaments identified and described in previous chapters. Other tactics are adaptable to alternative styles. Your personal technique and strategy should be developed with an understanding of the tactics explained in this chapter. In studying these tactics, try to understand when you may be reacting or responding emotionally rather than responding to the substance of the negotiation.

THE STAGES OF NEGOTIATION

As noted in the previous chapter, it is helpful to look at the process in five stages or phases—preparation, introduction, initiation, intensification, and closing. We addressed the preparation phase in the previous chapter. In this chapter, we address the remaining four phases. Note again, however, that you should not expect the process to proceed in five distinct stages. The stages overlap. The more complex the matter being negotiated, the more complex will be the process as well.

THE INTRODUCTORY STAGE

It may be helpful to think of the **introductory stage** of negotiation in steps:

1. Prepare.
2. Define the rules, and set the tone.
3. Focus on the issues.
4. Begin to persuade with appropriate tactics delivered in a style and technique that suit your strategy and personality.

An early step in the interaction is to set the **tone of the negotiation.** By tone, we refer to a competitive versus cooperative atmosphere that sets a tone for the process to be used as described in chapter 8. There will, of course, be an initial exchange of identification information—names, positions and/or professions, company or firm names and business, and so forth. In this introductory stage, you want to make *personal* contact and establish trust while you set the tone. You should convey a warm and cooperative attitude and treat the other person with dignity and respect.

At this early point, there may be attempts to establish legitimacy, expertise, popularity, and identification powers described in chapter 10. Educational background, name-dropping, and professional and negotiation experience are the types of information shared in an effort to establish these powers.

Demeanor and body language discussed in a prior chapter, as well as verbal statements, are cues to a person's attitude toward the negotiation. If both parties are attempting to set the same tone, things will begin to progress. Remember, however, that in a competitive negotiation, one or both parties may lose everything. If one party adopts a competitive tone while the other seeks a cooperative tone, the first matter to negotiate should be the tone that will prevail.

If you are trying to establish a cooperative tone, personalize the interaction. Use the person's first name unless a title of respect is appropriate, in which case you should wait until the person grants permission for more familiarity. Be warm and friendly. Try to talk about something you may have in common with each other. Talk about innocuous matters such as the furnishings or the city. Begin to speak of the need to find a fair and equitable solution to a mutual problem. If the physical setting is structured to intimidate or accentuate a competitive spirit, get up and walk around. Sit in a different place.

Psychological tips to show competitive vs cooperative atmosphere

Examples of uncomfortable and psychologically unbalanced settings are differences in chair height and lighting. If your chair is noticeably lower than the other party's chair, it is a tip-off to a competitive tone and an attempt to gain an unfair advantage by intimidation. Bright sunlight behind the other party that shines in your eyes is another tip. Using round tables, sitting side by side, or sitting at angles to each other are examples of arrangements conducive to a cooperative atmosphere and tone. Direct face-off positions from opposite sides of a squared table are more competitive arrangements. A cooperative setting requires that all parties perceive accommodations as equal. You should guard against being intimidated by any physical arrangement.

HOT TIP!
Watch for signs of games at this early stage.

Control how you respond – remember you are negotiating – ego-out!

If the other person's attitude changes to a more cooperative tone consistent with yours, you can proceed. However, maintain your guard with the knowledge that the other person may continue to internally view the situation as a contest. You may have to control your responses to various intimidating and manipulative tactics explained in succeeding paragraphs that may be used against you. In such instances, you will also have to make a concentrated effort to use tactics designed to emphasize that you have what the other person needs.

It is possible to transform the other person's competitive attitude into one of your powers. That person may believe that he or she is in the weaker position and cannot fairly get what he or she wants. The person's behavior may, alternatively, simply be reflective of personality or habit. Determine whether the other's behavior is caused by situational power. If so, you must deal with the real balance of power. In any event, maintain your personal control and stick to your parameters and goals established during your preparation, unless and until information comes to light that necessitates reconsideration of your strategy. Focus on content.

Your people helps establish and determine their position to do this

If the other person's attitude does not change to coincide with yours, you should terminate the negotiation. You may simply refuse to negotiate in the style dictated by the other side. You may terminate negotiations finally, or you may leave the matter open for another date and location on the condition that your requirements regarding tone, approach, and process will be met. This is where your preparation in knowing your alternatives to a negotiated agreement pays off big rewards. Having alternatives will ease your mental anguish about the failure of this meeting.

INITIATION STAGE TACTICS

Asking Questions

Questions are and should be used during all stages of the negotiation process. It is helpful to obtain as much information as
possible as early as possible. You want to ask what your counterpart wants. You also want to know your counterpart's
agenda. If your agenda differs from your counterpart's, you will
have to determine whether or not using his or her agenda helps
you or hurts you. If your counterpart has established an ordered
agenda, you may agree to follow it. As things proceed—and as
necessary—you can alter that agenda. In fact, doing so after the
process is well under way can sometimes give you an advantage. It may throw the other party off balance in cases in which
you begin to suspect a hidden agenda on the other's part. You
must also be ready to share information with the other side as
the negotiation proceeds. Strategic release of information as explained in previous chapters may be appropriate.

The type of questions used will affect reactive behavior.
Safe and manageable questions are broad, open-ended, or
leading. Cool questions—asking for specific facts, such as
mathematical calculations—are also safe. Asking for help and
asking how an idea feels or sounds are also safe questions. All
of the foregoing types of questions are techniques that tend to
be constructive and to integrate power. Asking direct questions is also manageable, such as asking exactly how much
something would cost. Asking narrow questions will not elicit
much information.

Loaded questions can be viewed as antagonistic and can
create conflict. Loaded questions suggest a preconceived point
of view on the other side or put the other person on the spot. A
question that begins with "Don't you think . . ." is probably a
loaded question. Loaded questions may be perceived as power-
over techniques, which are defined in a previous chapter. They
tend to have destructive effects by creating defensiveness.

Sometimes hypothetical questions are useful. A hypothetical question can be effectively used to propose a mutual solution. "If you do x, then I will do y" is an example of a
hypothetical question. When you receive a hypothetical question, you should evaluate it just as you would a direct offer.

Beginning with Big Issues or Small Issues

Whether you begin with the largest issue or with the smaller issues will depend upon the particular case and the particular individuals involved. Handling small items that proceed relatively quickly often provides momentum and goodwill, which are helpful when the big issues arrive on the agenda. On the other hand, resolving the biggest issue first may reduce overall anxiety. In most cases, the right choice is the one that facilitates communication and cooperation.

Tentative Resolution

It is advisable to confirm at the outset that the goal is for a complete agreement and that each issue or piece resolved is tentative until the entire matter is addressed. This tactic will reserve to all parties the flexibility to find solutions and trade-offs at the end. It will also protect a party from unscrupulous tactics by the other side. In most cases, the order of the agenda becomes less critical once this rule of **tentative resolution** is openly stated.

Making the First Offer

Do not make the first offer unless you cannot avoid it! Allowing your counterpart to open the negotiations usually results in your gaining information. Often, the other side's opening is better than you anticipated. If the other side is determined to follow the same philosophy, of course, there can be no beginning unless one gives in! When there is a standoff, the one who has the greatest need to resolve the matter will usually start, however reluctantly. After a couple of attempts to persuade the other side to go first, you should go ahead and start. Going second is not so important that it is worth disrupting a cooperative negotiating tone.

Starting High or Low

Prior to beginning the interaction, you should have established three positions on each issue. Your beginning or opening position in the negotiation session should be the best possible amount or position that you can reasonably support. *It should not be ridiculous.* If you start at your target—the position you think is the best you can probably obtain—you will have no room to negotiate and still attain your target. If you must err, be on the assertive, more positive side. You will never do better than your opening. The reference to high or low, of course, relates to your role in the transaction—seller or buyer, payor or payee.

Extreme Positions

The tactic of extreme positions rarely works when used on an experienced negotiator. If your counterpart presents an extreme position or exaggerates his or her position, *do not counter.* It is a competitive tactic designed to force the other side to make a move, and it may be used at any stage of the negotiating process. Do not take the bait! If the offer is outrageous or ridiculous, laughter is an appropriate response. If the other party makes no response, a countertactic is to ask for the basis or support for the party's offer. If your counterparts are seriously interested in negotiating, they will either offer their reasoning or amend their offer.

Note – laugh at ridiculous offers

Reluctance

Reluctance is the tactic of appearing hesitant—or less than enthusiastic—to enter into the negotiations. It is designed to make the other side believe there is little need to do what the other side wants. The party using this tactic hopes the other side will take actions or make offers to increase interest and thereby raise the stakes. The truth is that no one will (or should) negotiate unless he or she believes that there is something to gain that cannot be gained through other alternatives, as noted elsewhere in this book. Do not fall into the reluctance trap. It is a rather competitive technique of using reverse psychology or reactance theory (Brehm 1966) discussed in another chapter. Do not take the bait. Conversely, do not appear too anxious either! Take comfort in your prior preparations. You have alternatives.

Reverse psychology

The Squeeze

Telling the other side that he or she will just have to do better is **the squeeze.** It is designed to intimidate the other side into making another offer. One who falls prey to this tactic will be negotiating against oneself. An effective response is to ask for a counteroffer. Responding to this tactic with a concession is a common mistake. *common*

Negotiation against self

First and Final Offer

A first and final offer may be utilized successfully only by the party holding the greater situation power or general balance of power. An insurance company negotiating a settlement with its insured, for example, may employ this tactic. When you are on the receiving end of this tactic, evaluate the offer relative to your goal, range, and plan. Do not reject it just because of the manner in which it was offered. Ignore the word *final* in your evaluation. A quick resolution is fine—as long as it meets your requirements. When both sides take a direct approach, communicate effectively to understand each other, and make offers that solve the mutual requirements, negotiation can be that fast!

Bracketing

Bracketing is moving in the opposite direction from your counterpart's offer by the same amount of distance from your target. For example, you may make an offer that is an equal distance above your target as the other side's opening offer was below your target. Or, if you were the buyer in such example, you would make an offer an equal distance below your target as the other side's offer was above your target.

Once this maneuver is made two or three times, an alert counterpart will have a fairly accurate indication of the target. While there is nothing wrong with this, often the primary function of this tactic is to attempt to withhold information. As such, it is not very effective!

Many use this tactic in the hope of splitting the difference. In analyzing the offers and counteroffers and considering that the other side may be bracketing, you can make a reasonable guess regarding the other side's target. The move may allow you to retain your flexibility by not hitting too close to your target. As is noted later in this chapter, your concessions should decrease in size as the negotiation on an item progresses.

Flinching

Flinching is used throughout all stages of the negotiation process. It is often apparent, however, at the initiation stage in response to the opening gambit, which was defined in a prior chapter. Flinching is a behavioral reaction to an offer by the other side. Flinching may be surprise or laughter. The tactic is designed to make the other side make a move. If you are on the receiving end of this tactic, do nothing. Wait for the other side to make the next move. If the other side truly thinks that your offer was unreasonable, he or she should ask for support and reasons. If the tactic was a ploy, your silence and waiting should force the hand of your counterpart.

Blocking

Blocking is the act of ignoring all but a portion of a question or proposal. Blocking is also giving a broad answer to a narrow question or answering a different question than was asked. Answering a question with another question is another blocking tactic.

Good Guy, Bad Guy

The good guy, bad guy tactic may be used by a team of negotiators, as explained in the next chapter, or it may be used in reference to someone not present during the face-to-face interaction. This tactic may be used at any point during the process; however, it is usually employed in the beginning or at the end of negotiations. Do not be disarmed by this tactic. Smile at the bad guy. Deal with the good guy, and deal with what is on the table.

Counteroffers

The positions and parameters for the negotiation are established by the initial offers on each side. Once initial positions are established on each side, movements are referred to as *concessions*. Counteroffers are concessions. Counteroffers or concessions come in two basic varieties. You may adjust the item on the table—although not necessarily to the level requested by the other side. You may, alternatively, concede an adjustment but tie it to your counterpart's agreement to something else that you want. With the second variety, you give something and receive something in exchange. As stated elsewhere in this book, the positions should be principled, reasoned, and supported. Concessions are also discussed under intensification stage tactics and closing stage tactics later in this chapter.

INTENSIFICATION STAGE TACTICS

The tactics discussed in this section are most typically utilized during the intensification stage of the negotiation process. The intensification stage is when the momentum on an item or issue has increased, the parties are very involved, and the offers are getting closer to the targets.

Diversion

Diversion is an attack on the other side's weakest point. It is designed to divert attention from the counterpart's strengths when it is known that the strength of that position can be well supported. Rather than ask for support that will entrench the position, the other side attacks the weak and relatively irrelevant spots in the position. This tactic falls in the category of psychological games and may be considered disingenuous and manipulative. If you are the recipient of this tactic, recognize the strength of your position and do not be distracted or fooled.

Association

Association is bringing in another issue to negotiate in relation to and with the issue on the table. It is often helpful for both parties to use the second issue in trade. It can strengthen your overall position to tie an item that is small to you, but that may be important to the other side, to an item that *is* important to you. This is an integrative and constructive technique.

Forbearance

Forbearance is putting off a decision, not answering, or asking for time. Sometimes, if an impasse has been reached on an item, setting it aside and moving on to other items is the best course of action. If someone employs this tactic at the conclusion of negotiations, however, recognize that leaving the table means negotiations have failed.

Extrapolation

Extrapolation is to give enough information for members of the other side to draw their own conclusions without actually answering the question directly. It is sometimes helpful, because the conclusion is then *theirs*, not yours. Individuals who develop the effective exercise of this tactic are very successful negotiators. This technique is also the essence of persuasion.

The Intense Squeeze

The intense squeeze is a more intense version of the squeeze used during the initiation phase noted earlier. It is to allege that you have done the best you can do or that the other side has not done its best. It is employed to make the counterpart give in. When this tactic is used by your counterpart, guard against inappropriately increasing your concessions. An effective response is to ask for help—for information or reasons. You may also ask for a counteroffer.

Begging

When someone begs, you should ask him or her to explain and support factually and/or conceptually why you should accept the request. Similarly, if someone bemoans his or her lack of knowledge or ability to negotiate, do not do the job on that person's behalf! Make him or her state a position. Begging may be done honestly or as a psychological game. Your response need not be affected by the counterpart's motive.

Bullying

Bullying is one of the most obvious power-over techniques. Never try to engage a bully in a fight. Do not cave to a bully either. Stay calm. Restate your position and reasoned support with confidence. Lower the volume of your voice steadily. Finally, be silent or leave. Do not compromise with someone who is bullying you. If you move off of your position in response only to the bullying, you will be negotiating against yourself. Bullying is often used in a competitive negotiating style. It is also sometimes used by extremely negative or aggressive people who might have tried to begin the negotiation in a cooperative style but have lost self-control.

Limited Authority

A party may claim limited authority as an excuse in the hope that the other side will then concede. Again, you should endeavor to negotiate only with the person who has ultimate authority or authority equivalent to your own. Do not fall prey to this tactic. Summon the person with authority!

Anger

Anger is used to induce a concession by the other side. Do not be affected by outbursts or other displays of anger. It is an intimidation tactic. Stay calm. Lower the level of your voice. Thank them for their views, and proceed as you would have had there been no anger displayed. It is also sometimes appropriate to show offense or embarrassment for the other side. Feigned anger is sometimes used to intimidate. Remember that real anger precipitates the loss of control, which is very disadvantageous in negotiation.

Real anger is usually precipitated by some underlying fear. If you are the one angry, examine your fear and assertively address your real concerns. It is even okay to say that you are angry and that you are going to take a brief break. Try to indicate your desire for a mutual resolution. If the other party is genuinely angry, it is okay to acknowledge that person's anger and, again, to express desire to find a mutual resolution.

Threats

Like feigned anger, threats are attempts to use power aggressively, as discussed in chapter 10. Threats are used for the purpose of precipitating a unilateral and unpaid-for concession by the other side. Carefully evaluate whether or not the side delivering the threat has the power to execute it. If the other party cannot control the threatened outcome, there is no real threat! Carefully evaluate the likely consequences of the threat being carried out. If the consequences are not negative, there is no real threat. Remember that once the threat is executed, it loses all power over you.

Veiled Threats

Examples of veiled threats include "I never forget a face" and "I always pay my debts." These, along with the actual threats and feigned anger already noted, are competitive and aggressive intimidation tactics designed to make the other side cave from fear.

Handoff

The handoff is an attempt to make it the other side's problem. "It's up to you now" is an example of the handoff. Do not accept! The task is to find a mutually satisfactory solution. Bring the other party back to focusing on the fact that you *both* need to solve the problem.

Intensified Concessions

Do not give a concession unless the other side asks for one! When a stalemate exists requiring someone to make a move, a hypothetical concession is sometimes useful. If the other side says that your concession has no meaningful value, withdraw it. You can use it later. Do not be concerned about the number of concessions given or received. Keep your eye on your goal. It is the amount and substance of the concessions and progress toward your goal that matter. Many people employ bracketing (noted earlier) to structure concessions at one-half of the difference between the target and what is on the table. It is advisable to vary your practice so as not to be precise and not to be predictable.

Splitting the Difference

Unless the offer meets your needs and goals, your response to this tactic should be to treat the amount as the other side's new starting point. Because of the risk in how it will be received, you should avoid using this tactic unless you are very close to closing the deal and what you offer is, indeed, within your goal. Using the bracketing tactic creates an impulse on the other side to use the tactic of splitting the difference.

Equalizing

If the other side supports a position, you will be able to get movement only if you equally support your alternative position. This is known as **equalizing.** It is also consistent with the principles of persuasion. If your counterpart is unable to equalize your support, you are in the stronger position.

Narrowing

Narrowing is the tactic of resolving several issues sequentially in a pattern to narrow the disagreement to one issue. If you allow yourself to be put in this position and the remaining issue is a critical one for you, you may find yourself at the disadvantage of having run out of common ground. If the final issue is of equal importance to all parties, the order should not matter. Making it clear at the beginning of the negotiations that nothing is firm until all issues are resolved will protect you from the manipulative use of this tactic by your counterpart. If you find yourself in this position in negotiations in which you have employed tentative resolution, you can reopen any items necessary to use in trade.

Intermission

The intermission tactic is to ask for time to think. As noted in several other chapters, intermission may be used to cool off hot tempers. This tactic is often used ostensibly to consider the other side's proposal. The time may actually be used to garnish support for why the other side's proposal is *not* satisfactory! Therefore, prepare.

Persistence/Patience

Often, after demonstrating calm persistence and patience in a position that has been reasonably supported, you will find that your counterpart's objections were over a relatively minute portion of the proposal. Once your counterpart has made clear his or her concerns, the proposal may be modified to be agreeable to both sides.

> "He that can have patience can have what he will."
>
> *Benjamin Franklin*

CLOSING STAGE TACTICS

There are ten key tactics often effective at the closing stage. They are described in this section.

Creating Time Pressure

One side can exert time pressure on the other side by indicating an unavailability to hold additional meetings. Do not let anyone pressure you into agreeing to something you do not want!

Feinting

Feinting entails raising another issue. After some negotiation on that new issue, the party who raised it gives in. The tactic is designed to make the other side feel obligated to give in on the previous issue to close the deal. Sometimes the issue raised is one that was not actually in dispute! Be careful not to lose sight of your target and overall goal, and be sure you are negotiating the real issues.

Reversal

In reversal, a party reverses previous consent on a previous issue in response to not obtaining agreement on the proposal currently on the table. Provided the party has made it clear at the beginning of the process that nothing is final until all issues are resolved, it is possible to employ this tactic without losing credibility or acting unethically. The tactic can exert effective pressure to obtain closing.

Withdrawal

Everyone tends to want what they cannot have! With this tactic, the proposal on the table is withdrawn. Sometimes the intent is to make the other side want the thing taken away. This tactic is particularly effective when negotiations are nearly complete and there is relatively little difference in the positions. It often works to close the deal.

This tactic is an example of applying reactance theory (Brehm 1966), commonly referred to as *reverse psychology*, as discussed previously. Using the withdrawal tactic presents much less risk than other more direct or deceptive attempts at reverse psychology.

Closing Concessions

Generally, your concessions should be smaller the closer you get to closing an issue. You should try to make all of your concessions conditional on your receipt of a concession from the other side. You should give a concession in order to get something critical to your goal when you have exhausted efforts to general creative mutual satisfaction on an issue.

Silence

Silence is the hardest argument to refute. Silence is often preferable to many other potential responses. If your counterpart has not said either yes or no, do not suggest that he or she leave and think it over. Refute silence with silence. To avoid a deadlock at the conclusion of negotiations on all matters, however, you may use a question such as, "Is there anything we have not covered?" Other questions or comments to break the silence may be, "What will it take?" or "Make me an offer." The tactics of reversal or withdrawal described earlier may also be used.

Ultimatum

Delivering an ultimatum is a dangerous tactic, unless you are actually willing to end the negotiations and walk away. A mild ultimatum, such as saying that you cannot see any alternatives unless you are missing some facts or data, may be used without risking breaking off negotiations. If the other party delivers a firm ultimatum that does not meet your needs, do not accept it. You should present reasons and support for why you cannot acquiesce, and you should convey a desire to find a mutually satisfactory solution. A search for creative alternatives and shifting to another issue are appropriate responses to an ultimatum.

Walking Away

As explained in chapter 14 relative to preparation, you must be prepared to walk away if the matter cannot be resolved satisfactorily. It is natural to resist giving up after expending time and energy in the negotiation process. You are vulnerable near the end of the process. Guard against agreeing to something you do not want. If your counterpart walks out, do not be intimidated into agreeing. Do not agree to something you cannot honor.

> **HOT TIP!**
> "Better to remain silent and be thought a fool than to speak out and remove all doubt."
> *Abraham Lincoln*

"Victory belongs to
the most
persevering."

Napoleon

Creativity and Patience

Creativity and patience will be your most effective tactics in the toughest spots.

The Nibble

The nibble is asking for just a little more or one more thing after the parties have just finalized the entire agreement. Whenever possible, it is a good idea to save something to give away in order to finish the deal. It makes some people feel good to get the last word in this manner. An alternative response to a nibble is to chuckle and acknowledge it as a nice try and done in jest. A word of caution is warranted in doing the nibbling. There is a point of going too far. On occasion, asking for just one more little thing has broken the deal.

NEGOTIATING IN A REPRESENTATIVE CAPACITY

When you are negotiating in a representative capacity, it is often advisable to have the principal *not* attend. The principal's absence will reduce emotional vulnerability to the issues, and the representative's limited authority provides protection from hasty decisions.

Another special note is in order regarding authority. If you are negotiating on behalf of someone else—your client or employer, for example—you must establish clear limits on your authority and a clear understanding of what the principal wants you to accept and reject. You must remember that we all have different perceptions and needs. If you are an attorney, for example, and have rendered your legal advice, the client gets to decide what losses he or she is willing to take! Avoid confusing the roles.

Individuals negotiating on behalf of others must also be sure to keep the principal or client informed of all critical information, the views or positions of the other side, as well as the status of agreement and disagreement. You must guard against placing your goals, opinions, or ego above the needs and desires of the principal or client. Doing so may cause you to become competitive. A competitive negotiating style will limit your vision and cause you to risk losing all.

A Word on Deceptive Tactics, Differing Styles, and Ethics

Deceptive practices and emotional appeals may surface at any stage of the negotiations. You must be prepared for the other side to play certain psychological games that are discussed in chapter 10. Extreme positions, reluctance, the squeeze, bullying, anger, and threats are some of the tactics employed to play psychological games. You must also be aware of the other side's attempts to exert various types of power.

Some people will attempt to gain advantage or employ unfair tactics by initiating telephone negotiations. The person calling has the advantage of being prepared and finding you unprepared. It is easier to mislead on the telephone; expressions and body language cannot be observed. It is easier to reject an offer on the telephone. It is also easier to be a bully on the telephone. Do not allow yourself to fall into these predicaments. You should develop your assertion skills to the level of being able to refuse the interaction at that particular moment in time. However, self-disconnection has been known to occur. Some people will find it easier to hang up on themselves in midsentence than to say "no" to the telephone call! When the original caller calls back thinking that the disconnection was a technical glitch, the intended recipient does not take the phone. If you are on the receiving end of such a disconnection, you will have to set another negotiation date.

The cooperative/collaborative approach is the key to win-win negotiation. Certain situations, however, are ripe for using the aggressive, competitive negotiating style. Competition in negotiations can precipitate unethical behavior. One-time interactions in which the other party fears no repercussion from your dissatisfaction or from his or her unfairness are the ones in which to be most on guard. Most major purchases of durable goods—automobiles, furniture, stereos, and appliances—are prone to a win-lose style. In such settings, you can, nevertheless, keep your eye on your goals and your alternatives.

You must establish and maintain your own personal integrity. Some people think it is acceptable to take advantage of a party's weakened physical condition. Others think such conduct is unethical. Is it unethical to take advantage of the other side's fears?

Certain conduct in negotiations is clearly unethical. Any misrepresentation, false claim, or lying is unethical. Any form of deception is unethical. Is selective disclosure during negotiation unethical? What is the difference between puffery and lying? This is the area that is difficult to explain, but we all know in our hearts when our line has been crossed. If you are using discretion in the extent and timing of your disclosures, you are not acting unethically as long as you are not leading the other side to believe something you know not to be true. If I tell you what I want and withhold from you what I think I will accept, I am not being deceptive necessarily. I do not know what I will ultimately accept until I know all of the aspects of our full agreement.

Even though you maintain your integrity and refrain from misrepresentations and deceptions, you must not assume that the other side is necessarily playing by the same rules. You should also note that there are cultural differences in expected and accepted negotiation behavior, as discussed in chapter 7. You are well advised not to trust the other side too much, and you should get verification and support for important matters. If you find that someone has been unethical during the negotiation process, you may express your dissatisfaction or difficulty with the tone and conduct of the negotiations. If the other side repeatedly evidences unethical behavior, you can terminate the negotiations. You have options and alternatives!

Performance Checklist

✓ Negotiation begins with the introductory stage. The tone is established during the initiation stage. Process and style may be negotiated during this stage. Significant progress is made in sharing information and gaining momentum during the intensification stage.

✓ Behavioral patterns in negotiation may be understood in terms of tactics. There are no rules regarding when each tactic may be used. Some tactics are clearly competitive and manipulative, while other tactics are conducive to collaboration and integration. Some tactics are particularly helpful in closing the deal.

✓ When negotiating in a representative capacity, it is critical that negotiators clearly understand the limits of their authority and refrain from substituting personal goals and ego for the goals and needs of the principal.

✓ Negotiators must also establish and maintain their own personal integrity during negotiation.

Key Terms, Phrases, and Concepts

Introductory Stage

Tone of the Negotiation

Loaded Questions

Tentative Resolution

Reluctance

The Squeeze

Bracketing

Flinching

Blocking

Diversion

Forbearance

Extrapolation

Equalizing

Feinting

The Nibble

Review Questions

Mark each of questions 1 and 2 as True (T) or False (F) and answer questions 3 through 10.

T F 1. Taking extreme positions is a competitive tactic.

T F 2. The tactic of reluctance is compatible with all four major negotiation styles.

   3. Would a sensor or an intuitor be most comfortable with the tactic of bracketing? Why?

   4. Would an individual with high competitiveness with others likely be successful using extrapolation? Why or why not?

   5. How does your study of common mistakes made in negotiation prepare you to respond to certain tactics?

   6. Describe how you plan to set the tone in your next negotiation.

   7. How many signs of psychological games can you identify? Name them.

   8. Explain the difference between a loaded question and a safe question.

9. Why is it important to use the tactic of tentative resolution?

10. Explain the difference between feinting and blocking.

Case 15.1

Reviewing some international incidents will help you to identify many negotiation tactics. There are many scenarios to use for such a case study. Three are presented here. First, try to recall the events surrounding the Cuban missile crisis. Second, try to recall the sequence of events transpiring just before Desert Storm. Third, try to recall the sequence of events that transpired just before the United States began Operation Freedom in Iraq. For each case, address the following questions.

Case Discussion Questions

1. How many of the following can you identify: threats, ultimatums, bullying, blocking? What other tactics can you identify?

2. Did any party use bullying? If so, how? Did any party give in or make inappropriate concessions? If so, how?

3. Describe the strategy or strategies used by any of the parties in any of the conflicts.

Chapter 16

Team Negotiation

PERFORMANCE COMPETENCIES FOR THIS CHAPTER

- To learn the additional complexities presented by team negotiation
- To learn how to gain benefits from team negotiation
- To learn how to avoid detriments of team negotiation

> "Teamwork is a lot of people doing what I say."
>
> *Marketing Executive,*
> *Citrix Corporation*

Is the statement in the opening quotation true? Maybe! Does the statement describe the best way to gain benefits from teams? *No!* In this chapter, we describe special matters that must be considered when teams are involved in negotiation.

ADDITIONAL COMPLEXITIES OF TEAMS

As you have learned from the material presented thus far, human interaction between two individuals is sometimes difficult. Additional human beings add further interaction dynamics. Conflict between and among team members may present itself. Such conflict may arise from personality, style, perception, and communication differences. It may arise from differences in individual abilities. It may also arise from power differentials and from substantive issues. The complexities and difficulties increase with larger-size teams. Furthermore, the nature of the task may or may not be most appropriate for team effort. That matter and other group dynamics are discussed in the next section.

GROUP DYNAMICS

"Light is the task when many share the toil."

Homer, Iliad

When the issues are limited or finite, you are certain that you hold all of the relevant information and expertise, and time is short, individual negotiation is likely to be best, unless you seek to balance personality factors during the interaction with the other side. Those factors are discussed further in following sections of this chapter. However, when the negotiation presents many and complex issues requiring much and differing expertise, the use of teams is likely to be beneficial provided that group dynamics are effectively managed.

Your negotiation team is likely to be a relatively temporary task group that has been formed to accomplish your goals in collaboration with your negotiation counterparts. Much research has been conducted relative to work groups. Even though it may be a temporary group, you can expect the members to progress through **stages of team development.** These stages are (1) mutual acceptance, (2) communication, (3) motivation and productivity, and (4) control and organization (Bass and Ryterband 1979).

Time must be allowed for formation activities that culminate in preliminary mutual acceptance. The next step is for team members, through communication, to establish respective roles and rules or norms of behavior. During this step, team members begin to respect and trust each other. If conflict is being managed or resolved appropriately, the team will begin to address the task. Beginning to work together will increase cohesion and commitment to the common goals.

The extent of similarity among team members will affect the type and level of conflict. The more team members are alike, the less conflict will be experienced. More conflict will be experienced in diverse teams. However, as discussed in chapter 3, conflict is good! The basic purpose of using teams is to gain additional minds. That principle is evident in research on group productivity. A homogeneous group is likely to be more productive when the task is simple and quick action is necessary while a heterogeneous group is more productive when the task is complex and requires creativity (Bass and Ryterband 1979).

Care must be taken to maintain constructive conflict—sharing of differing points of view. If such conflict is avoided, the team is subject to the phenomenon of **Groupthink.** Groupthink is experienced when highly cohesive teams begin to place the value of their friendship or cooperation above the value of the task (Janis 1982). Groupthink will result in expressed consensus and failure to introduce conflicting thoughts and data—all to the detriment of task outcome. The introduction of constructive conflict in these situations may be accomplished by playing devil's advocate or suggesting hypothetical scenarios. Brainstorming is another technique that may stimulate individuals to voice thoughts openly. The only rule in brainstorming is that there are no rules! All thoughts are encouraged.

While conflict is necessary for effectiveness, destructive conflict is likely to polarize members (Moscovici and Zavalloni 1969). When members are polarized, communication ceases and effectiveness is destroyed. Without communication, the benefits of additional minds cannot be obtained.

Another aspect of group dynamics is that groups tend to be more willing to take risks (Wallach, Kogan, and Bem 1962). Therefore, care must be taken to reevaluate all positions.

> **HOT TIP!**
> Diversity can be used to increase constructive conflict.

GOOD GUY/BAD GUY

You may recall the good guy/bad guy tactic presented in a prior chapter. This is the primary tactic more easily used by teams than by individuals. Sometimes a team member is designated to play a role acting as the good guy. Playing roles sometimes works and sometimes does not work. The tactic of good guy/bad guy is particularly helpful when one negotiator on each side has difficulty communicating with one on the other side and the person designated as the good guy is able to reach the counterpart perceived as difficult. In such cases, one team member is perceived as the good guy; however, in reality, that person is facilitating communication by serving as somewhat of a mediator. If all team members are alike, this tactic is more difficult to use. The next section of this chapter addresses complementary choices.

COMPLEMENTARY CHOICES

Team diversity provides the greatest benefit in using teams for negotiation. Look for diversity in individual personality, style, and perspective. Also look for diversity in knowledge and expertise. A team may be built with individuals who have strengths in the areas of a single negotiator's weaknesses. In that way, team members complement each other and reduce the interpersonal difficulties encountered in one-on-one negotiation.

That having been said, note that diversity may also present difficulties. Team members must view the conflict presented from individual differences as positive and use that conflict constructively. If that diversity becomes divisive, using a team will be more detrimental than beneficial.

There are also personality characteristics discussed in other chapters that are more and less conducive to team participation. Individuals with high levels of openness, sociability, and emotional stability tend to be more willing to work in teams and, therefore, more effective in teams. Individuals with high needs for personal power, competitiveness, or authoritarianism tend not to work well in teams.

MAXIMIZING BENEFITS AND MINIMIZING DETRIMENTS

Person mix and positive use of constructive conflict are crucial to maximizing benefits that may be gained with team negotiation. In addition to balance in the team, you will need to negotiate with each other, prepare together, and share information and views with each other prior to entering into negotiation with the other side.

Failure to do so will invite detrimental team conflict during the negotiation process.

It is also a good idea to establish rules of conduct and roles to be served. Those rules may include a predetermined signal to be used by team members to signify a need for a team caucus during meetings with the other side. This will enable you to use each other to stop runaway enthusiasm or anger, or to avoid proceeding with erroneous assumptions, or to interrupt other inappropriate and detrimental behavior by a team member.

Sometimes teams are used for no purpose other than to outnumber and intimidate the other side. This is an aggressive and competitive approach. Recognize that it may be interpreted as just that. If your counterpart is going it alone, you most likely should do the same—unless you advise your counterpart ahead of time of your desire or need for additional negotiators. It is important that the other side know how many people will be involved and what the role of each is to be. It is important to allow the other side the same number of people.

Note that you may opt to use a team in preparation even in cases in which you will approach the interaction with the other side individually. In complex matters, effective teams will improve the work product.

> "... [I]f you ... click as a group, your teamwork and commitment may even be strengthened."
>
> *Joe Torre, manager, New York Yankees*

Performance Checklist

✓ Using teams in negotiation can often be beneficial. Teams may be utilized during preparation and/or during the interaction stages of negotiation. Teams are most beneficial when used to address complex matters to be negotiated in instances in which time is not short. Using teams will introduce additional complexities. All the matters of individual differences and sources of conflict discussed in previous chapters apply to interactions among team members. Teams develop through stages referred to as acceptance, communication, productivity, and organization.

✓ The more diversity—in terms of personality, style, approach, and perspective—that exists among team members, the more beneficial will be the outcome of using a team, provided that conflict is appropriately managed and resolved. Less diversity in team membership diminishes the ability to generate multiple views and creative solutions. If team conflict is avoided, groupthink may occur. If team conflict is mismanaged, division may result to the detriment of team productivity.

✓ Techniques of generating and maintaining an effective level of conflict and cohesion in teams include playing devil's advocate and sharing common goals. Rules of conduct and important signals should be established prior to commencing negotiation with the other party to the negotiation. The counterpart in the negotiation should be advised of the intention to utilize a team and should be allowed a reciprocal option.

Key Terms, Phrases, and Concepts

Stages of Team Development

Groupthink

Review Questions

Mark each of questions 1 and 2 as True (T) or False (F) and answer questions 3 through 10.

T F 1. When using team negotiating, it is necessary to negotiate with team members.

T F 2. Using teams in negotiation presents additional complexities and challenges.

3. Name the stages of team development.

4. When will a homogeneous group likely be more productive than a heterogeneous group?

5. When or on what types of tasks will a heterogeneous team be more effective than an individual negotiator?

6. Name three aspects of personality that are conducive to working effectively in teams.

7. Name three aspects of personality that are not particularly compatible with teamwork.

8. Why are teams more useful on complex matters than on simple ones?

9. Evaluate whether or not you are an effective team member. What are the reasons for your effectiveness or ineffectiveness? What can you do to become more effective in a team relationship?

10. When would you play devil's advocate? Would you be good at it?

Case 16.1

Adel works for a major airplane manufacturer in the Midwest. He must travel to Washington, D.C., to negotiate revisions to a contract with the U.S. military. The key issues presented are cost overruns due to complex engineering changes. He has two weeks to prepare for the meetings, which will run over a period of three days in Washington. His department is currently spread pretty thin working on several projects simultaneously. Adel's staff is a fairly homogeneous group, most with engineering backgrounds. His two senior people typically disagree on everything.

Case Discussion Questions

1. What factors should Adel consider in deciding whether or not to use a team for the negotiation?

2. What additional information would you desire before making your final decision on whether to take a team to Washington?

3. How should Adel decide whom to take to the negotiation?

Chapter 17

Negotiation in Leadership and Public Relations

"Leadership is the art of getting someone else to do something you want done because he wants to do it."

Dwight D. Eisenhower

PERFORMANCE COMPETENCIES FOR THIS CHAPTER

- To learn how leadership encompasses negotiation and persuasion
- To learn personal characteristics that affect leadership behavior
- To understand public relations as negotiation and persuasion

It is no accident that the opening quotation sounds very much like the negotiation tactic of extrapolation! This chapter explains how leadership encompasses negotiation and persuasion and how improving your negotiation skills will simultaneously improve your **leadership** and **public relations** skills. All of what you have learned in previous chapters applies to leadership and public relations.

Knowledge of self, personality, conflict, perception, and power is useful in leadership positions. Skill in conflict assessment, conflict management, and conflict resolution; the ability to identify interests and goals of multiple constituencies; the ability to find common ground and mutual solutions; and skill in effecting attitude change and inspiring others are all necessary for effective leadership and successful public relations. Public relations is an important component of organizational leadership. Understanding perception, influence, and persuasion is critical to managing public relations. All of the matters and skills addressed relative to effective negotiation are also important to effective leadership and public relations.

> **KEY POINT**
> Leadership =
> Negotiation;
> Public relations =
> Negotiation.

WHAT IS LEADERSHIP?

A variety of definitions exist for *leadership*. However, clear consensus exists that leadership is influencing human behavior. As we have previously said, to negotiate and persuade is to influence human behavior. Furthermore, leadership is just as individual as is negotiation.

WHAT MAKES A LEADER?

Researchers have investigated personal traits and specific behaviors associated with effective leaders. However, the research has not identified with certainty specific traits or behaviors applicable to all leaders or all situations. One item consistently recognized as relevant to effective leadership, however, is interpersonal skills. The most recent research and theories utilize a contingency approach that recognizes the complexities inherent in human interaction. Most authorities, including Warren Bennis (quoted at the beginning of this section), name people skills as key in making one a leader (Loeb 1994). Bennis also points to the need for candor in leaders (Loeb 1994).

> "... [L]eaders aren't born, they're made—mostly self-made."
>
> *Warren Bennis, Fortune, September 19, 1994*

WHAT SKILLS ARE NECESSARY TO LEAD?

> **"There is no training to be a CEO; it's an extraordinary thing."**
>
> *Gerald Levin, former CEO, AOL Time Warner, Inc.*

Since people skills are necessary for effective leadership, we should identify what comprises people skills. The short course in leadership, according to Bennis, is to be you (Loeb 1994).

As explained elsewhere in this book, to be yourself effectively, you must know yourself! You must know your strengths and use them. You must know your weaknesses, allow for them, and choose to develop yourself. The material presented throughout this book should assist you in learning to know yourself and others in ways that will help you to be a more effective leader.

In 1999 Andersen Consulting completed a worldwide survey of CEO leadership skills. Among what were considered the most important skills for leaders was the ability to foster teamwork, and the top sources for failures were identified to be lack of good listening skills and lack of empathy skills (What are the Skills, 1999).

Other skills for leadership include the ability to think systematically, creatively, and conceptually; the ability to analyze information and make decisions; knowledge of the organization you will lead; and knowledge of the organization's environment. Last but in no manner least leaders need skill in asserting themselves (Loeb 1994). As stated in other chapters, assertiveness and honesty are necessary to influence and persuade others. Your practice in identifying interests and goals and in preparing for negotiations will provide you the additional benefit of serving to build key skills necessary for leadership.

WHAT PERSONALITY CHARACTERISTICS AFFECT LEADERSHIP BEHAVIOR?

Intelligence, self-confidence, assertiveness, persistence, adaptability, and sociability are often found—or perceived—in leaders. Assertiveness, persistence, and adaptability aid in negotiation, as you have learned in previous chapters. Even though sociability may be relevant to leadership, introversion and extroversion seem not to be related by themselves to effective leadership except in situations where one or the other preference assists in interaction with the particular followers. However, other facets of personality discussed in previous chapters are relevant to both negotiation and leadership behavior.

The intuitive preference is consistent with the conceptualization and future orientation needed in establishing vision for negotiation and leadership. Those with a feeling preference in decision making may find it easier to build the skills of empathy and persuasion important to negotiation and leadership.

A high level of emotional stability is related to confidence and may, therefore, be a positive characteristic in being an effective negotiator and leader. Similarly, a high level of conscientiousness may provide the persistence that is beneficial for negotiation and leadership. A high need for social power, as well as a high need for affiliation, relates to the motivation to inspire and benefit others. As such, these characteristics are likely to be beneficial in leading. Personal charisma will always be a positive characteristic for influencing people in any situation, including leadership (Nadler and Tushman 1990). Some research exists on other personality characteristics as noted in the following paragraphs.

Both Type A and Type B behavior may either be helpful or provide obstacles to effective leadership, just as they impact negotiation. Type A leaders tend to be poor delegators, prefer to work alone, and like to maintain control (Miller, Lack, and Asroff 1985). Type A leaders are inclined to be intense and demanding and to set high standards. Competitiveness may be a detriment to leadership. Effective leaders are called upon to foster cooperation and collaboration. Nevertheless, some Type A individuals have certainly shown themselves to be effective leaders. Southwest Airlines' Herb Kelleher, former General Electric leader John Welch Jr., and Bill Gates of Microsoft® are described as Type A personalities (Nahavandi 1997, 56).

Self-monitoring has not been much explored relative to leadership. It seems likely that people rated high in self-monitoring, which is a characteristic helpful in leadership, would be more adaptable to situational, cultural, and interpersonal contingencies.

Locus of control has been addressed in some studies related to leadership. CEOs with an internal locus of control may be more likely to select innovative but risky strategies (Miller and Droge 1986). Individuals with an internal locus of control also tend to be more proactive and future-oriented (Miller, Kets, deVries, and Toulouse 1982). Key tasks of effective leadership are to have vision and to effect change.

High energy and internal motivation have been identified as leadership traits (Kirkpatrick and Locke 1991). Abilities to engage in systems thinking, to be open-minded, to communicate effectively, to maintain cultural awareness, and to possess emotional intelligence also emerge in the research as characteristics that make leaders effective (Block 1993; Wheatley 1994). As stressed in previous chapters, those abilities make for effective negotiators as well.

Individuals with high levels of Machiavellianism do not generally make effective leaders or negotiators. Their self-interest and dishonesty are obstacles to achieving legitimate goals. Those with high Machiavellianism may be personally successful in accomplishing their personal agendas. A low level of Machiavellianism should not be confused with lack of assertion or persuasion skills. Assertion and persuasion are skills that may be developed and are not necessarily related to Machiavellianism.

KEY CONCEPTS OF MASS COMMUNICATION FOR LEADING PUBLIC RELATIONS

Public relations can also be defined as influencing human behavior! As noted in the preceding discussion and elsewhere in this book, trust is critically important to negotiation. However, trust is also important in public relations. In fact, it may be that the essence of positive public relations is trust. The leader is ultimately in charge of public relations.

It seems that media personnel like conflict. The spin placed on reports is persuasive communication intended to influence attitudes. However, public relations is more than mere publicity. It is two-way communication.

"Leadership is about building . . . trust."

Anne Mulcahy,
Xerox chairman and CEO,
Fortune,
November 18, 2002

In considering public relations, you should ask yourself seven questions:

1. What do you want the public to know?
2. What do you want the public to think?
3. What does the public currently think?
4. What do you seek to change?
5. What alternative do you have for communicating your message?
6. How will you obtain feedback?
7. How will you evaluate your effectiveness?

If these questions sound somewhat like negotiation preparation described in another chapter, it is not your imagination! The processes are much the same.

When disseminating information for mass consumption, be aware of the perception difficulties discussed in previous chapters, including the fundamental attribution error (attributing causes to internal sources) and the negativity bias. Know that conflict made public will be perceived as worse than it is. Be aware of the public's suspicion of possible manipulation in your communication efforts.

Steps necessary in managing business crises or for positive public relations are similar to the steps set forth in earlier chapters on negotiating, influencing, and persuading. You must stay calm. You must diagnose the nature of the crisis, conflict, or problem and assess its effects. You must gather information, plan, communicate, and evaluate (Dominich 2001). In planning, you will identify interests and goals, identify options and risks, assess relative powers, assess benefits, and develop a strategy—the same process required for any negotiation preparation. The use of teams can be very beneficial in these tasks.

While the basic rules for effective and persuasive communication are applicable here, the medium used for public relations is often mass communication. Public relations professionals are expert in evaluating various media for specific purposes. Professionals should be utilized in selecting and coordinating the choice for disseminating your message.

Performance Checklist

✓ Leadership and public relations are, like negotiation, the acts of influencing human behavior. The same skills necessary for negotiation are necessary for effective leadership and public relations. Leadership can be learned or developed.

✓ Certain attributes of personality are often found or perceived in effective leaders. Personal characteristics affect leadership in essentially the same manner that they affect negotiation behavior. Trust is an important ingredient in negotiation, leadership, and public relations.

✓ The steps necessary to manage or resolve business crises or to gain positive public relations are substantially the same as the steps necessary in negotiation. The underlying conflict or challenge must be diagnosed and the repercussions must be assessed. Information must be gathered, interests and goals must be identified, alternatives must be identified, relative powers must be assessed, a strategy must be developed, and a persuasive message must be communicated.

Key Terms, Phrases, and Concepts

Leadership

Public Relations

Review Questions

Mark each of questions 1 through 5 as True (T) or False (F) and answer questions 6 through 10.

T F 1. According to many experts, leaders are made—not born.

T F 2. Credibility and trust are probably the most crucial ingredients to successful negotiation, leadership, and public relations.

T F 3. Top sources of leadership failure include poor listening skills and lack of empathy skills.

T F 4. Systems thinking has been cited as a necessary leadership skill.

T F 5. What an effective leadership style is varies by individual.

6. Describe five ways in which negotiation is the same as leadership.

7. Describe five ways in which negotiation is the same as public relations.

8. Is persuasion the ultimate goal of negotiation, or leadership, or public relations?

9. Identify three things you may do to improve your leadership skills.

10. Identify three things you may do to improve your public relations skills.

Case 17.1

You may recall that after Martha Stewart's criminal conviction in 2004, she announced that she would serve her prison sentence while awaiting the processing of her appeal. After making that public announcement, she sought the court's assistance in commencing her punishment.

Case Discussion Questions

1. Why do you think that Ms. Stewart made a public announcement rather than merely proceeding with her plans?

2. Critically evaluate Ms. Stewart's public relations during her ordeal. Was her public relations effort successful? What opinions or attitudes did she change?

3. Compare or contrast Ms. Stewart's public relations efforts and results with those of the former Enron executives.

Chapter 18

Third Party Intervention

"Here I stand; I can do no otherwise, God help me. Amen."

Martin Luther

Sometimes parties involved in a conflict are unable to manage or resolve it by themselves. The parties may be unable to agree on the process or approach to be used. Parties may be unable to reach agreement on the issues in dispute. Parties may be unable to find common ground necessary to come to agreement. Such obstacles may arise from a variety of causes. Style and communication differences, perception differences, cultural differences, and anger are typical causes. Parties may experience these problems when setting out to develop a new relationship, such as a new business venture or other business contract arrangement. These problems may also arise during the performance of contracts previously agreed to, and these problems may be encountered in trying to settle what both parties agree is a wrong done by one to the other. Impasse may arise at any point in the conflict, negotiation, and persuasion process.

When impasse occurs, a neutral third party may be able to facilitate agreement and resolution. Sometimes all that is necessary by the third party is to get the principal parties communicating. Using a third-party interventionist often alleviates the need to resort to formal litigation. Thus, the term used to describe that process is **alternative dispute resolution (ADR).** Sometimes third-party intervention is used in conjunction with litigation. Many written contracts specify an ADR for prospective disputes between the parties.

In this chapter, we discuss major types of third-party intervention along with tips and skills for using these processes.[1]

CONCILIATION

KEY TERM
Conciliation is a process to foster goodwill.

Conciliation is the least intrusive of third-party processes. A neutral person agreeable to all parties is selected to serve as **conciliator.** The conciliator serves as a go-between. Typically, the conciliator meets separately with each party in attempts to persuade the parties to proceed with each other. Thus, the conciliator's primary role is to reestablish or improve communication between the parties. The

---

[1] Nationally recognized formal certification or licensing in the field of conflict intervention does not exist. However, forty hours of study tends to be a generally recognized standard. Interested persons may contact state and local court offices for information regarding study and experience requirements for serving as conciliators, mediators, or arbitrators. Many institutions of higher learning offer programs of study in conflict and negotiation. Some private organizations provide such training as well. One organization known internationally is the Mediation Training Institute International. Information may be obtained from that organization at http://www.mediationworks.com/medcert2/faqs.htm.

conciliator is not expected to provide input on substantive matters. When the parties are too angry to speak with each other, a conciliator may be all that is needed. It is not uncommon for the conciliator to assist in process suggestions. The conciliator may make process suggestions to each of the parties regarding ways to facilitate communication. However, during conciliation, it is the parties who remain in control of negotiation.

MEDIATION

Mediation is a process that allows for substantive input by the third party. The mediator's role is to assist the parties in finding common ground and coming to resolution. The mediator may play the role of both conciliator and **mediator,** depending on the nature of the obstacles. The mediator may meet separately and jointly with the parties. With mediation, as with conciliation, the parties maintain control of resolution.

> "Make two grins grow where there was only a grouch before."
>
> *Elbert Hubbard,*
> *Pig-Pen Pete*

The role of the mediator is to actively assist in finding common ground and resolution. The mediator gathers information, evaluates issues, hears both sides, and makes suggestions. Private mediation is confidential and informal. When private mediation is used, the parties must agree on the choice of mediator. The purpose is to clarify interests and goals, to evaluate relative merit and strength of positions, to explore alternatives, and to explain repercussions of failing to agree. It is important for the mediator to have relevant knowledge of the business and issues, including legal requirements and liabilities involved in the dispute. Often a licensed attorney expert in the particular type of dispute is selected as the mediator.

Mediation is also often annexed to court proceedings. Courts differ in the formality of their ADR programs. At times, the court may direct the parties to find a mutually agreeable mediator and undertake the process. Often, the court will appoint the mediator or direct the parties to a particular formal ADR program. The purpose of the mediation and the role of the mediator remain as we have discussed.

KEY TERM
Mediation is a process to assist substantive resolution.

Mediation is the process used in federal, state, and local courts as an alternative to a settlement conference with the judge prior to commencement of the trial. In the federal system, a significant number of district courts and circuit courts use mediation programs. The mediators used are judges and lawyers. A large number of state court systems have also moved to formal mediation programs.

ARBITRATION

Arbitration may be a private process or annexed to a court proceeding. If the parties are in dispute regarding an existing agreement, that agreement may contain a clause in which the parties agree to submit to arbitration. Alternatively, when negotiations appear to be in a stalemate, the parties may agree to submit to arbitration. The key difference between arbitration and the other processes already described is that when the parties submit to arbitration, they relinquish their control over the outcome. An **arbitrator** serves all of the functions served by a mediator plus the function of resolution. The decision is made by the arbitrator.

KEY TERM
Arbitration is a process to decide.

When arbitration is part of a court system ADR program, sometimes the arbitrator will conduct an adversarial hearing and issue a nonbinding decision on the law and outcome. The parties then have a limited time in which to accept the decision or proceed to trial.

Note that when the parties proceed to arbitration, they are proceeding into a win/lose environment. Each party's perception of relative values and goals may or may not coincide with the perceptions of the arbitrator. Thus, it is not the optimum solution; however, it is usually more pragmatic and cost-effective than proceeding to full litigation.

LITIGATION

"The bow is bent, the arrow flies, The winged shaft of fate."

Ira Aldridge, On William Tell

Obviously, once the parties proceed to litigation, they lose control over the outcome. Like arbitration, this is a win/lose option. Litigation is also very costly and time-consuming. Unfortunately, it takes only one of the parties to land everyone in court! Therefore, sometimes litigation is unavoidable.

LABOR-MANAGEMENT NEGOTIATION

Labor-management negotiation refers to negotiation between organizations and unions representing employees. There are some special considerations to observe in such contexts. Several federal laws govern this relationship. These laws may, in a sense, be viewed as a third party in the negotiation because the requirements must be observed with as much or more care as one observes other interests in negotiation.

Such laws, among other things, prescribe subjects that *must* be negotiated. That is, negotiation is mandatory and a party cannot refuse to discuss (or avoid) such subjects. In addition, certain behavior, tactics, or practices are deemed to be unfair and violations of the law.

Aside from these additional and special matters, the principles and the processes discussed throughout this book apply to labor-management negotiations as much as to other negotiations. However, due to the legal issues, legal expertise should be sought in this context.[2]

REQUISITES FOR SUCCESSFULLY UTILIZING INTERVENTION

If you are at an impasse in a context in which you believe it is possible to attain an outcome better than any of your nonnegotiated options, then you should be ready for assistance. A high need for control as well as differences in individualist or collectivist cultural views may affect one's attitude toward using intervention. A person with a more collectivist orientation is likely to be more receptive to intervention.

Trying a conciliation or mediation presents a no-lose option. The parties remain in control and maintain all options. The cost for the process is usually a small price to pay for accomplishing your goals. Aside from that cost, the worst outcome from conciliation or mediation is that you gain another's opinions and, perhaps, discover additional options! Your approach for successful intervention should be win-win.

During conciliation, mediation, arbitration, and litigation, the parties (or their attorneys on their behalf) will, of course, continue persuasion efforts. It is important to recognize the potential detrimental repercussions of utilizing aggressive or competitive styles of behavior toward an arbitrator, judge, or jury. Credibility is paramount as well.

---

[2] Key federal laws governing the relationship between labor and management are as follows: Norris-LaGuardia Act, 29 U.S.C. Sections 101–115; National Labor Relations Act of 1935 (the Wagner Act), 29 U.S.C. Sections 151–169; Labor-Management Relations Act of 1947 (the Taft-Hartley Act), 29 U.S.C. Sections 141, 504; Labor-Management Reporting and Disclosure Act of 1959 (the Landrum-Griffin Act), 29 U.S.C. Sections 153, 1111.

SKILLS NECESSARY TO EFFECTIVELY INTERVENE

Independence is critical to being an effective interventionist. The parties must perceive the third party as independent, as well. Top-notch communication and persuasion skills, open-mindedness, creativity, empathy, emotional intelligence, and unlimited patience are key skills necessary to effectively intervene. Consider all of the challenges discussed throughout this book and multiply them by the number of parties you seek to assist! Intervention is, indeed, challenging! But it is very rewarding.

Performance Checklist

✓ The four types of third-party intervention are conciliation, mediation, arbitration, and litigation. The first three processes are called alternative dispute resolution (ADR) as alternatives to litigation. The parties maintain decision control of outcome in the processes of conciliation and mediation. The parties lose outcome control in the processes of arbitration and litigation. All four processes may be initiated by the parties. In many court jurisdictions, ADR is annexed to court proceedings and, as such, mandated to the parties. Court ADR systems may include both mediation and arbitration.

✓ Labor-management negotiation is a special context requiring compliance with several laws. In that context, legal expertise should be used along with application of all the principles and processes described in this book that apply to negotiation generally.

✓ Parties will likely derive the greatest success in using ADR when adopting a win-win attitude.

✓ Skills necessary for serving effectively as an interventionist include independence, patience, empathy, creativity, emotional intelligence, and top-notch interaction skills.

Key Terms, Phrases, and Concepts

Alternative Dispute Resolution (ADR)

Conciliation

Conciliator

Mediation

Mediator

Arbitration

Arbitrator

Labor-Management Negotiation

Review Questions

Mark each of the questions 1 through 5 as True (T) or False (F) and answer questions 6 through 10.

T F 1. All third-party interventionists should be neutral.

T F 2. The least intrusive third-party process is conciliation.

T F 3. Parties lose outcome control in arbitration.

T F 4. Mediators should help the parties find common ground.

T F 5. Arbitration is often ordered by a court.

6. List three typical causes for impasse between parties.

7. Name a personality characteristic that may frustrate the successful use of an interventionist.

8. Why would it be true that collectivist cultures are more open to interventions?

9. How are the skills necessary to be an effective intermediary different from the skills necessary to be an effective negotiator?

10. Assess your potential for serving as a third-party interventionist.

Case 18.1

You may recall the criminal trial of O. J. Simpson. Opinion regarding his guilt or innocence is sharply divided around the world.

Case Discussion Questions

1. Is this an ultimate example of effective persuasion skills? Why or why not?

2. How much of the trial attorneys' efforts was negotiation?

3. What public relations efforts were undertaken? To what effect?

Chapter 19

Using Your Personal
Negotiating Power

"What we learn
after we know it all
is what counts."

Alexander Pope

PERFORMANCE COMPETENCIES FOR THIS CHAPTER

- To integrate the material from previous chapters
- To identify tactics that likely will and will *not* work for *you*
- To learn how to develop your personalized negotiation strategies
- To learn how to deal with stalled negotiations
- To apply collaborative techniques in competitive and avoidance systems
- To apply your knowledge by practicing negotiation

In the foregoing chapters, we addressed the foundation of knowledge necessary to developing your personalized negotiation strategies. You have had the opportunity to assess yourself regarding your approach to conflict and negotiation as well as your natural style of interaction. You have had the opportunity to assess key aspects of your personality that further affect your negotiation temperament. You have learned principles of perception, power, communication, assertion, and persuasion. You have practiced diagnosing conflict and identifying interests and goals. You have learned basic rules to follow, common mistakes to avoid in negotiation, and the steps necessary to prepare for negotiation. You have learned several tactics used in negotiation. You have also learned principles for team negotiation as well as leadership and intervention roles.

The material in this chapter will assist you to hone your personal power by providing suggestions for matching tactics with personality and temperament, including tips for dealing with your opposites in negotiation. We also address special aspects of competitive and avoidant systems and stubborn counterparts. You will have the opportunity to assess what you have learned and tie it all together by tackling full-blown negotiation challenges.

DEVELOPING A PERSONAL NEGOTIATING STRATEGY

The one best style of negotiation that is most likely to result in consistent success and honored agreements is the win-win style of the cooperative/collaborative approach, as has been explained in previous chapters. There is not, however, one best temperament; nor is there a single best strategy that, by itself, provides the key to successful negotiation.

Your temperament affects the tactics you are best able to employ. You must look to your uniqueness as strength. In developing your strategy, you must use your personality characteristics as assets. The key is in knowing yourself and adapting to the circumstances, situation, and other personalities involved. Disputes, differences, and personality conflicts can be managed and resolved when you understand and use the concepts of human behavior explored in this book. Your knowledge of self and others is what provides your personal power to reach your goals.

QUIZ

The twenty-five questions in Box 19-1 will test your retention of some of the key concepts used in this chapter. You may use them as a review of prior material before you study the remainder of this chapter. Answers are provided at the end of this chapter.

Question 1
Which descriptive words are consistent with a positive, or constructive, view of conflict and negotiation?

Question 2
Might either Type A competitiveness or a high need for personal power be associated with a tendency to slip into any particular approach to negotiation?

Question 3
Which conflict approach would a person with a strong Type B characteristic find naturally comfortable?

Question 4
Think of a negotiation experience during which communication seemed relatively easy and requirements were clear. Try to identify briefly what contributed to the effectiveness of the communication.

Question 5
Have you experienced a negotiation during which communication was very difficult or, perhaps, so ineffective that the negotiation broke down with no resolution whatsoever? Try to identify briefly what may have contributed to the difficulties.

Question 6
If any portions of your answers to questions 4 and 5 relate to your counterpart's personality, temperament, behavior, or demeanor, try to identify whether or not those factors are similar or dissimilar to your personality, temperament, negotiating behavior, or demeanor.

Question 7
If you are at the negotiating table with someone who speaks in general terms and consistently looks at and refers to the big

picture, you are most probably dealing with one of which two temperaments?

Question 8
If you are at the negotiating table with someone focused on details, precision, and tangible results, you are most probably dealing with one of which two temperaments?

Question 9
Which temperament would you say has the greatest potential for losing big?

Question 10
How do you distinguish the harmonizer from the controller across the negotiating table?

Question 11
The Jungian preference describing how one takes in information is designated as which two opposite processes?

Question 12
The development of self-knowledge, self-management, self-motivation, and empathy will increase your ability to excel in human interaction and is known as what?

Question 13
What is the first rule for effective listening?

Question 14
What is filtering in negotiation communication?

Question 15
Name three aspects of negotiation that may differ with culture.

Question 16
What four types of goals should you identify in preparing for negotiation?

Question 17
What are the *ACES* for persuasive argument?

Question 18
How do you cross the *CREEK* to persuasion?

Question 19
Of the twenty steps in preparing for negotiation, which one would you name as most critical?

continued

Question 20
Do you need to worry if your counterpart thinks you are stupid? Why or Why not?

Question 21
In terms of perception, what effect does the fundamental attribution error cause?

Question 22
Is it true that individuals typically assume that others' cognitive structures are like their own and that our perception of others is colored by our self-perception? Why or Why not?

Question 23
State two important concepts about power in negotiation.

Question 24
In which negotiation cases are teams most appropriate?

Question 25
What is the primary source of your power?

THE INDIVIDUAL NATURE OF NEGOTIATION

HOT TIP!
Be yourself.

This section includes general comments on the use of certain tactics relative to temperament and other personal characteristics. Some tactics will feel natural to you, and others will not. If you choose tactics that do not come naturally, you will have to develop your ability to use them. Some tactics may never feel comfortable to you. It is best not to use a tactic that does not feel right for you.

Which tactics work well in combination with other tactics will depend on the particular negotiation subject and circumstances as well as the temperaments involved. The concepts and pointers presented here are intended to assist you in developing your personal negotiating skills. The principles apply equally to simple and complex negotiations. Complex negotiating tasks, however, will require increased preparation time and analysis as well as a longer interaction time.

MATCHING PERSONALITY AND TEMPERAMENT TO STYLE AND TACTICS

Although it is true that there is no one best temperament for negotiating success, it is worth noting key facets of personality that do provide an advantage when using the win/win approach. People who naturally seek harmony, such as individuals with a high need for affiliation, and those who use tact and diplomacy in interacting with others start out with a natural skill required to effect successful negotiations. Individuals with high self-monitoring tendencies and those with high levels of emotional intelligence also possess skills beneficial in negotiating.

Harmonizers—and controllers to a lesser extent—often possess these natural tendencies. Negotiators with very strong tendencies toward harmony should take extra care to be critical during the preparation stage. They should focus on goals and stick to the plan. Another caveat about harmony is that there remains the challenge of interacting with the personality on the other side. There are facets of each temperament that, if improperly managed, may impede coming to a mutually satisfactory agreement. The interpersonal skills generally known as tact and diplomacy will serve you well in minimizing conflict when dealing with your opposites.

It is more tactful, for example, to tell people that their product is ahead of its time than to say that their idea is crazy or that the product has no value! It is more diplomatic to say that you want to avoid costly litigation than to say you are going to sue for all you can get. The manner in which you say things and the manner in which you employ various tactics should be adjusted to suit the situation and the personalities.

Beyond using principles of effective speaking and listening and using tact, diplomacy, and principles of persuasion, tactics should be reviewed to determine fit. Some tactics are clearly identifiable with particular personality characteristics and negotiating temperaments. Other behavior related to personality should also be considered, as is noted in the following paragraphs.

KEY CONCEPT
One size does *not* fit all.

It is very likely that extroverts need to improve listening skills. It is very likely that introverts need to improve patience. However, introverts are likely to be very comfortable with the powerful tactic of silence. Those with Type A personality characteristics likely need to focus on resisting time pressure and developing patience as well. Those with a high level of competitiveness should work on asking questions with an open mind as a tactic for finding common ground.

Thinkers should guard against becoming rigid in thinking during negotiation. Feelers should guard against taking things as personal affronts during negotiation. Individuals seeking to develop their feeling preference should practice being open to alternative points of view. Individuals seeking to develop their thinking preference should practice detaching—trying to care a little less about what others think of them.

Individuals with low levels of emotional stability may be at a disadvantage in the negotiation process and should practice self-control. Such individuals may also have particular difficulty using the tactics of patience and calm persistence. Individuals with high levels of conscientiousness often are able to effectively utilize persistence.

Using distractive tactics will likely feel natural to a harmonizer or an action seeker because of their natural tendency to seek new information and to look at multiple issues simultaneously. The use of these tactics will not come as naturally to the controller or the pragmatist.

Pragmatists should take care not to overuse the tactic of bracketing and should work on maintaining flexibility. The pragmatist turned street fighter is likely to have little difficulty using the tactics of reversal or withdrawal. The street fighter is also most likely to use bullying tactics. Individuals with a high need for personal power or high Type A competitiveness may also be at risk for using competitive tactics.

Using the tactics of reversal and withdrawal will likely not feel natural to harmonizers because of their concern for the personal feelings of their counterparts. These tactics will usually not come naturally for the pragmatist or the controller because of their preferences for sequence, order, and resolution.

When negotiating with a controller or a pragmatist, the harmonizer should try to limit mental ruminations. Such may be interpreted as diversion tactics. The controller and the pragmatist are likely to be more comfortable delivering the first and final offer than they are being the recipient of the tactic. Harmonizers and controllers may feel natural with the blocking tactic. They should note its potential for creating offense, especially to the pragmatist.

PREDICTING BEHAVIOR

If we know someone's basic style of interaction and his or her motivation, we can predict his or her behavior. Thus, in negotiation, an understanding of a person's temperament, interests, and goals enables us to select effective tactics. If you are dealing with a preference opposite to yours and you evaluate the person's words and actions according to your preferences, communication will fail at best and conflict will arise at worst.

KEY CONCEPT
You should have seen it coming!

In developing your strategies for dealing with different temperaments, use the principles examined in previous chapters to anticipate how the other person will receive various tactics. For example, distractive tactics such as diversion and feinting will likely work when used toward a harmonizer or an action seeker but likely will not be as easily employed toward a controller or a pragmatist.

Harmonizers often perceive controllers as aggressive or overbearing. A harmonizer may view the tactics of reversal and withdrawal as personal affronts, unless they are delivered in a context of searching for alternative conceptual solutions. These tactics may be very effective, however, when used toward a pragmatist or a controller because of their penchant for order and need for closure. The tactics may also be effective on an action seeker due to his or her in-the-moment enthusiasm.

Order is much more important to individuals with a strong judging preference. Hence, interrupting order may cause disorientation for controllers and pragmatists.

Concession patterns may require adjustment for the personality of the other side, as well. For example, you can anticipate that the pragmatist will be somewhat stingy in his or her concessions. Therefore, you should slow the pace and the amount of your concessions.

The tactic of forbearance will be tough for a controller or a pragmatist to accept. Such reaction may mean that the tactic will be particularly effective in gaining a concession, or it may mean that use of the tactic will create conflict. The result will depend upon the manner in which it is used and the stage of the process in which it is used.

The tactic of extrapolation may be particularly helpful when negotiating with a controller or a pragmatist because of their strong opinions. Tactics designed to intensify issues or exert pressure will be received in different ways by different temperaments. Pressure tactics will usually not move the harmonizer to decision but may move the action seeker to decision. Pressure tactics may create excessive conflict with the controller or the pragmatist.

Harmonizers and action seekers are more susceptible to diversion tactics being effective on them. Harmonizers and action seekers will be less bothered being the recipients of the first and final offer tactic. Controllers and pragmatists may become angered by this tactic.

THE PROBLEM COUNTERPART

What if the other person will not cooperate? What if, despite all of your best efforts using what you consider to be the most effective tactics, the counterpart will not budge?

In situations of the latter type, breaking matters into smaller pieces or issues is often helpful. This technique is often called *fractionating*. *Reframing*—or stating your position with a different perspective—is another technique that is often helpful. Look for constructive ways to describe the situation, process, or issue in dispute. You may also try a different *ACE* in your persuasive argument.

If your counterpart indicates a desire to continue negotiating but cannot propose something that moves the process forward, you may also try a hypothetical. You may use your understanding of what benefits the counterpart and resolves the matter in describing what you would do in a hypothetical in which the counterpart provides what you desire of him or her.

In situations in which the other person appears to be the problem in that there is simply no effort being made, you have three good options: (1) disengage, (2) go to higher authority, or (3) assertively confront the person. Using assertive language, investigate the other person's feelings and positions as well as his or her fears. Words such as "I am having difficulty understanding exactly what your objections are" are appropriate. "I do not understand your position" is also appropriate. Ask questions in an effort to find common ground.

NEGOTIATING IN COMPETITIVE SYSTEMS

You may wonder how one uses a collaborative approach in a competitive system. Many legal systems present examples of competitive systems. The U.S. legal system is structured to be adversarial and envisions a winner and a loser in each case. Obviously, neither the attorneys nor the parties in a case have the power to alter the nature of the legal system. Because litigation is a win/lose option, it is usually the last resort to resolving conflicts. Nevertheless, until trial actually gets underway, the attorneys and the parties may continue to approach resolution in collaborative styles.

Once the parties arrive in trial, the focus necessarily must change to protecting oneself from loss. That does not mean, however, that aggressive tactics with the judge or jury are appropriate! Such tactics will not be met with pleasure. The system notwithstanding, the primary task to be accomplished once in litigation is to persuade the decision maker to your view.

The use of aggressive or manipulative communication will be no more persuasive in a courtroom than it will be anywhere else. Even though the outcome of the case is destined to be largely win or lose, the best chance of succeeding in getting what you want is to use all the *ACES* you can find along with the principles for crossing the *CREEK* as explained in an earlier chapter.

As noted previously, the arena of purchasing an automobile is another competitive structure that you have no ability to change. To be sure, you should prepare by investigating manufacturers' suggested prices, options, and alternative dealers and by following the steps for preparation described in a previous chapter. However, in these situations, your information will always be incomplete on the single most critical item—the dealer's bottom line. You have no way of knowing or verifying how long the dealer has held the car, or how much interest he or she has paid on the car, or what special arrangements or circumstances the dealer may have that affect the dealer's parameters. The best one can do in this arena is, again, to present *ACE* arguments, stress common ground of mutual desire for a sale, make an emotional connection, and stick to one's walk-away plan.

A competitive structure or system need not be synonymous with aggression or intimidation. Such tactics will further polarize the parties in a competitive system. The importance of preparation and evaluation of alternatives to negotiation is underscored in such cases; however, it is possible to pursue a collaborative approach within the constraints on both sides. The negotiation will be, nevertheless, conducted between human beings and subject to all of the phenomena addressed in previous chapters. Careful analysis of a competitive system is necessary for finding common ground and identifying what you have to offer your counterpart in negotiation.

NEGOTIATING IN AVOIDANT SYSTEMS

Just as is the case in competitive systems, the principles for effective interaction and collaborative negotiation apply in avoidant systems. Assertion and persuasion become particularly important in avoidant systems due to the structural inertia in acknowledging conflict. A positive, collaborative, win-win interaction is necessary to overcome negative attitudes toward conflict that are sustained by the system.

MINI NEGOTIATION EXERCISE

The mini negotiation challenges in Exercise 19.1 below will allow you to hone your diplomacy skills before you tackle the larger practice problems.

Exercise 19.1

Negotiation Challenges

SCENARIO 1

Place yourself in the position of department manager. One of the individuals in your department has worked all night to complete a report due this morning. When you look at the report, you see that one of the assumptions on which the report is based is in error. While you had discussed the premises and format thoroughly prior to the work, the report is now incorrect. How would you begin to negotiate in this situation?

SCENARIO 2

Place yourself again in your work environment. Assume that you are very close social friends with one of your associates and that at the end of the day he suggests going to a nearby restaurant. Another associate, whom you dislike and who the prior week placed you in a bad light with your boss, invites herself to join you. How would you begin this negotiation?

SCENARIO 3

Assume that you have just completed a task that you believe was expertly done. It constituted a complex written analysis and persuasive interaction requesting approval of a new project. Your presentation was to a committee of six individuals and required only majority consent for approval. Four committee members approved. Following the meeting, one of the individuals who disapproved of your proposal tells you that your data are in error and that the company is making a big mistake going forward. How would you begin a negotiation to win this person's approval?

Potential answers to the scenarios in Exercise 19.1 may be found at the end of this chapter.

PRACTICE

The best next step you can take following your study and understanding of what has been presented here is to practice. Then practice and practice more! Use case problems to integrate the principles studied in this book by applying them to formal negotiation processes.

You may practice by playing the role of a party in interest. You may, alternatively, practice negotiating in a representative capacity, either individually or in a team. You may also role-play as a conciliator or a mediator. Remember, however, that the best way to know yourself and, therefore, improve is to practice negotiating on your own account. Following each practice negotiation session, you should utilize the evaluation guidelines provided in the next chapter to assess your success and progress.

There are no "right" answers provided for these cases. The "right" answer in each case is the one that satisfies both parties and is within your appropriate goals. The evaluation questionnaires provided in the next chapter will assist you in evaluating your results.

The following summary steps may help you get started.

- Identify all components of the problem or transaction.
- Obtain as much information as possible.
- Get a *GRIP* on what you need and want.
- Assess the other side's wants, needs, and perceptions.
- Assess what you have.
- Assess the balance of power.
- Identify what is in disagreement and what is in agreement.
- Determine your alternatives to negotiation.
- Plan your strategy and agenda using your *ACES*.
- Establish trust.
- Meet the other's needs.
- Use the other's ideas.
- Make the interaction win/win.
- Hear the other.
- Talk the other's language to cross the *CREEK*.

SUGGESTIONS FOR CONTINUED DEVELOPMENT

As noted in the preceding section, practice is necessary for continued development of your negotiation skills. If you pay attention to your everyday interactions, you will find ample ground for applying your knowledge and practicing your skills. Practice every day on your own affairs. Practice thinking of negotiation as an opportunity—or as fun!

It is usually helpful to maintain a journal of your interactions. Make notes of your interpretation of and reactions to the characteristics and behaviors of others. Try to identify the negotiation temperaments of those with whom you interact. Make a list of the problems you encountered and the effort you must make in negotiations with your opposites. Try to assess how others perceive you. The hardest task in improving your negotiation may be in acknowledging how others perceive you. Remember also that the minimal features of conflict are values, meanings, perceptions, attributions, communication, and interdependence.

Know yourself.   Know Others.   Know The Situation.

Performance Checklist

✓ Effective negotiation is an integrated process of knowing yourself; correctly diagnosing conflict, as well as interests, needs, and goals; and communicating to the end state of mutual benefit. The style of negotiation most likely to result in consistent success and time-honored agreements is the cooperative/collaborative style. There is not one best temperament, nor is there one best strategy for all negotiations.

✓ Your temperament affects the tactics you are best able to employ. It is best not to use a tactic that does not feel right for you. Personality characteristics and temperament also affect reaction to certain tactics,

✓ Your personal strategies will include an effective combination of tactics, the selection of which depends upon the particular negotiation and individuals involved. In developing your negotiation strategies, you must use your personality characteristics as assets. Knowledge of self, others, and the situation provides your personal negotiating power.

✓ Fractionating and reframing are techniques helpful when encountering stalled negotiations. Three options for dealing with problem counterparts are to disengage, go to higher authority, or confront the counterparts.

✓ Competitive systems do not necessarily require aggressive tactics. Collaborative tactics aimed at finding common ground are important to negotiating in competitive and avoidant systems. Preparing assertive arguments loaded with *ACES* and following the principles of crossing the *CREEK* to persuasion provide the best chances for success in all systems.

✓ Integrating all that you have learned will require application through practice, practice, practice!

Key Terms, Phrases, and Concepts

Personal Negotiating Power

Predicting Behavior

Review Questions

Mark each of questions 1 through 4 as True (T) or False (F) and answer questions 5 through 10.

T F 1. It is possible to predict behavior.

T F 2. It is just a fact that some people are natural negotiators.

T F 3. Individuals should carefully consider which tactics fit them.

T F 4. Some tactics are distractive while others work to focus participants.

5. Identify at least two natural tendencies you possess that help to make you an effective negotiator.

6. Identify what aspects of your personality make you most vulnerable to errors in negotiation.

7. What knowledge is necessary to predict others' behavior?

8. Identify two areas in which you require the most improvement.

9. What will you do to improve your performance in the areas you identified in question 8?

10. What steps should you take when confronted with an uncooperative counterpart?

Case 19.1

Juan Braun works for an international accounting firm. He is a gentle soul. In fact, in one of the reviews that followed an auditing engagement, he was told that he is simply too shy and sensitive to succeed in public accounting. His technical reviews are outstanding. His clients praise him for his persistence, patience, and understanding. They also comment on his knowledge and intelligence. Juan has been accepted into law school. A colleague told him that the firm encourages only tax division employees to attend law school. Juan intends to remain in the audit division. Juan plans to

go to the partner in charge of the office and demand a revised schedule that will facilitate his attending and completing law school.

Case Discussion Questions

1. Critically evaluate Juan's strategy. Will it be effective? Why or
   why not?

2. What makes Juan most vulnerable in this case?

3. Design a new, more effective strategy for Juan.

Answers to Quiz in Box 19.1

✓ Answer to Question 1: Positive approach words include
interaction, mutual benefit, interdependence, opportunity,
difference, exchange, persuade, exciting, stimulating, and
challenging.

✓ Answer to Question 2: A high level of Type A competitiveness
or a strong need for personal power may cause one to be prone
to a competitive approach to negotiation.

✓ Answer to Question 3: A strong Type B person may find a collaborative approach naturally comfortable.

✓ Answer to Question 4: Key psychological and sociological factors that tend to enhance effective communication include good
listening, accurate self-awareness, self-control, adaptation of
approach, order, and presentation to meet the perception and
cognitive style of one's counterpart.

✓ Answer to Question 5: Key factors tending to diminish effective
communication and/or, depending upon their severity, tending
to result in conflict and/or total breakdown include interrupting; rigidity in plan, approach, and style; excessive repetition;
making assumptions; loss of control; offensive behavior or
words; and differences in personality and cognitive style.

✓ Answer to Question 6: What is sometimes viewed as an
offensive or difficult behavior is often merely a reflection of a personality comprised of components opposite to one's own. Abstraction and distraction to one are reflection and interrelating to
another. While one responds to approaching deadlines, another
sees no date or end. Annoying detail to one is the tangible substance of importance to another. What is justice to one is relative
and subjective to another. We tend to expect others to be like us.
We tend to take offense when someone does not act as we expect.

✓ Answer to Question 7: You are likely dealing with either a harmonizer or a controller.

✓ Answer to Question 8: You are likely dealing with either a pragmatist or an action seeker.

✓ Answer to Question 9: Both the high roller and the street fighter—both out-of-control temperaments—may have the potential for losing big.

✓ Answer to Question 10: They both present a broad and theoretical approach; however, the harmonizer will be open-ended while the controller will exhibit resolve to close.

✓ Answer to Question 11: Sensing (S) and Intuiting (I).

✓ Answer to Question 12: Emotional intelligence.

✓ Answer to Question 13: Talk less and listen more.

✓ Answer to Question 14: The two basic rules for filtering are (1) to know your prejudices, biases, and tendencies and allow for them; and (2) listen and speak to the other in his or her language.

✓ Answer to Question 15: Some of the key differences include time orientation, formality, power distance, context, Type A personality behavior, sensing and intuiting preferences, individualism and collectivism, dress, the acceptance of alcohol, and gift giving.

✓ Answer to Question 16: You should come to *GRIP* with substantive gain you desire (*G*), relationship goals (*R*), face-saving goals for yourself (*I*), and process goals for the interaction (*P*).

✓ Answer to Question 17: Appropriateness, consistency, effectiveness, and special things.

✓ Answer to Question 18: You persuade by using common ground (*C*), reinforcing your position with facts and data (*R*), making an emotional connection (*E*), being empathetic (*E*), and keeping your credibility (*K*). Your best chance of persuading is when you argue in the other person's latitude of indifference.

✓ Answer to Question 19: Obviously all twenty steps are important and necessary; however, knowing your alternatives to a negotiated agreement is critical to knowing whether or not to negotiate at all!

✓ Answer to Question 20: No! As long as you are *NOT* stupid, your counterpart's assumption that you are will work to your advantage!

✓ Answer to Question 21: We tend to ignore external causes and emphasize internal causes in attributing motives and traits to others.

✓ Answer to Question 22: Yes, both parts of the question are true.

✓ Answer to Question 23: Perhaps the two most important concepts to remember are that your personal power is the most critical component in negotiation and that the existence of power in others is largely dependent upon your perception of and acquiescence to it.

✓ Answer to Question 24: When the negotiation presents many and complex issues requiring much and differing expertise, the use of teams is likely to be beneficial—provided that group dynamics are effectively managed.

✓ Answer to Question 25: Your personal power comes from understanding yourself and using your interpersonal skills.

Potential Answers to Mini Negotiation Challenges in Exercises 19.1

Scenario 1: I appreciate your dedication and hard work. I really don't like having to say this but I have a huge problem. I need to know why this assumption was used and exactly what impact it has on the result. It was my understanding that the analysis was to be premised on X.

[Note the "I" words expressing your feelings soften the impact and reduce the likelihood of retaliatory aggression or defensiveness.]

Scenario 2: I need to talk with [friend's name] about some personal matters in private. I hope you will not be offended or think me rude but we will have to go alone this time. [If you cannot bring yourself to be open about a possible future time, the response will be diplomatic without that phrase as well.]

Scenario 3: I'm sorry that we disagree. I checked and rechecked my data several times. I believe I am correct. I would like specific support for your position so that I can reevaluate yet again. I want what I think we all want—the correct decision.

[Notice the expression of your feelings along with respect for the other and the link to common goals.]

Chapter 20

Post Negotiation Evaluation

PERFORMANCE COMPETENCIES FOR THIS CHAPTER

- To learn the indicia of a successful win-win negotiation
- To learn how to evaluate your negotiation effectiveness

"When you reread
a classic, you do
not see more in the
book than you did
before; you see
more in you than
there was before."

Clifton Fadiman

"Only mediocre
people are always
at their best."

Jean Giraudoux

There is always room for improvement in our interpersonal skills and in our negotiation skills. The questionnaires provided in this chapter should be used as often as possible following your negotiation experiences, both formal and informal. Remember that everyday negotiations provide ample opportunity to experiment and to practice.

ASSESSMENT TOOLS

As you assess yourself, decide which areas need your attention for further development. Characteristics of a successful win-win negotiation are provided in Box 20-1. Note which tactics and techniques did and did not work for you. Evaluate why you obtained the result you obtained. A post-negotiation evaluation questionnaire is provided in Exhibit 20-1. Try other tactics and techniques that seem to fit your personal style.

Box 20-1 Indicia of a Successful Win-Win Negotiation

✓ Both sides feel successful.

✓ Both sides are able to and intend to honor the agreement.

✓ In those cases that fail to conclude in agreement, both sides feel that the failure was the result of the issues and not the unreasonableness of or the tactics used by the other side.

✓ Neither side has any personal animosity toward the other side.

✓ Neither side fears any negative repercussion from the other side.

✓ Each side is amenable to dealing with the other in the future.

Exhibit 20-1

Post-negotiation Evaluation Questionnaire

1. Did the negotiation conclude in an agreement?

2. If the negotiation did not conclude in an agreement, was your decision to terminate efforts necessary or appropriate?

3. Did you terminate negotiations because it was not possible to resolve the matter within your acceptable range?

4. Were you remiss in not adapting to additional information or finding creative alternatives at the negotiating table?

5. Do you have an alternative that is more beneficial to you than the solution that was available to you at the time negotiations terminated or more beneficial to you than the agreement you made?

6. Did negotiations terminate because of a communication difficulty or because of a genuine disagreement for which you could not find an acceptable mutual solution?

7. If negotiations concluded in an agreement, did you resolve the matter reasonably close to your target?

8. Was your prenegotiation preparation adequate to prepare you for the interaction?

9. Did you adequately and accurately anticipate the other side's needs, strengths, and weaknesses?

10. Did you accurately assess your own needs, strengths, and weaknesses?

11. Did you set an optimistic enough target?

12. Did you reach your target because you set it realistically and supported it well? Or did you reach your target because you set your goal too modestly?

13. Were you surprised by any information?

14. Did you make the first offer? Was that necessary?

15. Was your pattern of concessions effective? Were the increments too large? Did you concede too often?

16. Was the total volume of concessions you made roughly equal to or lower than the total volume of concessions made by the other side? If not, is there good reason?

17. In your evaluation of concessions, was any significant difference between the parties' aggregate concessions a result only of the reasonableness of the parties' respective starting positions? Or could you have conceded less? Or did you do a particularly great job of withholding concessions?

18. Did the members of the other side support the position that you accepted from them?

19. What tactics did the other side employ?

20. How well did you control your reactions to the other side's tactics?

21. Which tactics did you employ?

22. Which tactics were comfortable for you? Which ones worked best for you?

23. What types of power affected you detrimentally?

24. What types of power did you use effectively?

25. What did you learn about your own personality and temperament?

26. What did you learn about interacting with different temperaments and negotiating styles?

27. Were both sides cooperative?

28. Did either side employ any unfair, deceptive, or unethical tactics?

29. Considering all of the circumstances, could you have done any better?

30. What would you do differently, if you could redo this negotiation?

CHECK YOUR PERSONAL EXCELLENCE PROGRESS (PEP)

KEY POINT
You won't do anything extremely well, until you do it poorly several times!

You may use the questions in Exhibit 20-2 to check your progress at developing more effective negotiation skills. The statements are presented in general form for periodic use. You should, however, also use the personal excellence progress (PEP) evaluation following every significant negotiation, whether that interaction felt easy or difficult. Simply read the statements with the particular negotiation in mind for those evaluations.

EXHIBIT 20-2

Personal Excellence Progress (PEP) Evaluation

Answer each question using the following scale:

1 = never, 2 = seldom, 3 = much, or half of the time, 4 = very often, 5 = always

1. I am aware of my typical behavioral patterns in interaction.
2. I maintain emotional stability during negotiation.
3. I believe that a mutual solution exists.
4. I notice behavioral cues from my counterpart that affect message meaning.
5. I adapt to the behavioral expectations of the situation and context.
6. I recognize information processing styles of my counterpart that differ from mine.
7. I resist any urge to view the negotiation as a contest.
8. I resist any urge to place time pressure on myself during negotiation.
9. I refrain from seeking personal credit for solutions.
10. I look for ways to share power with my counterpart.
11. I refrain from dominating, or power-over, tactics.
12. I believe that the end does not always justify the means.
13. My view of conflict is positive.
14. I look for constructive effects of conflict.
15. I analyze problems and conflicts with a systems perspective.
16. I am able to manage and sustain constructive conflict.
17. I think I know how my words and behavior are perceived.
18. I resist any urges to try to change the other person.
19. I focus my persuasive efforts toward the perceptions, opinions, and behavior of my counterpart.

20. I avoid negotiation only when the issue in conflict is unimportant, or emotions are too high, or the interaction is likely to produce more harm than benefit or no improvement over not negotiating.

21. I use accommodation when the relationship is more important than the substantive issues and collaboration fails.

22. I use collaboration as my first-choice approach.

23. I negotiate only with persons in authority to agree.

24. I maintain an open mind and flexibility during negotiations.

25. I negotiate only when I am prepared.

26. Prior to negotiation, I thoroughly analyze interests and goals of all parties.

27. I evaluate and rank my GRIP goals.

28. I identify and address my fears prior to negotiation.

29. I structure arguments with ACES.

30. Prior to negotiation I identify and analyze power held by all parties.

31. I express my feelings with I statements.

32. I have no fear of appearing stupid.

33. I am an effective listener.

34. I am able to walk away from negotiations at the appropriate times.

35. I am honest and ethical in my negotiations.

36. When my counterpart seeks a competitive process, I negotiate the process prior to beginning negotiation on the issues.

37. I refrain from assuming what the other side wants.

38. I refrain from countering to unsupported positions.

39. I support my positions with reasoning, facts, and data.

40. I allow my counterpart time to evaluate, answer, and decide.

41. Prior to negotiation, I know my options and establish a walk-away point.

42. I summarize the status of negotiation progress and results.

43. I ensure that the agreement is put in writing as soon as possible.

44. I am able to empathize with the other parties.

45. I use only tactics that are comfortable for me.

46. My counterparts perceive me as tactful and diplomatic.

47. I am able to recognize when my argument will not be accepted.

48. I am able to find common ground.

49. I am able to reframe arguments to reach my counterpart's latitude of acceptance.

50. I am persuasive.

Scoring:

Perfect	=	250 Keep up the great work!
Excellent	=	225 Keep up the good work. Focus on areas of lowest scores.
Very good	=	200 Continue building your skills.
Good	=	175 Continue building your skills.
Above average	=	150–174 Keep working!
Wake-up Call	=	Below 150 Begin study and practice.

The PEP is intended to check your current attitudes, approach, and general interaction behavior, as well as your effectiveness in particular negotiation efforts. Pay close attention to areas that repeatedly show less-than-optimal ratings. Focus your efforts on improving in those areas.

Performance Checklist

✓ There are six key indicia of a successful win-win negotiation. You may evaluate your negotiation results according to those measures.

✓ In this chapter, you have been provided with tools for assessing your negotiation conduct and personal effectiveness. Successful negotiation requires knowledge and practice. Studying the principles outlined in this book regarding human interaction and practicing effective communication are keys to becoming more effective in your negotiations.

Key Terms, Phrases, and Concepts

Post-negotiation Evaluation Questionnaire

Personnel Excellence Progress (PEP) Evaluation

Review Questions

Mark each of questions 1 through 4 as True (T) or False (F) and answer questions 5 through 10.

T F 1. Failure to agree always means that the negotiation failed.

T F 2. One sign of an unsuccessful negotiation is animosity on one or more sides.

T F 3. A mutually beneficial agreement is likely to be honored.

T F 4. Reaching your target always means you did things right.

5. What can you do to become more aware of your behavior?

6. How can you practice to become more flexible?

7. Name the three principal options available when confronted with something you do not like.

8. Why is it futile to try to change the other person?

9. Analyze whether you are afraid of appearing stupid in negotiation. What will you do with that fear?

10. How do you plan to assess and monitor how others perceive you?

Case 20.1

Emil is taking a course in conflict and negotiation. He has digested a great deal of information. As he lay falling asleep, he remembered a story his dearly departed mother had told him about when she left Czechoslovakia just before the Communist regime blocked it off for decades. His mother had lamented about having sold precious belongings for fractions of their worth and scraping up just enough money to reach America to start over penniless. Emil had known his parents as shrewd business people but he always thought they had been foolish to virtually give away their things. Now he could not help but wonder whether his parents were indeed smarter than he thought!

Case Discussion Questions

1. How would you advise Emil on evaluating the success of his mother's negotiations to sell her belongings?

2. What powers and/or fears were likely at play during the negotiations?

3. Can you identify anything in the case that was considered non-negotiable?

Happy Negotiating !

Appendix A

Personality and Behavior Assessment Resources

Tests and scales have been developed to measure nearly every aspect of personality and type of behavior. It can be difficult to find these instruments. The sources listed here should help in your search. Types of instruments and potential ways to find them are included.

TYPES OF TESTS

There are published and unpublished tests. The published tests are typically published by commercial organizations and may be obtained for a fee. Unpublished tests are less widely used and harder to locate. Generally, they are available only from the authors. There may not be data verifying the validity or reliability of such tests.

PUBLISHED TESTS

The *Mental Measurements Yearbook* (MMY) series dates from 1938 and provides information regarding the use of published tests and where to find them. The best place to find this series is in an academic library. The yearbook is organized alphabetically by test. Indexes available include the following: (1) Index of Titles, (2) Index of Acronyms, (3) Classified Subject Index, (4) Publishers Directory and Index, (5) Index of Names, and (6) Score Index.

The *Tests in Print III: An Index to Tests, Test Reviews, and the Literature on Specific Tests* (1938) contains references to commercially available tests. *Gary Groth-Marna's Handbook of Psychological Assessment*, 2nd ed. (John Wiley and Sons, 1990), contains references to widely used instruments such as the Wechsler intelligence test, the Rorschach test, and the Minnesota Multiphasic Personality Inventory.

UNPUBLISHED TESTS

Sources containing references to unpublished tests include the following.

Andruhs, Richard S. *Adult Assessment: A Source Book of Tests and Measure of Human Behavior.*

Beere, Carole A. *Women and Women's Issues: A Handbook of Tests and Measures of Human Behavior.*

Goldman, Bert A. *Directory of Unpublished Experimental Measures. Tests: A Comprehensive Reference for Assessments in Psychology, Education and Business.*

INTERNET SOURCES

A list of downloadable tests may be found at **http://www.ets.org/testcoll/pdflist.html.**

A personality assessment inventory may be found at **http://www.sigmaassessmentsystems.com/personality.htm.**

An online personality assessment may be found at **http://www.psycho services.com/personality.htm.**

Appendix B

Cases for Negotiation

Cases for your negotiation practice are contained in this appendix. You have already used portions of these materials as you studied various chapters of this book. As you utilize the cases for full negotiation practice, please observe the instructions set forth here. Part One of this appendix contains the full cases, and Part Two of this appendix contains supplemental case questions related to specific chapters.

For each case presented, there is one section describing the transaction or matter to be negotiated. That information is entitled "General Information." Following the general information is confidential information for each of the parties. Please do not read any of the material marked confidential for your counterpart. You are to read *only* the general information and the confidential information for the counterpart whose role you will play or whom you will represent. If you choose to practice a third-party intervention role, you should read *only* the general information. In such instance, the negotiation parties may share with you whatever information they choose.

Although the cases are drawn from real-life scenarios, all names have been changed. Any similarity to actual organization or individual names is coincidental. The scenarios do not report actual facts related to any real people or entities named. You may use the cases in any order; however, the fact patterns and issues become increasingly complex as cases are presented through this appendix.

In each case you are to adhere to the parameters and goals stated. After you have finished each negotiation session, use the post-negotiation evaluation questionnaire (Exhibit 20-1) and the PEP evaluation (Exhibit 20-2) in chapter 20 to evaluate your performance.

PART ONE: CASES
A Supply Order Case

General Information

Betty Buyerson is the vice president of purchasing for Maximize, Inc. Sophie Supplier is the vice president of production for Our-Parts-Are-Best, Inc. The parties have a history of doing business together. The typical quarterly order is $350,000. Due to repetition of business, prices have been approximately 2 percent below market alternatives. The parties are negotiating a new contract for a $500,000 order.

Confidential Information for Betty

Orders usually require ninety days for delivery. This time Betty wants delivery in sixty days. She knows that such a time frame may not be practical. Nevertheless, she believes that speeding the process will allow for more business and generate additional net profits this year in the amount of $60,000.

Confidential Information for Sophie

Betty has been generating 90 percent of Sophie's business. Sophie would like to increase sales to Betty. It is imperative that Sophie not lose Betty's business. It is not possible to increase sales by shortening delivery time.

A Charitable Contribution Case

General Information

Haas Gotbucks is the wealthiest person in the state where Investinus University is located. Freddie Fundraiser is the vice president of development for the university. Freddie is seeking a one-million-dollar contribution from Haas. The funds are needed for substantial renovation of a building. Freddie has arranged a meeting with Haas.

Confidential Information for Freddie

Freddie does not know the extent of Haas's financial holdings; however, Haas is well known in the community for contributing substantial funds to worthy causes. Freddie believes that, since Haas is a graduate of the university, a large contribution is likely.

Confidential Information for Haas

Haas has more money than he can ever spend. He is in the process of deciding where to place a two-million-dollar contribution this year. He is not fond of Investinus University. When he graduated from there, they refused to grant him high honors due to his failure to submit an administrative form requesting honors. His pet charitable cause is the prevention of cruelty to animals. The state's entire program has come to rely on his generosity. He plans to donate one million dollars to them again this year. He is considering giving the other million to the Red Cross.

A Discount Rate Case

General Information
Ken Clark is employed in the convention and conferences department of Luxury Hotel in the city slated for a company's awards conference. Bess Choice is in charge of making all travel and accommodation arrangements for the conference. Bess has identified three hotels that may be used for the function. Bess has traveled to the city to make her final selection and negotiate all fees.

Confidential Information for Bess
The three hotels Bess has identified with rooms available on the dates required are the Luxury, the Not-So-Grand, and the We-Try-Harder. The Luxury provides the most extensive and modern facilities, the most elegant rooms, and the best restaurants and is the preferred site. The Not-So-Grand is an old hotel that may have seen its better days but would fit the bill. Bess loves the charm of that hotel. The third choice provides all that Bess is looking for except that it is outside of town and would require conference attendees to travel by taxi for sightseeing and any enjoyment of the local culture. Bess has learned that the published room rates for the Luxury and the We-Try-Harder are substantially the same and range from $105 to $215. The Not-So-Grand runs approximately 10 percent lower. Food costs at all hotels appear to be the same. The We-Try-Harder has offered Bess a 5 percent reduction on its standard room, which will price each room at $100. They have also offered to provide shuttles to the downtown area at no added fee. Bess needs fifty rooms for five nights. Bess wants to get the best overall arrangements that will provide the maximum enjoyment for attendees at the lowest possible price. Her total budget for rooms, meals, and local transportation is $35,000.

Confidential Information for Ken
Ken is aware that the We-Try-Harder is competing hard with his hotel. He believes that his hotel is entitled to charge a premium price; however, he has been losing sales recently. Occupancy is not as high as his boss would like it to be. Published room rates for the

Luxury and the We-Try-Harder are substantially the same and range from $105 to $215. The Not-So-Grand runs approximately 10 percent lower. Ken is on a commission. He earns 5 percent on room rentals. He does not receive a commission on food sales. He has the authority to sell rooms at a 15 percent discount.

Purchase/Sale of Real Estate Case

General Information
Sylvia Seller's house has been on the market for sale for nine months according to listing records readily available. Patricia Purchaser has just entered the market. Patricia began looking at homes only two days ago. Patricia wants to purchase Sylvia's house. The house is owned by the estate of the prior owner, now deceased.

The listing price for the house is $399,900. There is no debt on the house. The price was just reduced from $465,000. The estate representatives have told Patricia that the asking price was reduced because the heirs want to have closure to the loss of their mother.

Homes in the neighborhood vary tremendously in size and style. The homes are all custom-built. Sylvia's is the smallest house in the immediate vicinity. Two nearby homes sold one year ago at $749,000 and $565,000. The parties have arranged a meeting to negotiate a contract.

Confidential Information for Sylvia
The estate of the prior owner includes three children who do not get along with each other. The house was a rather small portion of the estate. There is a large tax to pay; and the house, as well as two other properties, must be liquidated as soon as possible to pay obligations, especially taxes.

There is a problem with the lot. It sits low relative to bordering lots. Water collects near one corner of the house. Work is in progress to correct the problem, including corrective work in the crawl space. A sump pump has already been installed. The sellers are willing to agree to rectify the problem as a condition of sale.

Although it cannot be determined from the public records available to Patricia, the house has been on the market for sixteen months. The house was originally listed at $525,000. The market is generally bad from a seller's perspective. It is difficult to establish the market value of the house due to the variety of houses in the neighborhood. The house is two years old. The deceased owner expended $360,000 to construct the house. There is agreement among the heirs to sell the house for as low as $375,000. They will absolutely not take back any financing. The sellers want closing to occur within thirty days; however, they will be happy with a firm contract that will close within ninety days. The sellers are willing to pay up to $10,000 in closing costs for the purchaser.

Confidential Information for Patricia
Patricia is in love with the house. It is her dream house. It is also in the location she had targeted. Patricia is impressed with the neighborhood. She believes the house could justify a price of as much as $425,000. She would like to acquire the house for $360,000; however, she is willing to pay the asking price, if necessary. She does want to get the details on the work being done to the property. It appears to be a water problem.

If she must pay the asking price, she wants the sellers to take back a second trust in the amount of $20,000. Patricia does not want the second trust to be a deal breaker, though. Patricia has financing preapproved for her purchase up to the asking price. She has both a first and a second mortgage arranged to cover 95 percent financing of the property. Patricia requires that the sellers pay two points (2 percent) on the total amount of the sale price toward closing. Patricia requires that closing not occur for a minimum of ninety days.

A Contract Dispute Case

General Information
Ray has moved his business to a new address and has contracted with Dennis for landscaping at the new office location. The parties agreed on a decorative rock motif. It is extremely expensive, but it provides for low maintenance and year-round beauty. The parties have entered into a three-year agreement pursuant to which the base and a minimal number of trees and shrubs will be provided immediately with additional live plantings each of the next two years, including optional renewals. This morning, as Ray was checking on the job site, a load of rock was being delivered by Don. It was the wrong rock. Everyone can plainly see that the rock is full of clumps of dirt. From a block away, it looks like dirt in a barnyard. Ray requested that the rock be removed and returned. Don said that he had no authority and no equipment to remove the rock. Don also advised Ray that two hundred more tons were on order for delivery. The rock, including delivery, is billed at $30 per ton. Ray called Ken. Ken is on his way to the job site to meet with Ray and Don. All three individuals are the sole owners of their respective companies.

Confidential Information for Ray

The rock that Ray authorized was washed river rock that was quoted by Dennis at between $40 and $60 per ton. Trucking was estimated at $45 per ton, making the total cost approximately $85 to $105 per ton. After Ray selected the rock he wanted, Dennis came back with a small handful of what appeared to be what Ray wanted. Dennis said he had found another source for a price of $10 per ton. Ray had given his okay, provided that the rock was in fact the same as what he had previously selected. Ray wants the dirt removed from his property. Ray also wants the job done and does not want to overpay. Ray is not willing to pay any of the cost for the mistake.

Confidential Information for Dennis

Dennis ordered the rock because it is substantially cheaper than what Ray originally selected. Don showed Dennis a sample from which Dennis took another sample to show Ray. As far as Dennis is concerned, Ray approved the ordering of this rock. Dennis does not want to be left paying for the trucking and removal of this rock. He feels that although he ordered it, Ray should pay. Dennis does, however, want Ray's business on this three-year contract. Dennis feels that he was misled by Don and that Don should correct this error.

Confidential Information for Don

Don is livid. He feels as though he is the only one at risk here. He has incurred cost. He bought the rock. He trucked the rock. If he has to remove it, he will have to pay for equipment and labor to do so. He recalls the conversation with Dennis. He remembers telling Dennis that the rock was cheaper because it is unwashed. Don would like the contract for the correct rock, but he expects not to be left holding the bag on this one.

A Human Resource Needs Case

General Information

Katia has just had a huge project dropped in her lap due to the resignation of a colleague. The organization is experiencing a downsizing. The project has a very tight deadline. It is due in two weeks. Katia's department is not to be affected by the layoffs, but she does not have adequate numbers of staff to complete the work on time. The general feeling among people who have escaped the layoff is relief as well as fear of their number coming up soon. Roger, Katia's boss, has a reputation for never giving in to requests of any kind. A mere twenty-four hours have passed since the project landed on Katia's desk, but Roger has requested a meeting to discuss the status.

Confidential Information for Katia

Katia believes that her predecessor has had the project for a month already, even though it appears that virtually no work has been done on it. Roger was known to be very fond of Katia's predecessor, Ralph. Roger was grooming him as replacement when Roger moves up the ladder. Katia thinks that she might bring the project in on time if she gets authorization to hire temporary workers or to utilize people from another department who have already been given a ninety-day notice of termination. If none of those options work, then at a minimum she will have to figure out how to get her salaried staff to work excessive overtime, despite their fears of being let go. She wants assurances that she and her entire department will have continued employment for at least the coming year. She also wants to try to trade a promotion for getting this project done on time.

Confidential Information for Roger

Roger is in a pickle. He knows that Ralph, the employee originally assigned to this project, did not properly address it. He knows that Ralph was spending all of his available time looking for a job. Unfortunately, Roger's superior holds Roger responsible for the delays as well as for the loss of Ralph's productivity. Roger may very well lose his job if this project fails. However, no funds are available to hire contract employees on a temporary basis; nor are funds available to delay the layoffs. Roger thinks people should be thankful to still have their jobs and do whatever is required. Nevertheless, he will try his best to motivate Katia to succeed here. He plans to offer her a promotion if absolutely necessary.

A Contract Bid Case

General Information

General Contractors, Inc. (GCI) is in need of a subcontractor to complete work on a twenty-thousand-square-foot office building. The work required to be done is a small part of a big job already in progress. GCI had contracted with a small company because it got a very low price. The subcontractor went out of business and is unable to complete the job. Conti Construction Company (CCC) is able to perform the work and is interested in obtaining the subcontract.

The parties have already discussed the overall needs and timing for the job. They are in agreement regarding the estimated number of man-hours necessary to complete the job. Although they are in agreement regarding the overall size of the job, they do not yet have a full subcontract value because they have not yet agreed on unit price. They must establish cost and markup allowed. As soon as they come to an agreement on pricing, they should be ready to proceed. Gene Igor, president of GCI, and Carl Connor, president of CCC, have set a meeting to negotiate the price for the subcontracted work.

Confidential Information for Gene Igor, GCI

GCI's prime contract is a modified cost-plus-fixed-fee arrangement. The contract provides that, in the event costs escalate more than 5 percent above GCI's projections, GCI's fee will be reduced pro rata. GCI has had cost overruns in the early work on the project. GCI would like to make up as much of that deficit as possible on the remaining work. GCI is also behind schedule on the project. In the event that GCI does not meet its completion deadline, it will suffer yet another financial penalty, further reducing its profit in the job. GCI has worked with CCC in the past and knows that CCC is reliable and competent. GCI does not want to risk contracting with anyone other than CCC on this project. Gene must come to an agreement with Carl.

GCI budgeted $37.50 per man-hour for the work to be contracted with CCC. Because of the condition of the project, GCI would like to subcontract with CCC at $36.00 per man-hour. According to Gene's estimates, that would be a 15 percent markup, which would generate a 13 percent gross profit for CCC. Gene is figuring Carl's costs to be $31.25 per hour. Gene is willing to promise CCC another extremely lucrative contract that would begin in six months in exchange for CCC's reduction in price on this job. That next job is a firm contract, and Gene estimates that CCC will enjoy a 40 percent markup on that job.

Gene recognizes that his cost estimates may be in error; however, his goal is to limit Carl's markup to 15 percent on this job. As a last resort, Gene is willing to pay up to 30 percent over whatever Carl can establish as his costs in order to finish this job and avoid the additional penalty for failing to complete on time.

Confidential Information for Carl Connor, CCC

Carl is aware that Gene is in a bind. However, unbeknownst to Gene, Carl could really use this contract. He just received word last evening that a job he was counting on and that he expected to finalize yesterday has been postponed for three months. The last time Carl spoke with Gene, they both believed that Carl would have to add extra workers to take on Gene's job.

Carl still believes that, since he is the best contractor to pull Gene's feet out of the fire, he should receive a premium on this job.

Carl wants a 35 percent markup on the job. His bottom line is a 25 percent markup. He has enough small jobs and things in the pipeline, as well as time off he can schedule, that it is not worth his effort to perform under strained conditions for less than a 25 percent markup. Carl has never done a job for less than a 20 percent markup. Carl would be willing to give Gene a break if this were a larger, long-term job.

Carl employs a union shop. He pays $25 per hour; however, when employer taxes and benefits are added, his hourly cost is $33.75. At a 35 percent markup, he would charge Gene $45.56 per hour. At a 25 percent markup, he would charge Gene $42.18.

A Licensing Agreement Case

General Information

Tony Buyer is a certified public accountant in the process of establishing a private training company. Tony has been employed for many years in an executive position with Express Financial, a well-known financial services company. He has been responsible for the business-development division of that conglomerate. Andy Ledger, also a certified public accountant, is the senior partner in a midsize public accounting firm. Both parties live and work in the Washington, D.C., metropolitan area.

Tony and Andy have communicated with each other regarding a potential business arrangement. Tony made the initial contact by letter, explaining his interest. They have spoken by telephone as well. Tony is interested in purchasing or otherwise gaining the rights to use training materials owned by Andy's firm. Both parties understand that the training materials desired by Tony are to be directed at training small business owners and would-be entrepreneurs in financial and accounting concepts. Andy's firm has developed training courses that it has used to train new staff members. Tony has already reviewed the subject course material. Both Andy and Tony believe that Andy's course material is well-suited for Tony's purposes.

Tony's experience in establishing new lines of business, providing venture capital funding, and monitoring new businesses has convinced him of the need for his proposed training. No one in the area is providing such training. Both parties recognize that small business is the fastest-growing segment of the U.S. economy. Both parties recognize that training is the fastest-growing industry in the Washington, D.C., metropolitan area. Both parties believe that this type of training would be extremely valuable to entrepreneurs, many of whom fail because of improper or inadequate accounting knowledge.

Both parties are interested in establishing a business relationship. They have set a meeting to negotiate the terms of a licensing agreement for the use of Andy's materials. Both parties have authority to make the final decision.

Confidential Information for Tony Buyer

Tony's employment agreement prohibits him from conducting any business activities whatsoever for so long as he continues to be employed by Express Financial. Because of that restriction, Tony had to obtain permission to commence work on his new business plan. Two months ago, Tony began discussions to obtain that permission and negotiate an early retirement. As a result of those discussions, it may turn out that Express Financial will fund Tony's new venture; however, no final agreement has been reached. Tony has begun work on his new company. He has incorporated a new entity, prepared a business plan, registered trading names, and completed other preliminary chores. He has established a private, proprietary school pursuant to the applicable provisions of the *Virginia Code*. Also as a result of his discussions with Express Financial, however, Tony now has only six months of employment remaining. At the end of that time, he will retire.

Tony has identified two options for obtaining the necessary training materials. He can design and prepare them himself, or he can try to obtain a license to use materials that others may already have prepared. While he is personally capable of preparing the courses, he estimates that the task will require six months of his concentrated effort. His goal two months ago was to have his new business generating income within twelve months. Once the courses are in hand, he anticipates a time requirement of three months to market the first offering. He now has only eight months to meet his original target and only six months before his income gets reduced due to retirement. If he prepares the courses himself, the time line to begin generating revenue from the business is at least nine months. Cash flow is a concern, even though he will have a retirement income. He must post a $5,000 bond with the state authorities at the time he markets his first offering.

Tony believes that he can charge $1,000 tuition per student. Tony projects that the best he can hope for during his first year of operations is to enroll approximately one hundred students. During the first year, costs will be very high. Even with one hundred students, he anticipates net income of only $35,000. After the initial year, his projections increase dramatically as he plans to add instructors and expand into additional geographic areas. He believes that the net profits will be between $250,000 and $750,000 after the business is up and running, depending only upon how fast he is able to add instructors and locations.

Tony is anxious to come to an agreement with Andy because of the time it will save him. He must know immediately whether or not they have a workable agreement because he cannot delay starting his own course preparation. Tony has contacted each of the firms constituting the big ten accounting firms as well as all regional firms and several midsize local firms. No one except Andy was interested in talking to Tony about his proposal.

Tony has established the following as his absolute ceiling for entering into a licensing agreement: (1) an initial licensing fee of $7,500, which will grant him the right to use the courses for a period of two years, renewable after that at Tony's option; (2) annual renewal fees beginning with the third year of $2,500; and (3) a royalty fee of $15 per student. Tony figures that the income stream to Andy, conservatively, will be at least $60,000 in the first five years in total (or $12,000 per year on average), although he recognizes that it will be only around $9,000 during the first year. Tony cannot come up with more than $7,500 up front prior to starting operations. If he is required to expend more than some combination of those amounts in cash, he believes he will be better off in the long run to incur the delay of developing the courses himself.

Confidential Information for Andy Ledger
Andy is very enthused about Tony's new business proposal. Andy estimates that Tony's business will generate profits of $500,000 per year. Andy would like to enter the business himself. He really does not have the available time to divert from his accounting practice so he is not seriously considering jumping on Tony's idea.

Andy sees income potential for his firm, as well as public relations and advertising benefits. Andy also sees the potential for Tony to provide training to Andy's small-business clients. The firm has expended a substantial amount of time, energy, and money developing the training materials. They were developed over several years with input from several professionals. The material includes real-life practice sets, and the courses are excellent. Andy believes that it would be an extraordinary feat for a single individual to develop such courses from scratch.

Andy wants a minimum of $25,000 to let the courses out of his door. Andy has determined that his absolute minimum terms for an agreement with Tony are as follows: (1) a one-time licensing fee of $25,000, (2) annual renewal fees of $10,000, and (3) royalty fees at 5 percent of gross revenue. Andy figures that after the initial two years his firm's income stream will be approximately $25,000 per year. He is willing to be somewhat flexible in collecting amounts due during the first two years, because he recognizes the difficulties of start-up operations.

Purchase/Sale of a Business Case

General Information

Richard Lightning owns and runs an electrical contracting business. The business has been a tremendous success. Richard is very good at what he does. He is adept in obtaining business and performing his contracts and in personnel and business management generally. He started his business twenty years ago out of his home. Revenues increased steadily from the beginning. Within three years, he acquired office space. In each of the last ten years, his gross revenues have been $1,275,000. The net profit in each of those years was approximately $500,000. He employs five, full-time, regular employees and contracts for additional help as jobs necessitate. He funds bonuses, pensions, and profit-sharing plans for himself and his employees out of the revenues of the business. Eighty-five percent of his business is with the federal government. Richard now distributes to himself substantially all of the earnings each year. The book value of the company is $150,000, of which $100,000 is in cash.

Shorty Wireman is interested in acquiring a profitable contracting business. Shorty is in his early thirties and is employed in a management position with a large electrical contracting business. Shorty is disgruntled with his employer because he is unable to share in company profits. Shorty would like to work for himself; however, he would like to shortcut the process by buying into an existing operation.

Shorty is well aware of Richard's reputation for excellence and success. Shorty made the original contact. Shorty's late father had been a friend of Richard's and had served as Richard's CPA until his death two years ago. Shorty called Richard and asked if there might be any interest in a potential sale of the business. Richard said that he makes it a practice not to dismiss opportunities out of hand and that almost everything has its price. Richard indicated a willingness to discuss the matter. Richard has shared with Shorty the general financial information outlined in the preceding paragraphs (in exchange for an enforceable confidentiality agreement). Richard knows that Shorty's inheritance from his father's lucrative accounting and investment advisory practice has provided Shorty with the financial ability to make the purchase. Shorty possesses the requisite electrical certifications necessary to transition into owning and operating the business.

[In negotiating this problem, ignore any complexities of tax law.]

Confidential Information for Richard Lightning

Richard is in his late fifties. He has grown tired of the demands of his business. He really would like to sell and move on to other endeavors. He would especially like to have more leisure time to enjoy his two passions—golf and his Harley-Davidson motorcycle.

Richard knows that the success of the business is tied to him personally. His personal contact with various decision makers in the government agencies is what generates jobs. He anticipates that Shorty will want him to continue to consult, at least during the first two years after the sale. Richard has decided that he does not mind a minimal amount of consulting; however, he is not anxious to accept any agreement that requires full-time involvement over any extended period.

Richard has been concerned for several months about one major contract that generates 40 percent of his revenue. There is some risk that his firm will be replaced with a large management company. If that were to happen, Richard would have to make a substantial effort to obtain new contracts. Although he has been given verbal assurances, Richard worries. If the contract is renewed, the fee will increase by 5 percent.

Richard is also concerned that business will drop off generally after his sale. Therefore, he is adamant that the price not be tied to future earnings. He also believes that the $100,000 cash in the bank should be distributed to him prior to any sale and that Shorty should loan to the company whatever cash is necessary to operate. At the present time, Richard foresees no significant cash-flow shortages.

Richard thinks his business is worth two-and-one-half times earnings ($500,000 times 2 ½ = $1,250,000). However, since Richard takes a salary of $200,000 per year before the net earnings figure, he thinks that $700,000 should be used in the price calculation ($700,000 times 2 ½ = $1,750,000). Richard would like to receive $1,850,000 in the sale ($1,750,000 plus the $100,000 cash balance). All things considered, however, Richard would hand over the business for $1,000,000 in immediate cash. Richard is willing to consult if necessary for $100 per hour.

Confidential Information for Shorty Wireman

Shorty is very anxious to acquire Richard's business. Shorty is currently earning a salary of $70,000 per year. Richard has told Shorty that the business can afford to pay a salary of $200,000 per year and still generate a net profit of $500,000. Shorty recognizes that Richard's personal involvement is key to the success of the business, and he will require Richard to consult with him as a part of any purchase agreement.

Shorty believes that Richard's business should be valued at one year's expected earnings. (This would be a 100 percent capitalization rate or 1 divided by 100 percent.) Shorty believes that the value may be annual earnings of $500,000 plus the $200,000 expected salary to him; so Shorty would like to pay $700,000. However, in view of the reputation and good will, Shorty expects to have to pay a premium. Shorty is willing to go as high as a 25 percent premium. (This would be 1 divided by 1.25 percent, or an 80 percent capitalization rate.) Shorty will pay up to 125 percent of the amount it is expected the company will generate in net profits and salary to him during the first year, provided that Richard will consult for two years. That calculates as $700,000 times 1.25 percent, or $875,000. Shorty thinks Richard should consult in exchange for that premium price. If Richard will not agree to that, Shorty would be willing to reduce the price to $775,000 and pay Richard $100,000 to work full time.

Shorty wants to hold back 10 percent of the purchase price or the consulting fees payable to Richard, contingent on all existing contracts continuing for twelve months following his purchase. Shorty also wants to know whether the company anticipates any cash-flow problems that might require additional cash infusions. Shorty's ceiling on the amount of cash he is willing to pay immediately is $950,000, including the purchase price, cash infusions, and any advances to Richard. Shorty's other overall limitation is that expected cash flow (before tax) over the first eighteen months should equal his up-front cash investment.

Settlement Negotiation Case 1 Injury Accident

General Information

One Friday evening at approximately eight o'clock, Leroy Bell, a very successful stockbroker, was leaving City Hospital in his Cadillac. The hospital is located in the center of the busy downtown area. It was dark, and a light snow was falling. Leroy's wife was in the hospital suffering from cancer and recovering from surgery related to the cancer. Leroy was so concerned and distraught over his wife's condition that he had been drinking heavily all week. Many people, including hospital personnel, are aware of this.

Leroy was in a hurry to get home to his son who was very ill with the flu. As he was traveling up a one-way street, he had to swerve to miss a car that stopped suddenly in the right lane for no apparent reason. As he swerved to the left, he struck Sally Hide who had slipped from the passenger seat of a four-wheel-drive vehicle parked on the left side of the one-way street. Sally fell onto the snowy and slippery street into Leroy's path.

Sally's back was broken. She has become paralyzed as the result of the injury. Sally was thirty-six years old at the time of the injury, and she was an extremely successful corporate attorney. Police and ambulance personnel on the scene of the accident apparently did not suspect any alcohol. In any event, no suspicions were reported and no sobriety tests were administered. No tickets were issued.

Sally has sued Leroy for $7,500,000. The parties have set a meeting during which they hope to settle the claim without the need for prolonged litigation.

[As you negotiate this case, ignore any complexities of law with which you are not familiar.]

Confidential Information for Sally Hide

Sally Hide had been drinking heavily on the evening of the accident. Sally had been drinking excessively for several months. Her husband had urged her to seek help for her drinking problem. The reason Sally fell out of the vehicle that night is that she was reaching to the ground to gather snow to throw at her companion. In her intoxicated condition, she fell out of the vehicle. Her companion was not her husband. Her companion that evening was a professional associate with whom she had been having an affair for more than a year.

The foregoing notwithstanding, Sally and her attorney have questioned the people who were in the stopped car that Leroy swerved to miss. Those two people are ready to testify that Leroy was traveling too fast for the road conditions and did not have control of his car.

Sally is very concerned that her affair not be made public. Sally is also very concerned that her drinking problem not be made public. Both matters could destroy her professional practice, which she has managed to hold together despite her physical condition. Professionally, Sally has adapted very well to her paralysis. Disclosure of her affair will also destroy her marriage. The affair is now over, and Sally wants to remain with her husband. Her husband wants a divorce; however, he has not been able to file for one yet, due to Sally's condition.

Sally's medical expenses have totaled $250,000. Her net annual income at the time of the accident was $200,000, and her current net income is approximately $215,000 per year. Sally would be pleased to recover only her medical expenses and let the facts and details rest in private peace. She would be ecstatic to recover anything above $250,000.

Confidential Information for Leroy Bell

On that Friday, Leroy had three old-fashioneds between 3:00 and 6:00 p.m. before entering the hospital to visit his wife. Although he was very angry over the hand life had dealt, he believed that he was sober and in control when he left the hospital to drive home. Both Leroy and his attorney believe that the alcohol did not contribute to the mishap. Leroy recognizes, however, that his mind was not on his driving and that he was going a little too fast.

Leroy is aware of Sally's excellent reputation in the community. Leroy and his attorney are also aware that Sally had been in a bar that evening with an associate. Leroy is worried about any disclosure of his drinking. He is worried that a public trial would adversely affect his successful business. Leroy thinks that he will have to pay Sally at least $750,000. He is willing to go as high as $1,750,000 to settle the case.

[In your negotiation, ignore any complexities that may be added by the existence of insurance companies. Assume that Leroy is self-insured.]

Settlement Negotiation Case 2 Divorce

General Information

Mr. and Mrs. Endin are getting a divorce. They have been married three years. Wilma has been a successful attorney for twenty years. Manny retired one year prior to their marriage. Manny has a comfortable retirement income in which Wilma has no legal right or interest. The couple has been living in the home that belonged to Wilma prior to the marriage. Wilma purchased the home thirteen years ago for $650,000, paying $250,000 in cash and obligating herself to a mortgage in the amount of $400,000.

Wilma has not been very assertive with Manny in the past. Against Wilma's wishes, Manny moved in with Wilma two years before they were married. Manny's life style improved significantly with this move. Shortly after Manny moved in and prior to their marriage, Wilma transferred, without mortgagee consent and without Manny obligating himself to the mortgage, the title of her home so that they would own it jointly. Manny paid Wilma $50,000 for the transfer. The market value of the home at that time was approximately one million dollars. Currently, the market is depressed, making the value now closer to the original price of $650,000.

The parties signed a prenuptial agreement before their marriage. It merely states that each party will retain his or her separate assets and that Wilma waives all rights to support. One year ago, Wilma transferred the entire title to the home into Manny's name solely. The transfer was made only between the parties with no notice or consent by the mortgage holder. Wilma remains the only party obligated on the mortgage. There was no financial payment by Manny for the transfer. For a period of approximately two years and until six months ago, however, Manny made the mortgage payments in full. The monthly mortgage is $4,000.

The relationship deteriorated after the last title transfer. There have been two occasions on which police were called to the home when Manny lost control of his temper. Manny is under treatment for depression. He has left the home. Both parties want a divorce. Both parties want the home. They have set a meeting to resolve the dispute over the home and any other financial matters between them.

Confidential Information for Wilma

Wilma recognizes that she has made some mistakes. She was so in love that she did not recognize the signs of Manny's depression and emotional abuse until it was too late to undo the house transfers. She trusted Manny when he said that he had few financial resources and felt like the home was not theirs to share, prompting her to make the transfers with inadequate consideration.

Since Manny has been gone, Wilma has opened his mail. She learned that he has $250,000 in an investment account. She now suspects that Manny set out to take advantage of her from the beginning. Manny has been harassing her. He emptied the joint checking account to which only Wilma's money had been deposited. Manny has never added Wilma to any of his financial accounts.

Wilma is now in extreme financial distress. She has drawn down all of her lines of credit. Her cash inflow falls short of her mortgage payment and living expenses. Manny has refused to contribute to the mortgage payments in any way during the past six months.

Wilma would prefer to avoid prolonged litigation that would be necessary to prove misrepresentation and fraud against Manny. Such litigation would take two to three years, and she cannot hold on that long. She also recognizes that there is a high probability that the best outcome of such litigation would be for her to be awarded a one-half interest in the home. She may not receive an interest at all, given her prior transfers.

Wilma is emotionally attached to the home. She wants to return Manny's $50,000 in exchange for full title. She will go as high as $100,000 for a complete release by Manny of all interest in the home. She would like to defer payment to Manny for one year; however, the financing she has arranged will permit her to pay him now if necessary. If she cannot have the house, her second choice would be to have it sold. In any event, she wants Manny's financial share in the home reduced. She would agree to pay Manny $50,000 out of the sale proceeds, provided that she remains in the home until it is sold. She is willing to pay him $100,000 out of the sale proceeds if he pays one-half of the carrying costs until sale.

As a last resort, she will accept payment and allow Manny to stay in the house provided that he lists it for sale and actively markets it. She does not want him in the house in the long term. She believes that $125,000 would be an acceptable payment to her. She will take as little as $75,000 cash immediately as long as Manny becomes obligated on the mortgage and she is released. He is not willing to make payments to her contingent on sale of the house.

Confidential Information for Manny

Manny suspects that Wilma is opening his mail, and he wants her prosecuted for the offense. He is concerned about having withheld information from Wilma regarding his financial position. He fears that disclosure of that fact in court will void the prenuptial agreement. His attorney has advised him, however, that it is extremely unlikely that he would be required to share any assets with Wilma other than the home.

Manny wants a quick resolution. He does not have adequate income to qualify for a mortgage on the home. He wants the home sold. His theory is that a deal is a deal. The home was worth a million dollars when he first received an interest through superior negotiation. He urged Wilma to sell the home two years ago. If she had done that, his one-half interest would have generated him $200,000 after costs of sale. His investment is so low that the sale price now that he owns the whole thing is almost irrelevant. As long as he has full title, he is willing to pay the mortgage until it sells.

Manny is adamant about the following: (1) he will take no less than $200,000 to release his interest in the home; (2) he wants Wilma to release all claims to any of his other assets; (3) he will not pay any carrying costs of the house as long as Wilma is living there. His goal is to get $200,000 now and relinquish all rights to the house.

He believes that he will likely lose half interest in the house in litigation with Wilma. Therefore, he is willing to pay Wilma up to $75,000 at closing of the sale of the house, provided the house sells for no less than $800,000. He will go as high as $60,000 if the amount is not tied to the sales price. He thinks the house is worth $850,000 at this time. His attorney has explained to him the situation on the mortgage. He is willing to become obligated on it if he stays in the house.

Settlement Negotiation Case 3 Legal Judgment

General Information
Justin Holder is the attorney representing the deposit insurance fund of government X. Erica Right is the attorney representing one of the individuals against whom Justin's client holds a civil judgment. Five individuals as well as the corporate employer of Erica's client are jointly and severally liable for the judgment. That corporation is the ultimate parent holding company of a banking institution whose deposits are insured by government X.

The judgment is in the amount of $101,000,000 as the result of a jury finding a breach of fiduciary duty and mismanagement. Erica did not represent this client during the litigation. Erica has been retained for the settlement process, because litigation counsel is the holder of a $200,000 secured promissory note from the client for unpaid legal fees and has a conflict of interest in conducting settlement efforts.

All defendants have an appeal pending and believe that the trial court committed several reversible errors. One issue on appeal is the fact that no damages have yet been incurred by the plaintiffs. Another issue is that Erica's client was not an officer or director of the bank. She should have been dismissed from the case entirely. The lower court refused her motion to be dismissed, finding her to be a director in fact due to her position with the parent company.

The law permits collection efforts to proceed on the judgment despite the pending appeal. Justin has advised Erica that preferential treatment may be afforded to Erica's client in exchange for being the first to settle and drop the appeal. A meeting has been set for purposes of negotiating a settlement.

Confidential Information for Justin Holder

Justin believes that the errors by the trial court were significant and stand a chance of reversal on appeal. Although he believes that he will be sustained as to most of the defendants, he is concerned that he will lose his judgment against Erica's client. Such a loss presents further difficulty for him. He is also attempting to collect from the insurance company under the officer and director liability policy. Thus far, the company has taken the position that Erica's client was not an officer or director of the bank and was not insured. He anticipates prolonged litigation on the matter; however, a reversal of the judgment against Erica's client would defeat his claim before he can pursue it effectively. Justin seeks a quick settlement with Erica's client that will include a statement by her that she believes she is insured by the officer and director's policy.

Justin is adamant that Erica's client be left with no more than $50,000 in assets of any kind. He knows that she owns a home with a market value of $1,000,000, household belongings, two automobiles, and $25,000 cash. He will accept no less than a $300,000 settlement. He is willing to permit Erica's client to seek recovery or indemnification from the parent company that employed her.

Confidential Information for Erica Right

Erica's client has just received her final paycheck, because her client's employer has been forced out of business by the prolonged litigation. Her client owes a $200,000 promissory note to her former counsel for legal fees. Her home is encumbered with a $400,000 first trust plus the $200,000 second trust representing the legal fees. The value of her home is between $750,000 and one million dollars. She has only household goods, two automobiles, and $25,000 cash beyond the house.

Erica and her client believe in the merit of her appeal. Since the law permits execution of the judgment prior to decision on the appeal, Erica's client is facing the loss of her home. If the home were to be taken in judgment now, it would be very difficult to establish values and recoup the loss at a later time upon winning the appeal. She cannot afford to fund the appeal, in any event. If she does not come to a settlement, she will be forced into bankruptcy.

The primary goal is to buy time. Erica's client would like to settle for $100,000. She will go as high as $300,000 as long as payment is postponed for five years. Under no circumstances can she pay anything earlier than two years. She would also like Justin's clients to acknowledge that she committed no wrongful or unlawful acts.

PART TWO: SUPPLEMENTAL CASE QUESTIONS RELATED TO SPECIFIC CHAPTERS

Chapter 3

Select any case from Part One of this appendix, and read *only* the general information. Do *not* read either party's confidential information.

Diagnose the conflict.

Chapter 8

For practice, you may also select any negotiation case or cases at random from this appendix and read *only* the general information provided for each case selected. *Do not* read any party's confidential information when doing this practice exercise.

Come to *GRIP* with the selected case!

Chapter 9

As an additional exercise that will demonstrate the role of perception in negotiation behavior and decisions, you may try an experiment with one of the negotiation cases contained in this appendix. Find someone to pair up with and select a case at random. Read the general information for the problem individually and separately. You should both also separately read the confidential information for *one* of the parties while both of you place yourself in that same party's role. Each of you should separately assess your interests and goals in a potential negotiation of the matter. After you have each prepared, compare your assessments and determinations.

How do your perceptions differ? Why do your perceptions differ? How did your perception affect your goals and decisions about negotiating?

Chapter 10

Select a negotiation case from this appendix and read *only* the general information provided. Do *not* read either party's confidential information. Practice identifying and assessing the powers available to both sides in the case.

Chapter 14

For practice, you may select a case from this appendix. Read the general information and decide how you would complete the twenty steps for preparing to negotiate.

References

A

Anderson, N. H. 1965. Averaging versus adding as a stimulus-combination rule in impression formation. *Journal of Experimental Psychology* 70:394–400.

Atkinson, J. W., and J. O Raynor. 1974. *Motivation and achievement*. Washington, DC: Winston.

B

Bandura, A. 1977. *Social learning theory*. Upper Saddle River, NJ: Prentice Hall.

Bass, Bernard M., and Edward C. Ryterband. 1979. *Organizational psychology*. 2nd ed. Boston: Allyn and Bacon.

Batson, C. D. 1975. Rational processing or rationalization? The effect of disconfirming information on stated religious belief. *Journal of Personality and Social Psychology* 32:176–84.

Bem, D. 1967. Self-perception: An alternative interpretation of cognitive dissonance phenomena. *Psychology Review* 74:183–200.

Bem, D. J. 1972. Self-perception theory. In vol. 6 of *Advances in experimental social psychology*, ed. L. Berkowitz, 2–62. New York: Academic Press.

Berlo, D. K. 1960. *The process of communication*. New York: Holt, Rinehart and Winston.

Block, P. 1993. *Stewardship: Choosing service over self-interest*. San Francisco: Berrett-Koehler.

Borisoff, D., and D. A. Victor. 1989. *Conflict management: A communication skills approach*. Englewood Cliffs, NJ: Prentice Hall.

Brehm, J. 1966. *A theory of psychological reactance*. New York: Academic Press.

C

Cacioppo, J. T., and G. G. Berntson. 1994. Relationship between attitudes and evaluative space: A critical review, with emphasis on the separability of positive and negative substrates. *Psychological Bulletin* 115:401–23.

Cavanaugh, John C., and Fredda Blanchard-Fields. 2002. *Adult development and aging*. 4th ed. Belmont, CA. Wadsworth/Thomson Learning.

Chapman, L. J., and J. P. Chapman. 1959. Atmosphere effect reexamined. *Journal of Experimental Psychology* 58:220–226.

Checkland, P. 1981. *Systems thinking, systems practice*. New York: John Wiley and Sons.

Christie, R., and F. L. Geis. 1970. *Studies in Machiavellianism*. New York: Academic Press.

Cohen, Herb. 1980. *You can negotiate anything*. Secaucus, NJ: Lyle Stuart.

Conger, Jay A. 1998. The necessary art of persuasion. *Harvard Business Review* Volume 76 (3); pages 84–96 (12).

Coser, Lewis A. 1977. *Masters of sociological thought*. 2nd ed. New York: Harcourt Brace Jovanovich College.

Craver, Charles. 2002. Gender and negotiation performance. *Sociological Practice: A Journal of Clinical and Applied Sociology* 4 (3): 183–93.

D

Dahl, R. A. 1957. The concept of power. *Behavioral Science* 2:201–15.

Darley, J. M., and P. H. Gross. 1983. A hypothesis-confirming bias in labeling effects. *Journal of Personality and Social Psychology* 44:20–33.

Davies, M., L. Stankov, and R. D. Roberts. 1998. Emotional intelligence: In search of an elusive construct. *Journal of Personality and Social Psychology* 75 (4): 989–1015.

Day, D. V., D. J. Schleicher, A. L. Unckless, and N. J. Hiller. 2002. Self-monitoring personality at work: A meta-analytic investigation of construct validity. *Journal of Applied Psychology* 87 (2): 390–401.

Digman, J. M. 1990. Personality structure: Emergence of the five-factor model. In *Annual Review of Psychology* 41, eds. M. R. Rosenzweig and L. W. Porter, 417–40. Palo Alto, CA: Annual Reviews.

Ditto, P. H., and D. F. Lopez. 1992. Motivated skepticism: Use of deferential decision criteria for preferred and non-preferred conclusions. *Journal of Personality and Social Psychology* 63: 568–84.

Dominich, Joseph R. 2001. *Dynamics of mass communication*. 7th ed. McGraw-Hill. New York, NY.

Dunn, C. W., and C. M. Tucker. 1993. Black children's adaptive functioning and maladaptive behavior associated with quality of family support. *Journal of Multicultural Counseling and Development* 21: 79–87.

Dyrud, Marilyn A. 1997. Focus on teaching. *Business Communication Quarterly*, June 1997 v 60n2 p. 124–135 124 (11).

E

Eagly, A. H., and S. Chaiken, 1993. *The psychology of attitudes*. Harcourt Brace Jovanovich College. Fort Worth, TX.

Edwards, K., and E. E. Smith. 1996. A disconfirmation bias in the evaluation of arguments. *Journal of Personality and Social Psychology* 71 (1): 5–24.

F

Felder, R. 1996. Matters of style. *ASEE Prism* 6 (4): 18–23.

Festinger, L. 1957. *A theory of cognitive dissonance*. Evanston, IL: How, Peterson.

French, J. R. P., and B. H. Raven. 1968. The basis of social power. In *Group dynamics*. 3rd ed., eds. D. Cartwright and A Zander. New York: Harper and Row.

Friedman, M., and R. H. Rosenman. 1974. *Type A behavior and your heart*. New York: Alfred A. Knopf.

G

Geller, E. S., and G. F. Pitz. 1968. Confidence and decision speed in the revision of opinion. *Organizational Behavior and Human Decision Processes* 3: 190–201.

Gilbert, D. T. 1989. Thinking lightly about others: Automatic components of the social inference process. In *Unintended thought.* J. S. Uleman and J. A. Bargh. New York: Guilford Press.

Gilbert, D. T., and E. E. Jones. 1986. Perceiver-induced constraint: Interpretations of self-generated reality. *Journal of Personality and Social Psychology* 50: 269–80.

Gudykunst, W., and S. Ting-Toomey. 1988. *Culture and interpersonal communication.* Beverly Hills, CA: Sage.

H

Hathaway, W. 1995. A new way of viewing dispute resolution training. *Mediation Quarterly* 13:37–45.

Heider, F. 1958. *The psychology of interpersonal relations.* New York: Wiley.

Heine, S. J., T. Takata, and D. R. Lehman. 2000. Beyond self-presentation: Evidence for self-criticism among Japanese. *Personality and Social Psychology Bulletin* 26 (1): 71–78.

Hicks, L. E. 1985. Is there a disposition to avoid the fundamental attribution error? *Journal of Research in Personality* 19 (4): 436.

Hofstede, G. 1980. *Culture's consequences: International differences in work related values.* Beverly Hills, CA: Sage.

Hovland, C. E., O. J. Harvey, and M. Sherif. 1957. Assimilation and contrast effects in reactions to communication and attitude change. *Journal of Abnormal and Social Psychology* 55:244–52.

Hurtz, G. M., and J. J. Donovan. 2000. Personality and job performance: The Big Five revisited. *Journal of Applied Psychology* 85 (6): 869–79.

I

Ito, T. A., J. T. Cacioppo, and P. J Lang. 1998. Eliciting affect using the International Affective Picture System: Bivariate evaluation and ambivalence. *Personality and Social Psychology Bulletin* 24:855–79.

Ito, T. A., J. T. Larsen, N. K. Smith, and J. T. Cacioppo. 1998. Negative information weighs more heavily on the brain: The negativity bias in evaluative categorizations. *Journal of Personality and Social Psychology* 75 (4): 887–900.

J

Janis, Irving L. 1982. *Groupthink.* 2nd ed. Boston: Houghton Mifflin.

Jaycox, L. H., and R. L. Repetti. 1993. Conflict in families and the psychological adjustment of preadolescent children. *Journal of Family Psychology* 7:344–55.

Jones, D. C. 1992. Parental divorce, family conflict and friendship networks. *Journal of Social and Personal Relationships* 9:219–235.

Jones, E., and K. Davis. 1965. From acts to dispositions: The attribution process in person perception. In vol. 2 of *Advances in experimental social psychology,* ed. L. Berkowitz. New York: Academic Press.

Jung, C. G. 1968. *Analytical psychology: Its theory and practice.* New York: Vintage Books/Random House.

K

Kanouse, D. E., and L. R. Hansen. Jr. 1972. Negativity in evaluations. In *Attribution: Perceiving the causes of behavior,* eds. E. E. Jones,

D. E. Kanouse, H. H. Kelley, R. E. Nisbett, S. Valin, and B. Weiner, 47–62. Morristown, NJ: General Learning Press.

Keirsey, David, and Marilyn Bates. 1978. *Please understand me*. Del Mar, CA: Prometheus Nemesis Book Co.

Kelley, H. 1973. The process of causal attribution. *Amercian Psychologist* 28:107–28.

Kirkpatrick, S. A., and E. A. Locke. 1991. Leadership: Do traits matter? *Academy of Management Executives* 5 (2):48–60.

Koehler, D. J. 1993. The influence of prior beliefs on scientific judgments of evidence quality. *Organizational Behavior and Human Decision Processes* 56:28–55.

Kolb, D. 1984. *Experiential learning: Experience as the source of learning and development*. Englewood Cliffs, NJ: Prentice Hall.

Kolb, D. 1985. *LSI learning style inventory: Self-scoring inventory and interpretation booklet*. Boston: McBer.

Kolb, D., and L. Putnam. 1992. The multiple faces of conflict in organizations. *Journal of Organizational Behavior* 13:311–24.

Kroeger, Otto, and Janet M. Thuesen. 1988. *Typetalk*. New York: Dell.

Kunda, Z. 1990. The case for motivated reasoning. *Psychological Bulletin* 108:480–89.

L

LaTour, S. 1978. Determinants of participant and observer satisfaction with adversary and inquisitorial modes of adjudication. *Journal of Personality and Social Psychology* 36: 1531–45.

Lemert, Charles, ed. 1993. *Social theory: The multicultural and classic readings*. Boulder, San Francisco, Oxford: Westview Press.

Lewicki, R. J., and B. B. Bunker. 1996. Developing and maintaining work relationships. In *Trust in Organizations*, eds. R. M. Kramer and T. R. Tyler, 119–24. Thousand Oaks, CA: Sage.

Lind, E. A. 1992. The fairness heuristic: Rationality and "relationality" in procedural evaluations. Paper presented at the Fourth International Conference of the Society for the Advancement of Socio-Economics, Irvine, CA.

Lind, E. A. 1994. Procedural justice, disputing, and reactions to legal authorities. ABF Working Paper No. 9403, American Bar Foundation, Chicago.

Lind, E. A., C. T. Kulik, M. Ambrose, and M. V. De Vera Park. 1993. Individual and corporate dispute resolution: Using procedural fairness as a decision heuristic. *Administrative Science Quarterly* 38:224–51.

Loeb, Marshall. 1994. Where leaders come from. *Fortune*, September 19, 241.

Lord, C. G., L. Ross, and M. R. Lepper. 1979. Biased assimilation and attitude polarization: The effects of prior theories on subsequently considered evidence. *Journal of Personality and Social Psychology* 37:1098–2109.

M

McClelland, D. C. 1961. *The achieving society*. New York: Van Nostrand Reinhold.

McClelland, D. C. 1975. *The inner experiences*. New York: Irvington.

McGonagle, K. A. R. C. Kessler, and I. H.Gotlib. 1993. The effects of marital disagreement style, frequency, and outcome on marital disruption. *Journal of Social and Personal Relationships* 10:385–404.

Mead, G. 1934. *Mind, self, and society*. Chicago: University of Chicago Press.

Miller, D., and C. Droge. 1986. Psychological and traditional determinants of structure. *Administrative Science Quarterly* 31:539–60.

Miller, D., M. F. R. Kets de Vries, and J. M. Toulouse. 1982. Top executive locus of control and its relationship to strategy-making, structure, and environment. *Academy of Management Journal* 25 (2): 237–53.

Miller, D., E. R. Lack, and S. Asroff. 1985. Preferences for control and the coronary-prone behavior pattern: "I'd rather do it myself." *Journal of Personality and Social Psychology* 49:492–499.

Moreno, J. L. 1947. Contributions of sociometry to research methodology in sociology. *American Sociological Review* 12:287–92.

Moscovici, S., and M. Zavalloni. 1969. The group as a polarizer of attitudes. *Journal of Personality and Social Psychology* 12 (2): 125–35.

N

Nadler, David A., and Michael L. Tushman. 1990. Beyond the charismatic leader: Leadership and organizational change. *California Management Review* 32 (2): 77–97.

Nahavandi, Afsaneh. 1997. *The art and science of leadership*. Upper Saddle River, NJ: Prentice Hall.

Nisbett, R. E., and L. Ross. 1980. *Human inference: Strategies and shortcomings of social judgment*. Englewood Cliffs, NJ: Prentice Hall.

P

Peeters, G., and J. Czapinski. 1990. Positive-negative asymmetry in evaluations: The distinction between affective and informational negativity effects. In vol. 1 of *European review of social psychology*, eds. W. Stroebe and Hewstone, 33–60. Chichester, England: Wiley.

Peterson, P. D., and D. Koulack. 1969. Attitude change as a function of latitudes of acceptance and rejection. *Journal of Personality and Social Psychology* 11:309–11.

Petty, R. E., and J. T. Cacioppo. 1981. *Attitudes and persuasion: Classic and contemporary approaches*. Dubuque, IA: Wm. C. Brown.

———. 1986. The elaboration likelihood model of persuasion. In vol. 19 of *Advances in experimental social psychology*, ed. L. Berkowitz, 123–205. San Diego: Academic Press.

R

Ralston, D. A., D. J. Gustafson, R. H. Terpstra, D. H. Holt, F. M. Cheung, and B. A. Ribbens. 1993. The impact of managerial values on decision-making behavior: A comparison of the United States and Hong Kong. *Asia Pacific Journal of Management* 10 (1): 21–37.

Ralston, D. A., D. J. Gustafson, F. M. Cheung, and R. H. Terpstra. 1993. Differences in managerial values: A study of U.S. Hong

Kong and PRC Managers. *Journal of International Business Studies* 2:249–75.

Raymark, P. H., M. J. Schmidt, and R. M. Guion. 1997. Identifying potentially useful personality constructs for employee selection. *Personnel Psychology* 50 (3): 723–36.

Reardon, Kathleen K. 1991. *Persuasion in practice.* Newbury Park, CA: Sage.

Ritzer, George. 1992. *Contemporary sociological theory.* 3rd ed. New York: McGraw-Hill.

Rogan, R. G., and R. Hammer. 1994. Crisis negotiations: A preliminary investigation of facework in naturalistic conflict discourse. *Journal of Applied Communication Research* 22: 216–31.

Ross, M., and G. J. O. Fletcher. 1985. Attribution and social perception. In vol. 2 of *Handbook of social psychology,* 3rd ed., eds. G. Lindzey and E. Aronson. New York: Random House.

Ross, L., D. Green, and P. House. 1977. The "false consensus effect": An egocentric bias in social perception and attribution processes. *Journal of Experimental Social Psychology* 13:279–301.

Ross, L., and M. R. Lepper. 1980. The perseverance of beliefs: Empirical and normative considerations. *New Directions for Methodology of Social and Behavioral Science* 4:17–36.

Rotter, J. B. 1966. Generalized expectancies for internal versus external control of reinforcement. *Psychological Monographs* 80 (609).

S

Schwarz, N. 1999. Self-reports. How the questions shape the answers. *American Psychologist* 54 (2): 93–105.

Senge, P. M. 1990. *The fifth discipline: The art and practice of the learning organization.* New York: Doubleday.

Shapiro, D., B. H. Sheppard, and L. Cheraskin. 1992. Business on a handshake. *Negotiation Journal* 8 (4): 365–77.

Sherif, C. W., and M. Sherif, eds. 1967. *Attitude, ego-involvement, and change.* New York: Wiley.

Sherif, C. W., M. Sherif, and R. E. Nebergall. 1965. *Attitude and attitude change. The social judgment–involvement approach.* Philadelphia: Sanders.

Sherif, M., and C. T. Hovland. 1961. *Social judgment: Assimilation and contract effects in communication and attitude change.* New Haven, CT: Yale University Press.

Skowronski, J. J., and D. E. Carlston. 1989. Negativity and extremity biases in impression formation: A review of explanations. *Psychological Bulletin* 105:131–142.

Snyder, M. 1987. *Public appearances/ private realities: The psychology of self-monitoring.* New York: W. H. Freeman.

T

Tannen, D. 1991. *You just don't understand: Women and men in conversation.* New York: Ballentine Books.

Tannen, D. 1993. *Talking from 9 to 5.* New York: William Morrow.

Thibaut, J. W., and L. Walker. 1975. *Procedural justice: A psychological analysis.* Hillsdale, NJ: Lawrence Erlbaum Associates.

Triandis, H. C. 1980. *Handbook of cross cultural psychology.* Boston: Allyn and Bacon.

Tyler, T. R., and E. A. Lind. 1992. A relational model of authority in groups. In vol. 25 of *Advances in experimental social psychology,* ed. M. Zanna, 115–91. New York: Academic Press.

W

Waldman, David A., and Francis J. Yammarino. 1999. CEO charismatic leadership: Levels-of-management and levels-of-analysis effects. *Academy of Management Review* 24 (2): 266–285.

Walker, L., S. LaTour, E. A. Lind, and J. Thibaut. 1974. Reactions of participants and observers to modes of adjudication. *Journal of Applied Social Psychology* 4:295–310.

Wallach, M. A., N. Kogan, and D. J. Bem. 1962. Group influence on individual risk taking. *Journal of Abnormal and Social Psychology* 36 (2-A): 75–86.

What are the skills of tomorrow's global manager? 1999. Asia Pacific Management News, August 4. http://www.apmforum.com/news/ap040899.

Wheatley, M. J. 1994. *Leadership and the new science: Learning about organization from an orderly universe.* San Francisco: Berrett-Koehler.

Wilmot, William W., and Joyce L. Hocker. 2001. *Interpersonal conflict.* 6th ed. New York: McGraw-Hill.

Wilson, S. R. 1992. Face and facework in negotiation. In *Communication and negotiation,* eds. L. L. Putnam and M. E. Roloff, 176–203. Newbury Park, CA: Sage.

Wittrock, Merlin C., ed. 1977. *Learning and instruction.* Berkeley, CA: McCutchen.

Y

Yarbrough, E., and E. Wilmot. 1995. *Artful mediation: Constructive conflict at work.* Boulder, CO: Cairns.

Young-Eisendrath, P. 1993. *You're not what I expected.* New York: William Morrow.

Selected Bibliography

A

Abelson, Herbert I. 1959. *Persuasion.* New York: Springer.

Ajzen, Ecek, and M. Fishbein. 1980. *Understanding attitudes and predicting social behavior.* Englewood Cliffs, NJ: Prentice Hall.

Altman, E., and D. Taylor, 1973. *Social penetration: The development of interpersonal relations.* Holt, Rinehart and Winston. New York, NY.

B

Brehm J. (1966). A Theory of Psychological Reactance. New York: Academic Press.

Brenner, Charles. 1982. *The mind in conflict.* International Universities Press. Madison, CN.

Bruhn, John G., and Howard M. Rebach, eds. 1996. *Clinical sociology: An agenda for action.* New York: Plenum Press.

C

Cavanaugh, John D., and Fredda Blanchard-Fields. 2002. *Adult development and aging.* 4th ed. Belmont, CA: Wadsworth/ Thomson Learning.

Chapman, A. H. 1968. *Put-offs and come-ons.* New York: G.P. Putnam and Son.

Charns, M. P., and M. J. Schaefer. 1983. *Health care organizations: A model for management.* Englewood Cliffs, NJ: Prentice Hall.

Craig, Neil. 1985. *The mindbenders.* Glasgow: Westland.

D

Deich, A., and P. Hodges. 1978. *Language without speech.* New York: Brunner/Mazel.

Dyer, Wayne W. 1976. *Your erroneous zones.* New York: Funk and Wagnalls.

E

Elkins, Arthur, and Dennis W. Callaghan. 1979. *A managerial odyssey: Problems in business and its environment.* 2nd ed. Reading, MA: Addison-Wesley.

F

Fast, Julius, and Barbara Fast. 1979. *Talking between the lines.* New York: Viking Press.

Feyereisen, Pierre, and Jacques-Dominique de Lannoy. 1991. *Gestures and speech: Psychological investigations.* Cambridge: Cambridge University Press.

Fisher, R., and W. Urg. 1981. *Getting to yes!* New York: Houghton-Miflin.

G

Galbraith, J. R. 1973. *Designing complex organizations.* Reading, MA: Addison-Wesley.

Gergen, K. J. 1971. *The psychology of behavior exchange.* Reading, MA: Addison-Wesley.

H

Heider, Fritz. 1958. *The psychology of interpersonal relations.* New York: John Wiley and Sons.

I

Ilich, John. 1973. *The art and skill of successful negotiation*. Englewood Cliffs, NJ: Prentice-Hall.
———. 1992. *Dealbreakers and breakthroughs*. New York: John Wiley and Sons.

J

Jung, C. G. 1974. *Analytical psychology: Its theory and practice*. New York: Vintage Books/Random House.

K

Karp, David A., and William Yoels. 1993. *Sociology in everyday life*. 2nd ed. Itasca, IL: F. E. Peacock.
Karrass, C. L. 1974. *Give and take: The complete guide to negotiating strategies and tactics*. New York: Thomas Y. Crowell.
Kroeger, Otto, and Janet M. Theusen. 1988. *Type talk*. New York: Dell.

L

Laing, R. D. 1975. *Self and others*. Penguin Books. Baltimore, MD.
Laird, Donald, and Eleanor Laird. 1951. *Sizing up people*. New York: McGraw-Hill.
Luscher, Max. 1981. *Personality signs*. Warner Books. New York, NY.

M

Maslow, A. 1954. *Motivation and personality*. New York: Harper Brothers.
McKeachie, Wilbert James, and Charlotte Lackner Doyle. 1966. *Psychology*. New York: Addison-Wesley.

Morris, Michael W., Larrick, Richard P., and Steven K. Su. 1999. Misperceiving negotiation counterparts: When situationally determined bargaining behaviors are attributed to personality traits. *Journal of Personality and Social Psychology* 77 (1): 52–67.
Murnighan, J. Keith. 1992. *Bargaining games*. New York: William Morrow.

N

Nierenberg, Gerard I. 1981. *The art of negotiating*. New York: Simon and Schuster.

P

Pizer, Vernon. 1978. *You don't say: How people communicate without speech*. New York: Putnam
Poiret, Maude. 1970. *Body talk*. New York: Award Books.
Porter, M. 1980. *Competitive strategy: Techniques for analyzing industries and competitors*. New York: The Free Press.
Pruitt, D. B. 1981. *Negotiating behavior*. New York: Academic Press.

R

Rubin, T. I. 1980. *Reconciliations*. New York: Viking Press.

S

Schein, Edgard H. 1969. *Process consultation: Its role in organization development*. Reading, MA: Addison-Wesley.
Schelling, T. C. 1966. *The strategy of conflict*. London: Oxford University Press.

Schneider, David J., Albert H. Hastorf, and Phoebe C. Ellsworth. 1979. *Person perception*. Reading, MA, and CA: Addison-Wesley, Menlo Park, CA.

Shafer, John B. P. 1978. *Humanistic psychology*. Englewood Cliffs, NJ: Prentice Hall.

Shaffer, David R. 1989. *Developmental psychology*. 2nd ed. Pacific Grove, CA: Brooks/Cole.

Shuter, Robert. 1979. *Understanding misunderstandings*. New York: Harper and Row.

Smith, Charles P., ed. 1992. *Motivation and personality: Handbook of thematic content analysis*. Cambridge: Cambridge University Press.

Spangler, W. D. 1992. Validity of questionnaires and TAT measures of need for achievement: Two meta-analyses. *Psychological Bulletin* 112 (1): 140–54.

Stuart, R. B., ed. 1977. *Behavioral self-management*. New York: Brunner/Mazel.

T

Thompson, J. D. 1967. *Organizations in action*. New York: McGraw-Hill.

Tysons Corner, VA. Unpublished

W

Warshaw, T. A. 1980. *Winning by negotiation*. New York: McGraw-Hill.

Wilson, J. R. 1992. Face and facework in negotiation. In *Communication and negotiation*, eds. L. L. Putnam and M. E. Roloff, 176–205. Newbury Park, CA: Sage.

Wright, Leah N. 1935. *Getting along with people*. New York: Whittlesey House/McGraw-Hill.

Y

Yukl, Gary, and David D. Van Fleet. 1992. Theory and research on leadership in organizations. In vol. 3 of *Handbook of industrial and organizational psychology*, eds. M. D. Dunnette and L. M. Hough, 148–97. Palo Alto, CA: Consulting Psychologists Press.

Z

Zartman, I. W., and M. Berman. 1982. *The practical negotiator*. New Haven, CT: Yale University Press.

Index

Credits

p. 1, Robert Kneschke/Shutterstock

p. 11, Stephen Coburn/Shutterstock

p. 32, Alexander Raths/Shutterstock

p. 54, wavebreakmedia/Shutterstock

p. 72, Kzenon/Shutterstock

p. 85, Pressmaster/Shutterstock

p. 101, Monkey Business Images/Shutterstock

p. 110, Robert Kneschke/Shutterstock

p. 121, © AVAVA/Fotolia.com

p. 136, © pressmaster/Fotolia.com

p. 151, © pressmaster/Fotolia.com

p. 162, © ots-photo/Fotolia.com

p. 166, © Kzenon/Fotolia.com

p. 184, © Adam Gregor/Fotolia.com

p. 192, © Kzenon/Fotolia.com

p. 203, © AVAVA/Fotolia.com

p. 223, © AVAVA/Fotolia.com

p. 230, © decisiveimages/Fotolia.com

p. 237, © Kzenon/Fotolia.com

p. 244, © pressmaster/Fotolia.com

p. 261, © goodluz/Fotolia.com